Surviving Large Losses

Surviving Large Losses

FINANCIAL CRISES,

the MIDDLE CLASS,

and the DEVELOPMENT OF

CAPITAL MARKETS

Philip T. Hoffman

Gilles Postel-Vinay

Jean-Laurent Rosenthal

THE BELKNAP PRESS OF
HARVARD UNIVERSITY PRESS
Cambridge, Massachusetts
London, England
2007

Cataloging-in-Publication Data available from the Library of Congress
Library of Congress catalog card number: 2006041275
ISBN-13: 978-0-674-02469-4 (alk. paper)
ISBN-10: 0-674-02469-9 (alk. paper)

Contents

Acknowledgments

WE OWE AN ENORMOUS DEBT of gratitude to the institutions that have supported our work and to the individuals who have shared data, read what we have written, or offered us suggestions, advice, and criticisms. The institutions we wish to thank are the California Institute of Technology and the John Simon Guggenheim Foundation, for Hoffman; the Ecole des Hautes Etudes en Sciences Sociales and the Institut National de la Recherche Agronomique, for Postel-Vinay; and the Ecole des Hautes Etudes en Sciences Sociales, the Ecole d'Economie de Paris, the Institut National de la Recherche Agronomique, the John Simon Guggenheim Foundation, and the University of California, Los Angeles, for Rosenthal. The individuals to whom we are grateful include Mike Alvarez, Peter Bossaerts, Jerome Bourdieu, Federico Echenique, Mordechai Feingold, Oscar Gelderblom, Peter Gourevitch, Rod Kiewiet, Morgan Kousser, Naomi Lamoreaux, John Ledyard, Juliette Levi, Mark H. Madden, Mark Rubenstein, Joseph Ryan, Kenneth Sokoloff, Akiko Suwa-Eisenmann, R. Bin Wong, the Harvard University Press readers, and especially Ann Hawthorne and Michael Aronson.

Le souvenir se présente à l'imparfait . . .

Memory appears in the imperfect . . .

—Francis Ponge, "Proèmes"

Introduction

HAVE YOU EVER WORRIED about the chances of a financial disaster? Ever lost sleep over the possibility that your savings might be gutted or your investments wiped out? Maybe you haven't, because you are smart and savvy and have taken all sorts of steps to defend yourself. Or maybe you are simply confident that modern financial markets and government safeguards will always protect you.

But that protection doesn't always work. Just ask Sandra Stone or any one of the 20,000 or so other former employees of the Enron Corporation whose pensions and savings were swallowed up when their company went bankrupt late in 2001. Stone could have been speaking for any one of her colleagues when she exclaimed: "I'm livid, absolutely livid. I have lost my entire friggin' retirement to these people."[1]

No one wants to end up like Sandra and her coworkers. But the sad fact is that she and her colleagues are by no means alone. Financial crises have struck repeatedly for centuries, leaving countless victims in their wake. Some of those victims were so noted for their brilliance that we think they surely ought to have known better: Isaac Newton sustained losses in an early English stock market bubble;

Voltaire, who had speculated to great advantage, dropped a sizable chunk of his profits in a government debt default; and the brilliant economist Irving Fisher saw his fortune annihilated in the Great Crash of 1929.[2] If geniuses like these proved so vulnerable, what's the outlook for everyone else?

Hindsight often persuades us that the crises could easily have been avoided. Yet the truth is that financial crises are virtually inevitable, like earthquakes or hurricanes. Indeed, despite all the reforms they have inspired, they continue to batter us, as we can see from the collapse of the Asian banks and stock markets, the bursting of the Internet bubble and subsequent wave of bankruptcies, and the corporate scandals of the late 1990s. Nor do they show any signs of abating, despite government programs offering new ways for investors to shelter their holdings.[3] Fears about possible financial debacles are in fact constantly bubbling up in the media. Will they arise from mutual fund scandals or insolvent company pensions in the United States, from rollercoaster real estate prices in prosperous countries such as Britain or Australia, or from some rapacious government just about anywhere in the world?

What makes the crises so important—beyond the painful losses they entail—is that they often prove to be turning points in the evolution of financial markets and long-term economic growth.[4] Some of them, obviously, have ended up shackling economic growth. The 1929 stock market crash and ensuing epidemic of bank panics in the United States is perhaps the most familiar example.[5] Yet others have had a very different effect. Indeed, a number have actually helped foster long-run growth by reshaping financial institutions. In 1719–20, a stock market bubble in Paris ruined many investors. But it also gave birth to a new financial market, which raised unparalleled amounts of capital for private investment. And even the crash of 1929 helped bring about beneficial reforms that improved financial institutions, both in the United States and elsewhere. Crises thus seem to have the potential not only to do harm but also to wipe the slate clean, leaving actors free to design new institutions that better resist trouble in the future. Innovation and financial failure may thus be inseparable—a financial parallel to a process sketched long ago for technology by the economist Joseph Schumpeter.

Since financial crises will inevitably recur, we must explore their causes and long-run consequences and in particular how they shape the evolution of financial systems. The crux of the matter is determining how crises affect—and are in turn affected by—the development of financial institutions. Are there institutions that attack the causes of crises and make it less likely that they will strike? Are there institutions that prevent crises from crippling a financial system when they do hit? Are there institutions that keep crises from hobbling financial development and economic growth or make it more likely that they are followed not by stagnation but by beneficial reforms? And under what conditions will such institutions arise?

Both the causes and consequences of crises play out over a span of years, decades, or even generations, as do economic growth and the development of financial institutions. It is therefore impossible to study the relationship between crises and financial development by examining contemporary evidence alone. Only a study of longer periods can reveal the linkages among crises, institutions, and financial development. Only history can give us the necessary perspective.

Imagine, for example, that you had lived through the financial crisis at the beginning of Great Depression. The economic distress had just opened the door to new political leaders—among them, Roosevelt in the United States and Hitler in Germany. At that moment, in the opening months of 1933, could you possibly have foreseen all the political and economic ramifications of Roosevelt's presidency or Hitler's dictatorship, if you had only taken into account what was known at the time? Even if you had considered only financial development and economic growth, could you have known that New Deal legislation would shape financial markets in the United States for the rest of the century or that regulations from the Third Reich would influence the German economy into the 1980s?[6]

History helps us to understand the relationship among crises, institutions, and financial development. But we also need the tools of political economy to appreciate all that history tells us. Despite a great deal of excellent work, no one has yet combined history and political economy in a way that explains why financial crises are virtually inevitable or why they can have such strikingly different long-run consequences—why some are destructive while others turn out to be creative.[7] Nor has anyone determined what institutions are likely to help a financial system surmount crises and continue its development. Yet these issues are not mere academic questions; they demand our attention, and not simply because the savings, investments, and retirements of so many people today are at stake. Future generations are at risk too. Financial markets are an extraordinary engine for promoting investment and innovation and for making economies expand. They can finance an education or help entrepreneurs start businesses in countries rich or poor. When ineffective financial systems prevent individuals from borrowing, investing, or diversifying their holdings, then the economy as a whole suffers, and later generations are poorer than they would otherwise have been.[8] That is true whether the country is wealthy or impoverished.

Definitions

Before we go any further, we should make several things clear, beginning with what we mean by a financial crisis. A number of definitions are possible—a sudden drop in market values might qualify, as would sheer volatility of prices—but for our purposes we have chosen something slightly different. For us, there is a crisis when a large number of financial contracts are suddenly broken. The simplest case would involve a number of borrowers defaulting on their loans, but a wave of corporate bankruptcies that wipes out shareholders will also count.[9] So too will a government's decision to renege on its debts or to pay its bondholders in money made worthless by inflation or devaluation. And one can think of other examples as well. Imagine that a hedge fund sells scores of investors insurance against adverse events such as a drop in the stock market. If the stock market tumbles but the hedge fund is unable to pay off on the insurance, then that too would constitute a crisis—one that, as we shall see, came perilously close to happening in 1998.

The crises that meet our definition are often triggered by sudden shifts of value or sharp changes in incomes, revenues, or costs—what economists and other social scientists call shocks. Because shocks often provoke crises, the two concepts may seem practically synonymous, but they do in fact differ. To take a concrete illustration, suppose that farmers borrow to buy land and machinery when agricultural prices are high and interest rates low. If prices then drop and interest rates soar, that will constitute a shock, but there will be a crisis only if a large number of the farmers default on their debt, as happened in the 1980s in the American Midwest. Fortunately, institutions can sometimes keep shocks from unleashing crises or diminish the havoc that crises wreak. The key lies in trying to create such institutions and ensuring that they also promote financial development and economic growth.

When we speak of institutions, we also have a specific meaning in mind: for us, institutions are rules, along with some means of enforcing them. The rules may be laws, regulations, or contracts upheld by courts; rules of this sort, which are enforced by the state, we call formal institutions. But the rules may also simply be regular patterns of private behavior kept in place not by the state, but by expectations about what other people will do—for instance, an investor's decision to follow the advice of a trusted financial adviser rather than listening to some unknown broker who telephones him out of the blue. Rules of this type we will call informal institutions. We have to ask why some crises bring on formal institutional change—that is, modified laws and government regulations—and why others alter private patterns of behavior.

What Lies Ahead

What, then, do history and political economy reveal about the causes and consequences of crises? What do they divulge about the relationship between crises, institutions, and long-run financial development?

What they show is that three factors are critical for the development of financial institutions: the level of government debt, the size of the middle class, and the amount of information that is available for parties to perform financial transactions. To illustrate the enormous impact that these factors have, we turn to financial dramas acted out in the capital markets of Europe, Asia, and North and South America—some recently, and some long ago. These dramas are illuminating histories that we probe with the tools of political economy to help make clear under what circumstances our three factors will promote financial development and keep crises from taking too heavy a toll, and when it is that they will unfortunately do the reverse. They also demonstrate that no financial institution is optimal for all times and places: an institution that seems best one day—a bank or a stock exchange—can easily falter or crumble as our three factors change. In contrast to what short-run statistical evidence has led many observers to believe, there is simply no one single best specific mix of banks, markets, and other institutional arrangements for financial transactions.

These dramas and stories are thus our evidence. In nearly every case, they could be supported with quantitative evidence and formal economic models, but to make things easy for readers we have chosen to limit ourselves to our analytical stories. They are the most effective—and certainly the most interesting—way to make our points.

We start with a look at two of the major causes of crises: predatory behavior by governments and problems with information that bedevil all financial transactions. Both of these causes can in turn be traced back to our three factors, for informational problems reflect the different information that parties to financial transactions usually have, and governments are usually driven to prey on capital markets when they have run up too much debt. We then examine the demands for institutional change that arise in the wake of crises, show how these demands are shaped by our third factor—the size of the middle class—and then see how they can be met, whether by the government or by private entrepreneurs. Throughout, we ask what institutions will make financial markets more effective, by encouraging financial development and limiting the harm that crises can do.

In tying financial development and crises together, we do not mean to imply that stronger financial markets are just a terrible danger. Such a claim might fit the common belief—particularly on the left—that financial markets are purely evil, but it would mean blinding oneself to the immense good that they do. The trouble is that economies cannot enjoy this good without running the risk of having crises. In that sense, the truth about financial markets is reminiscent of what the seventeenth-century philosopher and mathematician Blaise Pascal said about human beings: they are neither angels nor beasts and thus are neither completely good nor completely evil. The virtue of financial markets is that they enable transactions that make people better off, by boosting investment, providing protection against risk, and fostering innovation and economic growth. The downside is that financial development often brings crises in its wake. The stereotypes of the left are thus mistaken, as are equally unrealistic assertions made by observers on the right, who overlook crises and blithely assert that financial markets never do any harm.

Our ultimate goal is to understand financial development, which has long been of deep importance in countries rich and poor. Financial development matters for us all, but to grasp it, we must study the causes of crises and their unforeseen consequences, which only history can unveil.

CHAPTER 1

The Political Economy
of Financial Crises

IMAGINE THAT YOU are an investor, a cautious one. Why might you be wary? Perhaps you recently dropped a sizable bundle in the stock market. Perhaps accounting scandals or terrifying world events make you fret about the future. Or perhaps advancing age leaves you with little time to recoup losses before you retire. In any case, you are anxiously seeking a safe haven for your savings.

If you are fortunate enough to live in a country like the United States in the early twenty-first century, or in certain other Western democracies, you will have many ways of assuaging your fears, from buying inflation-indexed treasury bonds to socking your money away in a government-insured bank account. Sure, terrorists may still strike, and companies may continue to doctor their books. But there is at least one nightmare that will not make you toss and turn at night—namely, the threat that the government itself will trample on the guarantees protecting your money. The federal government of the United States will simply not default on its bonds or get rid of indexing. Nor will it renege on the insurance payments owed you if your bank goes under. It just does not behave that way. If anything, when the U.S. government intervenes in financial markets, it strives to protect investors: recall how in 1998 the Federal Reserve Bank bailed out the hedge fund Long Term Capital Management in order to avoid a market panic that would have harmed not just the rich but many middle-class investors as well.[1]

Elsewhere, however, you might not be so lucky. Suppose, for example, that you had the misfortune to be living in Argentina late in 2001, and had to invest your savings there, perhaps because, as a small-scale middle-class investor, you could not easily open an offshore bank account or buy foreign bonds or money fund shares.[2] Since you could not send your money abroad, your options would be grim. Argentine government bonds would be too risky. On the market they were in fact plummeting to a quarter of their face value because of concerns (justified, it turned out) that the government would default outright or would repay the bonds in devalued Argentine currency. Bank accounts would terrify you, too. Indeed, from July on, panicking Argentines were rushing to yank their money out of banks because they were alarmed that the government would in effect loot the country's banks. They wanted to get their money out and if possible convert it to dollars, a move that would also protect them against a likely currency devaluation. Faced with a bank run, the government finally froze savings accounts and imposed a ceiling on withdrawals from checking accounts. Had you put your money in a bank, it would have been stuck there.[3]

As an investor, you would clearly do worse in Argentina than in the United States, at least at the end of 2001. Blame for your woes in Argentina could in large part be laid at the government's feet. But Argentina is not the only country whose government mistreats investors. There are many others that do the same, just as there are many besides the United States that nurture investors. What is it that makes a government protective of investors? And what makes it predatory? What, in short, turns some states into Argentinas, and others into countries like the United States?

An answer to this question has proved elusive, even though the issue should interest all investors, not just timid ones. Indeed, the question should concern not just investors, but anyone with a stake in financial markets. At the very least, that means all people with savings; and because healthy financial markets have been linked to rapid economic growth, it actually means virtually everyone, rich and poor alike.

Even so, no one yet seems to know why some states end up like Argentina, and others like the United States. Economists, historians, and political scientists who have investigated the matter have tried to connect the type of governments that prey upon financial markets to certain political characteristics—above all else, the lack of democratic institutions, such as representative assemblies.[4] But by themselves, representative assemblies cannot guarantee that governments will leave financial markets unscathed: after all, in 2001 Argentina itself was a democracy.

What this argument leaves out are the wars, recessions, and other misfortunes that can leave a government desperate for funds and wreak havoc on its policies—in other words, real economic shocks. They can push even a staunch democracy to plunder financial markets. When faced with a shock, political leaders will act in a way that reflects not just the state's political system, but its financial health—in particular, the debt it already owes and the new taxes it can raise without enraging the citizenry.

The amount of government debt is critical here. If, like Argentina, a state labors under a huge debt load, then it will be tempted to meddle in capital markets to reduce its financial burden, tempted even to repudiate its debts or to plunder the financial system, just as Argentina did. Although such drastic tactics may provoke a crisis and handicap markets for decades, they may be less painful politically than an unpopular tax increase or cut in spending, and they will be all the more appealing when government debt is large. And if government debt is massive, then any state will consider victimizing financial markets attractive.

It would be wonderful if there were some simple rule that would tell us where this danger zone begins—one that might place it, for instance, at a certain threshold level of debt relative to the size of the country's economy or the amount of taxes the government collects. The unpleasant arithmetic of government budgets might conceivably give us some sense of where the threshold could lie, because over the long haul what the government spends has to equal what it takes in.[5] The trouble, however, is that both government expenses and government revenues are determined by a political process shaped by a host of political and economic factors, from the nature of the political system to the distribution of income and the strength of economic growth. The threshold will therefore vary from state to state. It will reflect the nuances of a country's history, the incentives its political leaders face, and the pressure that lenders can apply in order to be repaid. By bringing statistics and economic models to bear on contemporary data, one can determine where the threshold is likely to be in a set of similar countries, but the rule that such an exercise produces will never generalize to other places or other periods. A level of government debt that causes alarm in a developing country today—more than twice the government's annual revenues, for instance, as in Argentina at the end of 2001—may therefore not raise any fears at all in a rich democracy, particularly if the democracy happens to be at war and has generous allies or if the lenders who advance the government money happen to be powerful politically. At the end of World War II, for instance, Great Britain could sustain a public debt that exceeded six times the government's revenues.[6]

There is thus no way to tell precisely where the danger zone starts in every country. Nevertheless, political leaders in any given country will have an idea where it begins, as will lenders; and social scientists who pay close attention to an individual country's peculiarities can make the same inferences as leaders and lenders. In addition, there is at least one rule that holds in general: massive debt (particularly when measured relative to politically feasible tax revenue) will increase the odds that a country is approaching or has even entered its own peculiar danger zone. Even if the country is not already in its danger zone, a shock can easily push it there, causing financial markets to suffer. On the other hand, if its debt is far from such an extreme, it will be less likely to be in its danger zone and less likely to prey on financial markets.

No state can escape this iron logic, which derives from the constraints on government finances and the changing political costs of raising taxes and cutting expenditures. It has in fact played itself out over and over again, both today and in the past. In previous centuries, for instance, some states did not borrow regularly, unbelievable though that may seem to us today. Imperial China is one such example. Other states—notably eighteenth-century England—borrowed a great deal, but they kept from piling up huge amounts of debt relative to the taxes that were politically acceptable. If the logic is correct, both sorts of states should have had little incentive to maul their financial system, and the historical record bears out this contention. Financial crises might still erupt, but at least governments had not caused them. The story is strikingly different, however, in states whose public debt levels have climbed to extremes. Typically, a shock drives the government to unleash a crisis that hobbles capital markets for years—the grim fate that often awaits the Argentinas of this world.

Many countries ran this gauntlet of public debt in Europe between roughly 1500 and 1800, when repeated shocks from wars pushed many states over their thresholds. Although their experience may at first glance seem remote from us, it actually has considerable relevance for the governments today that run the highest risk of provoking crises by borrowing too heavily—the governments of developing countries and of nations emerging from communism. For the early modern European states and these nations today, the same logic applies: the logic of public debt levels and of danger zones determined by politics, fiscal systems, and the strength of the economy. The experience of the early modern states lets us see how that logic plays out. In developing countries it is still at work, while in Europe the long-run consequences are still visible.

Public Debt and the Government's Role

Public debt plays the starring role in the drama of governmental predation on financial markets. If a state has little or no debt, then it can usually borrow if it goes to war, plunges into recession, or confronts some other shock that necessitates a hefty increase in government spending. Lenders need not worry that current debt payments will prevent the government from repaying any new loans. It will of course help if taxes are low (or at least not so high that tax increases would make the public squawk), for then the state can levy additional taxes to fund the new loans. In any case, the state will be unlikely to unleash some devastating financial crisis by victimizing the financial system. Crises will of course still occur, but they will not be the result of the government's depredations.

A government-induced crisis will become more likely if public debt rises to extremely high levels, for then it will be harder for the state to cope with a war, a recession, or some other shock. If the state can still raise taxes, it may be able to sign new loans to pay for troops or to fund benefits for the unemployed, but eventually the tax increases will ignite political resistance. At that point, the state will be close to its danger zone, if it is not already there. Default will then become easier politically than spending cuts or further tax increases. After all, if you are fighting a war, you cannot take money for the troops and give it to bondholders. And cutting unemployment benefits

in a recession is likely to be political suicide, at least in a modern democracy.[7]

It is here that a shock can make predation attractive. It may take
the form of defaulting on the government's existing debt. A default
can free up money for essential expenditures (paying troops or unemployment benefits, for example) and yet carry few political costs, particularly if the bondholders are foreigners or members of a powerless
group. It may even be possible to stiff the old bondholders and then
use the money saved to fund loans from a new set of lenders. The
huge Spanish empire tried that strategy back in the sixteenth century; so did developing countries in the 1980s. And the government
need not stop there. States can, for instance, decide to print money;
such a move can unleash inflation and (if the inflation comes as a surprise) redistribute wealth from creditors to debtors, who can pay back
their loans in unexpectedly cheap paper. States can also force banks
or savers to extend new loans to the government. Argentina resorted
to such tactics in 2001; so, in the sixteenth and seventeenth centuries,
did scores of European rulers. And by the nineteenth century, default
had become a global phenomenon.

Once a state decides to plunder the financial system, capital markets are likely to suffer lasting harm. The government will have a difficult time borrowing anew, because even if it promises to pay high
interest rates, lenders will worry that they will not be repaid. And
with new loans impossible (or exorbitantly expensive), each additional shock will risk bringing further government pillaging. Investors may then shun financial transactions altogether: why deposit
money in banks, for example, if the government is likely to seize it?
In the worst possible case, the whole financial system will wither, not
just the market for government bonds. That is how a government-induced crisis can shackle the financial system for years. France (as we
shall see) learned this bitter lesson after its revolution in 1789, and it
may also be the fate in store for countries that behave like Argentina.

The common themes here—of shocks and indebted governments forced to make dire choices—have surfaced in nation after nation, both now and in the past, even in states that borrowed little or nothing. From the sixteenth through the early nineteenth centuries, for example, the Chinese empire took out practically no loans, in contrast to European states, which during the same period borrowed furiously to finance wars. The European states devoted as much as 60 to 80 percent of their budgets to chronic armed conflict (and even more if war debt and subsidies to allies are taken into account); imperial China spent perhaps only half of what was proportionally a smaller budget on warfare, which in its case was episodic and short-lived, and more on what we might call public welfare. China devoted far more of its resources to famine relief, for instance, than did European states. It maintained public granaries, tried to predict when famines would occur, and moved grain to areas of shortage; European governments never attempted something on this large a scale.[8]

Imperial China not only shifted food from province to province; it also had developed a tax bureaucracy that transferred tax revenues on a scale unheard of in Europe. If a shock struck—a crop failure, for instance—the government did not borrow; rather, it shipped food from a prosperous province to the affected area. If money was required, it could be conveyed via the tax system, and if necessary taxes could be temporarily raised.[9] The empire was large enough that transfers between regions took the place of borrowing. China could thus redistribute resources from province to province—in other words, over space—instead of pushing them off into the future by taking out loans. It thus had less of a reason to borrow.

Most European states were too small to take advantage of this sort of geographic redistribution. If a war erupted, for example, they would have a hard time finding a province that was unaffected. In addition, even the large European states lacked the tax bureaucracies that could raise taxes quickly and transfer resources from one province to another. Moreover, even where bureaucracies were in place, tax increases and the transfer of resources typically aroused daunting political resistance. Thus the nominally absolute rulers of seventeenth-century Spain had great difficulty getting troops and tax increases from regions other than Castile (the heartland of their kingdom, where their authority was strongest), especially when the soldiers and the men were to be sent abroad or to other parts of the Spanish empire.[10] As a result, the Spanish kings borrowed.

Taking out loans enabled European states to rearrange their expenses over time. Imperial China, by contrast, redistributed them geographically. With no significant public debt before the nineteenth century, China had little reason to intervene in financial markets, much less to prey upon them. True, it occasionally tampered with the currency, but this behavior seems trifling by comparison with that of European monarchies, which were much more likely to rely on currency manipulations for emergency revenue. In contrast to many European states, imperial China never defaulted on the public debt—it by and large had none—nor did it plunder banks or financial markets.[11] Indeed it essentially had no opportunity to do so, for large banks and financial markets simply did not exist in China before the late nineteenth century.[12] In Europe, capitalist organizations of this sort had often been ushered into being by government borrowing, at least in the states that did not prey on markets.

If a state borrowed but kept the public debt from rising to extremes, it could do even better than China. By borrowing, it could nurture capital markets, and as long as its debt remained below its danger zone, it would have little reason to plunder the markets it was encouraging. It could end up with a thriving financial system and the ability to borrow to cope with shocks. It might still experience financial crises, but they would not be provoked by government predation.

Eighteenth-century England was such a country. It borrowed to fight wars and raised taxes afterward to pay the interest on the loans.

Parliament could impose new levies if necessary, and the English tax administration collected the money efficiently. If a war broke out, England floated short-term loans to meet the immediate military expenses and then converted these short-term bills into longer-term securities (such as the 3 percent Consol, created in 1751) that were easily sold on the London Stock Exchange. Investors appreciated the liquidity of the government securities and also their minimal risk, for despite all the borrowing, the English loans remained generally safe investments from the 1720s on—evidence that England remained well below its danger threshold. One sign of their safety was the low rate of interest the English government had to pay: at least 2 percent less than what the king of France had to promise on even the least risky of his government's loans—a difference due in large part to the French king's regular habit of defaulting. The existence of these secure and easily traded English securities furthered the development of the London capital market, making it the financial center of Europe by the early 1800s.[13] Crises did occasionally arise, but they did not begin with a government default or some other act of state plunder.[14]

Whereas England remained safely outside its danger zone, other states in early modern Europe were not so prudent, particularly when their debt levels were already extremely high. They piled on more and more debt, ultimately pushing themselves into the danger zone and beyond. Spain is a prime example. The kings of Spain fought war after war in the sixteenth and seventeenth centuries. They battled (not always successfully) to put down rebellions; to weaken their bitter enemies, the kings of France; and to hold together a far-flung empire, which stretched west to Mexico and east as far as the Philippines. By the late sixteenth century, these monarchs expected abundant long-term revenues, including mountains of silver shipped from mines in Mexico and Peru; but the wars demanded immediate financing. They had to borrow, and borrow they did, running up short-term debts with domestic and international bankers—first Germans, then Genoese, and ultimately Portuguese. They also sold negotiable long-term bonds *(juros)*. All this debt was to be repaid with treasure from the Americas, but unfortunately, output from the mines there proved disappointing, and Spanish silver ships sometimes sank or fell victim to pirates and enemy fleets. Faced with such shocks, the Spanish kings suspended payments on the short-term debt and entered into negotiation with the bankers. The outcome, typically, involved giving the bankers long-term bonds in return for their short-term debt—a form of debt consolidation.[15]

The suspensions—there were ten of them between 1557 and 1662—might be considered crises, but it could be argued that the bankers knew what they were getting into, at least initially. They knew the short-term debt was risky. They might earn a high return on it, or they might end up with a suspension. In the latter case, however, they would at least get long-term bonds, which were relatively secure and easily sold. They accordingly charged an appropriately high interest rate on the risky short-term debt—as with junk bonds today—and consoled themselves with this risk premium and the security of the long-term bonds they would get in case payment was suspended on the short-term debt they owned. The suspensions would thus be one of the expected risks of doing business.[16]

The bankers' expectations began to prove radically wrong early in the early seventeenth century, when the long-term bonds themselves became risky. Declining revenues from taxes and the silver mines pushed the Spanish government toward desperate fiscal measures to cope with shocks, such as currency manipulation and tax increases that provoked rebellion.[17] With a government now willing to endure heavy political costs, the long-term bonds suffered too. The government withheld payments due on these and also cut the interest rate, thereby defaulting not just on the bankers but also on the numerous Spanish elite who had purchased *juros* as a safe investment.[18] A suspension now threatened losses far worse than anything the bankers had ever expected, and henceforth any long-term bonds they received after a suspension would be harder to peddle to the public. Although one can debate whether the earlier suspensions were crises, there is no doubt that the events of the seventeenth century qualified, and that the government bore responsibility for them. Spain had now clearly entered its danger zone.

As the crises in Spain spread from the market for public debt into the market for private credit, they wreaked havoc well beyond the holders of government bonds. One of the casualties was the financial nerve center of sixteenth-century Spain—the fairs in the city of Medina del Campo. Merchants and bankers from throughout Europe met twice a year at these fairs to finance extensive domestic and international trade in goods such as wool, which was a crucial raw material in the early modern economy. The bankers also handled money for the government and extended it credit. The crises, however, drove the frightened bankers and merchants away and reduced the Spanish fairs to insignificance.[19]

France provides an even clearer example of how a government-triggered financial crisis can harm not just the market for public debt, but an entire financial system. The crisis in France ended up crippling a major financial market—the Parisian market for long-term credit—for nearly two generations. The crisis began in 1788, when public debt accumulated as a result of years of warfare pushed the government to the brink of bankruptcy and forced Louis XVI to convene the Estates General, a gathering of elites that had not met in nearly two centuries. The meeting of the Estates General marked the beginning of the French Revolution, for within months the delegates were transforming the polity and society of their country. At the outset, the king merely wanted the Estates General to vote a tax increase, but many delegates desired constitutional reforms, such as the creation of a national representative assembly that would meet regularly. Realizing that if they granted the king a tax increase they would lose their political leverage and not get the reforms they wanted, they enacted only stopgap fiscal measures and in fact outlawed a number of existing taxes to prevent the king from raising revenue on his own. For good measure they devised and approved a complicated scheme of tax reform requiring a survey of all land that would take years to complete. With this move they ensured that the king would remain dependent on the representative assembly for a long time and be unable simply to disband it.[20]

The revolutionary government did manage to avert bankruptcy, but its finances worsened in 1792, when a newly elected assembly declared war on Austria, opening a conflict that would convulse nearly all of Europe until 1815. Although Louis XVI was deposed several months later, the hostilities required money immediately, but the revolutionaries had still not put the new tax system into place, and even if they had, collection of taxes would have been problematic because of counterrevolutionary revolts in the provinces. Their revolutionary ideals prevented them from cutting back on spending—doing so would have meant surrendering to the forces of reaction—and borrowing seemed out the question.

In this dire situation, it is hardly surprising that they chose to print money. The revolutionaries controlled the presses that printed the paper money (the revolutionary *assignats*), and they could churn out more *assignats* without pacifying the provinces or creating a bureaucracy of tax collectors. Printing money unleashed inflation, cutting the value of the French currency by 99 percent between 1791 and 1796, but it was their only choice if they wanted to fight a war and remain in political power.[21]

Private borrowers in France took advantage of this situation to pay off their debts in devalued paper money. For legal reasons, nearly all debt in France was nominal—in other words, loan contracts were not indexed against inflation—and most lenders (particularly those who

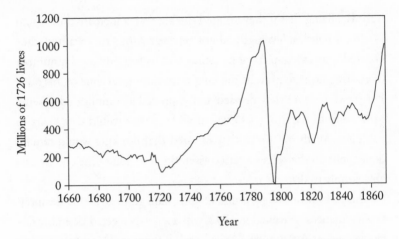

FIGURE 1.1 Outstanding private notarial debt in Paris, 1660–1870. (*Source:* Hoffman, Postel-Vinay, and Rosenthal 2000; the graph, © The University of Chicago, is reproduced with the permission of the publisher, the University of Chicago.)

had made long-term loans) had no way to protect themselves against repayment in *assignats*. As inflation progressed, private debtors could not resist the temptation to repay their loans at a fraction of their original cost. Thus the government financial crisis spread to private markets, and investors in private debt suffered losses far beyond what they ever had considered possible.[22]

The damage was particularly heavy in Paris, where the level of outstanding loans plummeted in the 1790s as borrowers extinguished their debts with worthless *assignats* (Figure 1.1). There, the crisis not only provoked catastrophic losses but also destroyed the very institution that had sustained a thriving market in long-term credit before the Revolution. This institution was an informal one in which a group of financial intermediaries arranged long-term loans by trading information with one another about potential borrowers and lenders and then finding the best match. The intermediaries were the city's notaries, who drew up loan contracts and other legal documents and managed people's wealth. The crisis did not eliminate them, but the threat of still further inflation made potential lenders reluctant to make long-term loans to anyone. That fear, plus continued governmental instability in the nineteenth century, made matching borrowers and lenders practically impossible. As a result the long-term credit market remained crippled until the 1850s.[23]

Financial crises are not always so devastating as the one in Paris, which played itself out like some disaster film. One might even be inclined to dismiss it as atypical, since it occurred in the midst of a political revolution. But in fact nearly all crises have enduring consequences, even when no revolution is under way, because they nearly all lead to long-lasting institutional change. As in Paris, they may destroy old institutions or give birth to new ones, which may be created for political reasons or may arise spontaneously from the reactions of borrowers and lenders. Alternatively, the crises themselves may provoke political reforms, which are particularly likely if the government has triggered all the problems. But once the crisis passes, further institutional reform will be costly or politically difficult, and the institutions put in place after the crisis will influence the economy for years and possibly create still other problems.

One of the causes of the financial crisis in Argentina in 2001, for instance, was a government currency board set up ten years earlier to cope with a crisis of government-induced hyperinflation. Establishing the currency board helped stop raging hyperinflation by pegging the Argentine peso to the dollar, but it hampered Argentina when several shocks battered the country in the late 1990s. The first was a rising dollar, which carried the peso higher and priced Argentine goods out of foreign markets. Then neighboring Brazil devalued its currency, making Brazilian goods a bargain and further cutting demand for Argentina's exports. The loss of export markets exacerbated a recession already under way in Argentina and ultimately helped push the country to default on its public debt.[24] One response, obviously, would have been to devalue the Argentine peso, but the institutional reform adopted after the previous crisis—the currency board—ruled that out. The previous reform limited what the government could do and in that sense contributed to the next crisis, in 2001. The long-term consequences of the 2001 crisis are still unknown. Argentina's economy did recover enough by the end of 2005 for the government to repay its debt to the International Monetary Fund. But this repayment has left the government with fewer restraints on its spending and paying a higher interest rate on the new loans it has taken out. In the meantime, Argentina has still not solved its persistent fiscal problems; thus the door remains open to new crises, which will be particularly likely if commodity prices fall.[25]

What happens when a government has amassed debts so massive that investors assume it will prey upon financial markets? If predation is expected (and impossible to insure against), investors will not lend to the government, no matter what interest rate it promises. What good is a high rate of interest if the government defaults and pays neither the interest nor the principal? The promise of high interest is simply not credible once the government reaches this extreme, for then investors know that default will be a tempting way to deal with shocks—more tempting at least than raising taxes or cutting spending. At the very least, the market for public debt will shrivel up, and private capital markets may wither too, if investors fear that continued government predation will threaten private contracts in ways that cannot be insured against. Suppose, for example, that lenders expect the government to unleash inflation. If usury laws and other legal restrictions keep them from indexing loans or charging a higher interest rate, then they will cease lending to private borrowers, and the private credit market will suffer. That was the situation in France in the early nineteenth century. Similarly, in Argentina in 2002, the freeze on bank accounts (and accompanying restrictions on foreign currency transactions) temporarily wiped out the short-term credit that sustained business dealings. The supply of goods dried up, particularly if they were imported, such as medicine. Even hospitals ran short.[26]

When a government mauls the public debt market it can thereby easily injure private capital markets too. Government predation will not always cause such harm, but the effects of its pillaging will endure, in both the public and private markets. The reason is that the government spoliation will trigger a financial crisis, and the crisis will, in most cases, be followed by reforms. The reforms will change the institutions governing financial markets, and the new institutions will be difficult to modify until the next crisis strikes. Worse yet, the reformed institutions may even help provoke the new crisis, because they will be designed to prevent the past crisis, not the one to come.

Since crises can do so much harm, obviously states should avoid the massive levels of public debt that make financial debacles likely. One might perhaps wonder whether a state should avoid debt altogether, for then it would have great leeway to borrow to deal with any shocks that strike. But if a state refrains from borrowing altogether, its capital markets may never develop, and the private economy will suffer.

The danger clearly lies at the extremes. As we shall see, that is often the case with financial markets. In this instance, one extreme is to refrain from borrowing altogether, which prevents financial markets from developing; the other extreme is to pile up enormous levels of government debt, which raises the odds that political leaders will prey upon investors. There are a variety of ways to avoid these two extremes, but political leaders may have little incentive to do so, particularly when they are confronted by a shock that demands an immediate solution. No leader wants to lose a war or be voted out of office in a recession, and when faced with such a shock, he may decide to borrow more or even to attack the capital markets, regardless of the long-term consequences for others.

Political Regimes and Moving a State's Danger Zone

So far, our argument has turned on the level of public debt—in particular, how close the debt level is relative to a danger zone that is peculiar to every state. If public debt rises into the danger zone—if, in other words, it veers toward one of our extremes—then the state will prey upon financial markets. It may default on its debt, tamper with currency, or interfere with financial transactions in other ways. In short, it will provoke a financial crisis, as in Argentina, with consequences that may endure for years.

But what if the state's danger zone moves? It certainly can move if a state takes steps to raise taxes, cut spending, and reassure its creditors. The trouble, however, is that these steps must convince potential lenders that their loans will be repaid and that they will not become victims of inflation, confiscation, or some other financial disaster. The key here is changing the incentives political leaders face, so that they will not be tempted to prey upon financial markets, at least until government debt rises to a much higher level than in the past. Such incentives necessarily rest on political change—political change that will induce leaders to repay government loans or discourage them from defaulting on the state's debts. Typically, they involve reforms that render tax increases or expenditure cuts less painful politically. But they may also involve ensuring that the cash from tax revenues or expenditure cuts actually goes to pay off government loans—perhaps by raising the political costs of government default.[27]

Change of this sort is rarely easy. Argentina might have avoided its crisis, for instance, if the provincial governments had been forced to reduce spending; they, after all, were running up much of the public debt. Doing so, however, would have meant crossing powerful state governors and laying off provincial employees—actions with heavy political costs.[28] Nor are such difficulties peculiar to recent times. In 1713 the cost of repeated wars had driven the Dutch Republic to suspend interest payments on its debt—a sign of a looming financial crisis. To avert the crisis, the republic could have moved its danger zone further away by hiking taxes and then using the increased revenue to pay off the government's creditors. But boosting taxes would have required a centralized tax authority and the enforcement of uniform tax rates—controversial steps in a country that was actually only a federation of nearly autonomous provinces. The uniform, centralized tax system frightened provinces that had long ducked their fair share of taxation, and when they blocked the fiscal reforms, the republic had to cut back its greatest expense—the military. Thanks to the military cuts, it dodged the financial crisis but paid a heavy price, for it tumbled from the ranks of the dominant European military powers.[29]

Nonetheless, some states have managed to move their danger zones further away. They then run less of chance of having a shock catapult them toward the extreme levels of debt where victimizing financial markets becomes attractive. England was one of the first, in the aftermath of the Glorious Revolution (1688–89), which deposed King James II and established parliamentary supremacy over legislation and taxation. Before the revolution, English monarchs were often unable to get lenders to make loans voluntarily. Afterward the English government could borrow huge sums of money, all at lower and lower interest rates: between 1695 and 1730, its outstanding debt rose 647 percent, while the risk premium on its loans disappeared. The political changes had clearly moved back the boundaries of England's danger zone, but the country's financial revolution required more than just a mightier Parliament that could now prevent the crown from preying on lenders. It necessitated higher taxes as well and an effective fiscal bureaucracy to collect them. England expanded and professionalized its fiscal bureaucracy, and with Parliament legitimizing higher taxes, the government's income more than doubled between 1690 and 1714. The financial revolution also depended on keeping Parliament itself from abusing lenders. Here the key was a political party—the Whigs—in which government lenders played a noteworthy role. The Whigs helped ensure that tax revenues would go to repay loans and convinced lenders that the state's promises to repay its loans were credible.[30]

Other states in western Europe pushed back their danger zones in the early nineteenth century, under pressure (at least initially) from nearly constant warfare during the French Revolution and the Napoleonic Empire. The staggering cost of the fighting impelled states, most of them absolute monarchies, to increase taxes, and there were two ways to do so. One was for the monarch to cede enough control over taxation and spending to a representative assembly. Although the assemblies were not democratic, they legitimized taxation and had an easier time imposing new levies. In the process, the monarch of course lost some of his authority, but in return he boosted the state's potential income and hence the possible military resources at his disposal.[31] The other path to increased tax revenue was to reform the fiscal bureaucracy and make it levy taxes uniformly across the various principalities that European monarchs typically ruled. Here too the state's net revenue rose.[32]

One might expect that the new tax revenue would have fanned the flames of war. But wars actually became rarer and shorter in nineteenth-century Europe, after Napoleon was gone. The principal European powers were at war 60 percent of the time in the seventeenth century and 36 percent of the time in the eighteenth century, but only 29.5 percent of the time in the nineteenth, and much of that involved Napoleon before 1815. Furthermore, the wars fought in the nineteenth century ended much faster than they had in the eighteenth, and as a result battlefield deaths relative to the population dropped sevenfold.[33]

One reason war had subsided was that the costs of defeat were now higher, particularly for the monarchs and royal appointees who still directed foreign policy. In the seventeenth and eighteenth centuries, kings who lost wars retained their thrones; from the revolutionary period on, they stood a much higher chance of being deposed.[34] It is no wonder then that they were willing to sacrifice some power in return for resources that could be used to defend their thrones. A second reason for the declining severity of war was the political change that had shifted danger zones in states across western Europe. Kings whose ancestors had reigned absolutely now shared power with representative assemblies, and in many ways these constitutional monarchies were little different from republics. States of this sort may simply have been less prone than absolute monarchies to fighting one another.[35]

The lesson of all this European history is this: if enough states move the boundaries of their danger zones by adopting representative institutions, then the very shocks that bring on financial crises will grow rarer, at least when the shocks are wars. The political change needed to move a danger zone is, of course, never easy. It incites opposition: to higher taxes, to reduced expenditures, and to constitutional changes that rein in the authority of absolute monarchs, provincial governors, or other powerful political leaders. The essential thing is getting the incentives right, so that leaders are no longer tempted to prey upon financial markets, at least until government debt rises to a much higher level than in the past.[36]

Although these historical examples may at first glance seem irrelevant to the modern world, the politics of debt levels is by and large the same today, particularly in developing countries. The shocks may differ—today they are less likely to be wars than recessions or shifts in commodity prices—but the political logic of extreme debt levels and movable danger zones retains its iron grip. We have seen as much in Argentina, but a similar story could be told about the impoverished countries of sub-Saharan Africa, which desperately need to develop effective bureaucracies that can furnish the public services needed for modern economic growth, from courts and schools to reliable power and transportation networks. Governments, after all, need not just prey upon capital markets; as we shall see, they can do good as well, and the public services they furnish are often essential for economic growth. Sadly, in many current African states, government bureaus are filled with political appointees, who do not provide the roads, education, electricity, and legal decisions that would spur growth. Worse, they and their politically influential patrons will resist if money is taken from their wages to pay for these public services, and the cost of their salaries boosts the pressure on governments to loot capital markets when shocks strike.[37] It is all reminiscent of the troubles European states had in establishing bureaucracies to funnel taxes to the public service that mattered most in early modern Europe—a strong military.

CHAPTER 2

Information and Crises

Ａs stocks plummeted from their 2000 peak, American business was rocked by a wave of corporate scandals. Perhaps the most notorious one struck the Houston energy trader, Enron, which filed for bankruptcy late in 2001, having exaggerated its profits by what the company's board later claimed was nearly a billion dollars. Deceptive dealings and misleading accounting had exaggerated Enron's earnings, and they soon attracted a swarm of congressional subpoenas and criminal investigations. Nor was Enron alone. In July 2002 the telecommunications giant WorldCom collapsed amid similar charges, edging Enron aside for dubious distinction as America's largest corporate deadbeat. Serious scandals pounded other firms as well, from Xerox and Tyco to Adelphia Communications. Meanwhile scores of public traded companies in the United States restated their earnings downward: 233 in the year 2000, and 270 in 2001, up from only 116 in 1997.[1]

Even professional investors felt deceived, all the more so since top executives at Enron and WorldCom had unloaded shares in their companies before the price collapsed. "You had highly promotional CEOs saying things were great yet selling just massive amounts of stock," said one portfolio manager, a contradiction he considered "virtually impossible to reconcile."[2] Lower-level employees, many of whom had invested their life savings in company shares, felt they had been misled, even though one would normally expect them to be particularly knowledgeable about their employers. As a former Enron human resources executive who had lost nearly all of his two-million-dollar pension account explained, employees had not been "properly informed" about what was "going on" at Enron and so could not make "intelligent decisions" about investments in the firm. In his words, "If we were given the proper information, which we weren't, . . . about earnings and the internal happenings in the company, we would have made a totally different decision."[3]

Foreign investors found the doctored accounting and meretricious information spread by rogue corporations particularly shocking. As one German portfolio manager declared, "There is unanimous agreement that the U.S. is not the best place to invest anymore."[4] Americans had bragged that their accounting standards were superlative; if the rest of the world wanted to enjoy a stock market boom and similar economic growth, they should get on the bandwagon and adopt the same accounting rules. Large companies and foreign investors had bought the argument and flocked to the United States.

As the stock market collapsed and the scandals surfaced, investment professionals in the United States began to fret over the toll the scandals were taking on the country's financial markets and its reputation as a safe haven for capital. To restore faith in American corporations, the legendary investor Warren E. Buffett called for an end to the most deceptive accounting practices, and in a similar appeal for reforms, the chief executive of the investment firm Goldman Sachs argued that CEOs should be required to hold on to their company stock so that they could not profit from insider information.[5]

The recurrent theme in all the scandals was information—information that not all investors held. The complaint against the corporate executives who sold company stock was that they had known the true situation, whereas other investors—and even their own employees—had been left in the dark. Such unevenly held information—"asymmetric information" in the jargon of economics—also lay at the bottom of the accounting scandals. Earnings reports and other accounting data have of course never been exact and are always subject to manipulation. But the doctoring had now reached unexpected proportions, casting an unparalleled burden of doubt on corporate financial reports and distressing even sophisticated portfolio managers and investment bankers.

Such problems with information are hardly peculiar to the United States; similar scandals have rocked Asian and European companies, such as Ahold in the Netherlands, Parmalat in Italy, and Vivendi in France, which, if the charges are true, deserves a prize for cheekiness for pressuring its auditors to fire an accountant after he objected to the way the company reported its earnings.[6] Nor are scandals of this sort a novelty of the twenty-first century. Asymmetric information worried investors long ago in medieval Europe, and informational problems have repeatedly provoked financial crises: in the London South Sea Bubble of 1720; in the Latin American mining stock crash of 1825; in the collapse of mortgage lenders in nineteenth-century France, America, and Australia; and in a host of other panics and financial disasters that have shaped the evolution of capital markets down to our own day. These dramas from history actually prove to be extraordinarily illuminating here. Indeed, they give us a firmer grip on the role that information plays in financial crises, because they have taken place long enough ago for us to see their long-run consequences. They thus reveal eventual truths still hidden in contemporary crises, whose effects are as yet unseen.

The first step here is to understand why information has always mattered so much in capital markets. That understanding leads, quite naturally, to two questions. First, what sort of financial markets are most likely to be battered by informational problems and the crises they bring on? Second, how do crises redirect people's attention from one kind of information to another? The answers to these questions will teach us two lessons. In the first place, we will learn that problems of asymmetric information worsen as capital markets grow in size, even though larger markets bring a number of benefits. The advantages that the large markets offer certainly outweigh the drawbacks, but the two are inseparable—an instance of the good and bad that are always bound up in financial markets. As a result, although a small market is usually an extreme to avoid, a large market is more likely to witness a crisis brought on by informational problems. Furthermore, the lessons that borrowers and lenders or investors and entrepreneurs draw from a crisis are likely to be quite different in a large capital market than in a small one.

We will also learn that financial crises alter the value of information in ways shaped by the accidents of history. Crises can drastically reduce the value of some information, driving investors to pull back from certain investments. But they can also make the reputation of firms that manage to survive a crisis without breaking their financial commitments. They can do the same for financial intermediaries whose advice enables investors to escape disaster. These intermediaries can then help a financial market to overcome a problem stemming from asymmetric information and allow it to expand beyond its old boundaries. Each financial disaster will thus privilege certain intermediaries and investments and ruin others, and as the market evolves, its shape and workings will reflect its own unique history of crises.

Asymmetric Information in Financial Markets

Nearly all investments are risky. Even a deposit in a savings account carries some risk: banks can collapse or lose track of money, and insurance for depositors may not exist. Withdrawing funds can be difficult too if (as in Argentina at the end of 2001) the government freezes bank accounts or the bank shuts its door because it has suddenly become insolvent. The investor is then vulnerable to losses from inflation or devaluation. The chance of loss is of course even greater with other investments.

The trouble is that investors do not know what the return on their investments will be. In other words, they do not know whether the money they have advanced will be paid back, or whether they will earn any profit on it. In most cases, all they can rely on are estimates of the chances for high or low rates of return, or even for a negative return if they lose some of the money they have put up. The estimates, which may derive from subjective hunches or from extensive research, will all be based on information that the investors consider relevant to their decisions: a company's earning reports, a stock market analyst's recommendations, or an entrepreneur's collateral and his track record of repaying previous loans. That is why information matters so much in financial transactions, for without it, investors are in the dark.

Investors do have some remedies here. They can diversify their holdings—investing in a mutual fund, for example, rather than owning shares in a single company—and they have in fact been doing so for centuries. Modern financial theory has developed sophisticated techniques for helping investors diversify their portfolios in an optimal way, but doing so requires information about the likely returns on all the holdings an investor might own. Without accurate information, any estimates are valueless.[7]

Ideally, all investors will have the same information. Yet difficulties can crop up even when they do. As work in experimental economics has shown, investors can all acquire the same information yet still be hobbled by erroneous beliefs. For instance, even if they all know what the fundamental value of a financial asset is, they may believe that other investors will pay more for it. That belief can then drive the price up above the asset's fundamental value, generating a speculative bubble and a subsequent market crash.[8]

As a practical matter, however, relevant information is almost never evenly shared. An entrepreneur, for instance, usually has a better idea of whether he will repay a loan than does the bank that lends him the money. A CEO of a publicly traded company usually knows more about his company's earnings than most shareholders. This sort of asymmetric information in fact provokes many crises and generates enormous trouble for financial markets, and, as we shall see, it explains why financial intermediation is so important.[9]

To see how serious such problems can be, consider the complaints that American executives have enriched themselves at the expense of uninformed shareholders—complaints that have grown ever louder during the recent corporate scandals. Executives at Enron engaged in such behavior—so the firm's board eventually admitted—and their actions triggered more than two dozen indictments and numerous criminal convictions.[10] Yet the trouble, as the business press noted, extended well beyond Enron and infected companies untainted by scandal.[11] In particular, it cast suspicion on the practice (which grew increasingly common in the United States in the 1990s) of paying top executives by awarding them stock options. Typically the options give an executive the right to purchase his firm's stock at a predetermined price. If the value of the firm's stock rises above this price, the executive can realize a huge profit by being able to buy shares at a discount. The goal of the options is to align the executive's interests with those of his shareholders. Since he benefits when the stock rises, he would seem to have an incentive to maximize his shareholders' wealth.

That is the way the options plans are supposed to work, at least in theory. But in practice they have typically had a number of curious features that cast doubt on their effectiveness. Perhaps the most notorious is the policy, common to most options packages, of rewarding an executive for a rise in his company's share price whether or not the increase has anything to do with his actions. In particular, the executive will benefit if his company's share price jumps during a bull market, even if he is not responsible for the increase, and even if his company is lagging behind its competitors.[12] This anomaly and others like it have led some experts to argue that the options grants are really designed not to maximize shareholder wealth, but rather to allow executives to siphon off an inordinate share of profits without outraging shareholders. Many shareholders are in the dark about the details of the option plans, the critics maintain; others are satisfied by the appearance it gives of creating proper incentives. The result is that shareholders end up being ripped off because they have less information. And their losses can go well beyond the excess compensation the executive receives, because he will not be working under a contract that encourages him to maximize shareholder wealth.[13] He will therefore devote too many resources to dubious projects that disguise his malversations and too few to true profit maximization.

Informational problems of this sort, which involve duplicitous behavior by a manager, have a long history, and one potential solution, since at least the Middle Ages, has been to write a contract for the executive that keeps him from defrauding shareholders or other investors. The options packages themselves, however, were supposed to be precisely this sort of contract: they were supposed to ensure that the management would work in the shareholders' interests. What kept them from working properly were the very details that many shareholders overlooked, particularly during a bull market. One remedy would be to give experts all the necessary information and have them watch over the shareholders' interests. In American corporations, the board of directors has this duty, but the directors themselves—so some observers complain—tend too often to defer to management.

Management that is knavish in its pursuit of self-interest is not the only informational problem facing investors. Indeed, even if the management works in investors' interests, asymmetric information can still cripple financial markets. Consider, for instance, what happened to credit markets in France at the beginning of the nineteenth century, in the aftermath of the devastating inflation of the French Revolution. Lenders, as we know, feared that inflation would return, and they consequently limited their lending to borrowers whom they knew well, and most refused to make long-term loans. Many of the borrowers, however, wanted long-term loans to fund construction projects and capital-intensive industrialization. Local lenders could not raise enough money for their projects, and even if they could, the short-term loans that they offered imposed a huge risk on borrowers of having funds dry up in, say, the middle of a huge construction project.

In this situation, nearly everyone agreed that it was worth creating a new bank, the Banque Territoriale, which would raise money at the national level and lend it out via long-term loans. Established in 1799 and based in Paris, the bank mobilized capital by selling long-term bonds and attracting depositors. It then made long-term loans to anyone in France it deemed worthy of credit. The new bank seemed to have a bright future, but after expanding rapidly, it failed within only a few years. What in fact toppled it was asymmetric information. The bank, it turns out, lacked the information needed to do a good job of evaluating its borrowers' creditworthiness. In particular, it had no access to the credit histories that were used by local lenders and by the loan brokers who screened potential borrowers for them. This state of affairs left local lenders and loan brokers able to retain the borrowers who were trustworthy while foisting all the poor risks onto the Banque Territoriale. With a loan portfolio full of deadbeats and dubious collateral, it is hardly a surprise that the institution failed.[14]

The informational problem here stemmed from what we might call blindness or ignorance—in this case, the bank's inability to tell what sort of lenders it was dealing with. The problem was not insurmountable, for a mere half-century later, an innovative French bank, the Crédit Foncier de France, succeeded where the Banque Territoriale had failed. Like the Banque Territoriale, the Crédit Foncier both raised money nationally and made loans nationally, yet the details of its strategy were different. In particular, the Crédit Foncier demanded that its borrowers register the mortgages on the collateral backing their loans with the state lien authority, and it used the lien authority's records to inspect its borrowers' credit histories and thus determine whether they were good credit risks. Use of the mortgage registry imposed a fixed cost that was prohibitive for small borrowers, and the policy on collateral and credit histories restricted lending to those who were the best credit risks. But the Crédit Foncier could attract these sterling borrowers because it could make large loans for long durations. The crucial difference between the Crédit Foncier and the earlier Banque Territoriale was better information.[15] Its success spawned imitators elsewhere in Europe and in Latin America.

Could the Banque Territoriale have survived simply by charging higher interest rates to make up for the losses on its risky loans? Probably not. Although higher rates would have driven away creditworthy borrowers who could get loans at lower rates from local lenders, they would not have affected deadbeats, who had no intention of repaying either the principal or interest on their loans. Higher interest rates could thus have actually worsened the Banque Territoriale's situation, by driving away its best customers and attracting more of the worst. In this instance, charging higher interest rates would not have made up for the lack of information.

At one extreme, the sort of troubles with asymmetric information that the Banque Territoriale faced can be so formidable that markets simply do not exist.[16] At the other, the problems are negligible. Usually, though, the situation lies somewhere in between, at least in financial markets: the market in question does function, but information is imperfect, crises arise periodically, and institutional innovators (such as the Crédit Foncier) emerge to solve the informational problems that caused the previous crisis.

It is easy to see how crises can strike such markets and why lenders have fallen victim to such problems time and time again. Imagine, for instance, that along with several other investors you are making loans to entrepreneurs, some of whom are the sort of deadbeats who bedeviled the Banque Territoriale. Imagine as well that neither you nor the other lenders can tell the deadbeats from creditworthy borrowers. If the number of deadbeats is not too large, then you and the other lenders will simply raise the interest rates you charge to compensate yourselves for the occasional losses from the deadbeats, and the credit market will function as normal. Suppose, however, that you alone among the lenders suddenly develop the ability to distinguish deadbeats from good credit risks. You can therefore limit your business to borrowers who are certain to repay and push the bad credit risks off on your competition. If you slough off enough of these miserable credit risks, the other lenders will be driven out of business as the bad credit risks borrow from them and then default. With mass defaults and lenders exiting or going bankrupt themselves, you can easily generate a crisis.

The tie between asymmetric information and crises is one of the major strands of the literature on problems in capital markets. It is also one of the major strands of our argument. As this and later chapters will show, asymmetric information is not just a major cause of financial crises; it is also a significant impetus for innovation in capital markets. Many financial institutions arise precisely in order to resolve troubles with asymmetric information, often just after a crisis has belted a capital market. It is then that actors fashion institutions to overcome informational obstacles and prevent crises in the future.

There are an enormous variety of informational problems and an even wider variety of possible institutional responses. Economic theory cannot prescribe a unique antidote for asymmetric information, for as yet it cannot tell us what institutions perform best in real-world financial markets. And even if it could do so, the advice it offered might fall on deaf ears, particularly if no one could capture the benefits from creating a better institution. Yet despite all the variety, historical solutions for informational problems have often had several common features. One frequent remedy is to write a new contract that provides better incentives. The corporate scandals in the United States, for instance, have already prompted a search for better ways to write contracts for executives—all in the hope of reducing management double-dealing in the future.[17]

A second common remedy, particularly when ignorance is the root of the problem, is to screen investment projects before advancing any money. That was one of the tactics adopted by the Crédit Foncier: it sifted through potential borrowers' credit histories, just as credit card companies do with retail borrowers today. The screening rules then become institutions themselves, since they too impose constraints on behavior.

A third antidote is to monitor investments after they are made in order to provide investors with updated information about what is happening to their money. Today auditors and securities analysts furnish this sort of information to banks and to stock market investors. These informational specialists help overcome asymmetries by collecting information and funneling it to uninformed actors. Other information specialists (such as modern credit reporting agencies and the officials who compiled the credit histories used by the Crédit Foncier) can help with screening. Whatever they do, their advantage is that they can provide information at lower cost precisely because they specialize.

In financial markets, the informational specialists often turn out to be financial intermediaries. In both eighteenth-century France and eighteenth-century England, for example, most mortgage loans were brokered by legal officials who had information about land and other collateral. The legal officials—notaries in France, attorneys and scriveners in England—knew which borrowers had enough collateral to be good credit risks, and their legal business also brought them into contact with potential lenders. They began by drawing up the loan contracts but eventually ended up bridging the information gap between borrowers and lenders and arranging the actual loans.[18]

One potential risk with all these specialists and intermediaries is that they themselves may exploit the very informational problems they are supposed to solve and take advantage of uninformed individuals who use their services. Obviously, double-dealing of this sort creates yet another asymmetry. A major complaint during the corporate scandals in the United States was that auditors were too accommodating toward companies like Enron that provided them with millions in nonaudit business. The auditors hesitated to object to dubious accounting if it threatened their fees from this other business, and they were therefore willing to certify financial statements that they knew were misleading. Or, worse yet, they eagerly participated in such financial legerdemain because of the big fees it brought in. Similar charges were made against securities analysts who touted the stocks of corporations like Enron or WorldCom. Expressing skepticism about those stocks would have endangered business that these corporations gave to the investment banks employing the analysts. One of the rare analysts who dared to raise doubts about Enron did in fact soon find himself without a job.[19]

Duplicitous information specialists can do more than simply accelerate the collapse of the stock market, as seemed to happen with the American corporate scandals in 2001 and 2002. Over a century earlier, similar misbehavior had in fact laid low the mortgage market in western America, putting hundreds of mortgage companies out of business and making it far more difficult and costly for American farmers to take out long-term loans, as the economic historian Kenneth Snowden has shown.[20] The informational obstacle at the time was distance. Although the western farmers offered their land as collateral to secure their loans, the distance between potential lenders and potential borrowers made it costly for the former to verify an appraisal. Negotiating with a farmer who defaulted on his loan was costly too, as was foreclosure.

In the late nineteenth century, mortgage companies and then insurance firms slowly surmounted this obstacle and started to move funds west. Both had local loan agents appraise collateral and take responsibility for negotiations or foreclosure proceedings with delinquent loans. When the land market boomed in the 1880s, however, more mortgage lenders entered the business, and some began hiring inexperienced agents and approving poorly secured loans. Competition drove even the better companies to follow suit, lest they lose customers and loan agents. The key information specialists—the agents—were now ignoring the information they held about the value of collateral in order to earn higher fees, and their lax behavior was stuffing loan portfolios with dubious mortgages. When drought finally punctured the land boom in the late 1880s, borrowers defaulted in droves. Although the insurance companies survived, the crisis drove nearly all the mortgage companies out of business and left the western mortgage market in shambles.[21]

There are a variety of ways of keeping information specialists in line and reducing the problems associated with their misbehavior. The right contract may induce an information specialist to do a diligent job. A loan agent in the American West, for instance, earned no commissions if his mortgage company rejected potential borrowers he had screened, and he personally bore the costs of dealing with defaults and foreclosures for delinquent loans. If he walked away from bad loans, he risked losing future commissions from his original mortgage company and difficulty getting any other company to hire him. His contract thus motivated him to screen loan applicants carefully. Such seemingly perfect incentives broke down, however, during the land boom, when new entrants to the mortgage business lowered their standards. Companies that did not approve poorly secured loans began losing customers and agents, and eventually the agents themselves stopped screening carefully, knowing that dubious loans would be approved and that other mortgage companies would still hire them if their borrowers defaulted.[22]

Information specialists and financial intermediaries can also be made to toe the line if misbehavior will cost them heavily in the future. The cost can be forfeiture of a bond or, if the misbehavior can be proved in court, payment of damages to plaintiffs in a lawsuit. It can be a ruined reputation and the loss of future business. Arthur Andersen, the accounting firm that audited Enron, confronted both sorts of penalties, which ultimately ruined it. It faced lawsuits from Enron's shareholders and creditors and, even worse, the flight of clients after it was indicted for obstruction of justice.

Information specialists may also fear government sanctions if they misbehave. It was the indictment, after all, that started Andersen's collapse by frightening away its clients.[23] But government policing and regulation can themselves entail still other informational problems. Although investors (and borrowers too) may want public officials to act in their interests, a politician or bureaucrat may end up listening instead to the information specialists he is supposed to regulate. Before the wave of corporate scandals in the United States, American accounting firms had successfully lobbied against regulations that would have limited their fees from providing nonaudit services to corporate clients—fees that were one of the principal reasons why the accountants certified the dubious financial statements.[24]

Nonetheless, the services provided by financial intermediaries and information specialists can be extremely valuable, provided all the potential problems can be held in check. After all, it would be wasteful for each saver to collect information on his own investments, if only because scores of investors would then be repeating the same information search. Furthermore, information specialists can gather the information cheaply because they specialize. Setting them up does of course entail a significant up-front cost. Loan agents in the late nineteenth-century American West had to be hired and trained, as did the notaries who arranged loans in eighteenth-century France. The same holds for modern accountants. This up-front cost will be prohibitively high in a small capital market, but it can easily be defrayed in a large one, where it can be spread over numerous investors and entrepreneurs. The same holds for other remedies for coping with asymmetric information in financial markets, such as screening investments or monitoring entrepreneurs and corporate managers.

Asymmetric information thus bedevils financial markets, and scores of institutions have arisen to cope with the resulting problems—and each institution has its own difficulties. Troubles with asymmetric information are in turn compounded by the tendency of investors to learn slowly in the short run and to learn too well in the long run—in other words, to underreact initially and to overreact in the long run. In particular, they are likely to relax their information requirements when markets are booming and then demand much more information once a crisis is past. Journalists detected such a trend in the United States once corporate scandals were past and stock markets began to revive, and surveys of investors seemed to bear out their suspicions. Investors had been deeply worried when the scandals broke and the market was collapsing. But as the market climbed in 2003, one journalist remarked that "many investors already seem less concerned about whether the executives running their companies are back on the straight and narrow. Rising stock prices, after all, hide a multitude of sins."[25]

This tendency may reflect the time it takes market participants to correct mistaken beliefs even when there is no asymmetric information—a finding of recent work in experimental economics.[26] Or it may stem from the stubborn psychology of human learning and the inclination many of us have to take a striking event like a crisis as representative of a new future trend. A salient event like a crisis whips us to attention, particularly when it is being bandied about in the news. But when markets are rising and public discussion has moved on to other topics, the memories of past crises may be shouldered aside by more recent events and by the confidence produced by a sustained market boom.[27]

In any case, difficulties with informational asymmetries will not be swept away by better technology. Newspapers, packet boats, rapid stagecoaches, and telegraph and telephone lines all cut the time it previously took to move information from one individual to another, just as Internet connections have in more recent years. But none of these technological advances ever eliminated financial crises. Price gaps between one region of the globe and another may have diminished, and crises may be resolved faster today, but informational differences—between corporate insiders and uninformed shareholders, for instance—persist. While we may all know more than our ancestors, the information at our disposal is still only partial and unevenly shared. Ignorance and double-dealing troubled investors centuries ago, and the remedies they turned to—incentive-laden contracts, screening of collateral, monitoring of agents and entrepreneurs, and the use of information specialists and financial intermediaries—resemble those we utilize today. The details will be different in distinct financial markets, but one constant remains: none of the antidotes has ever driven painful financial crises into extinction.

Crises in Large Markets

Are there any financial markets that are untainted by asymmetric information? Yes, but nearly all are small. By itself, small size cannot guarantee protection against difficulties with asymmetric information. If it could, you would happily lend money to any perfect stranger; and, once bound by a loan, the two of you would form the tiniest market possible, one with only two participants. But some diminutive financial markets do escape informational asymmetries, simply because they are so tiny that information flows freely, all the participants know one another, and asymmetries quickly disappear.

A situation like this arose in the local building associations that were an important alternative source of mortgages in nineteenth- and early twentieth-century America. Unlike the mortgage companies that mobilized capital in Europe and on the East Coast and then moved it west, the building associations raised their money in the very communities where they made their loans, rarely straying beyond the neighborhood where they operated. Members of the associations pooled their savings and lent one another money, and they then made sure that all borrowers repaid what they owed. They knew the value of the local property that served as collateral and could judge whether fellow members would be able to keep up with loan payments. They had little problem with management misbehavior either: the officers and member committees that took care of administering the loans faced social retribution if they failed to do their jobs.[28]

Minute credit markets of this sort were not peculiar to nineteenth-century America. Similar markets exist today in developing countries—in Nigerian villages, for instance, where they provide not mortgages but short-term loans that tide villagers over in bad times. Here too information flows freely. Borrowers and lenders know one another well, with 97 percent of the funds lent passing between neighbors and relatives.[29]

Because they are uncontaminated by informational asymmetries, such markets may sound positively idyllic; yet they inevitably have severe limitations, which make them an extreme that one would normally want to avoid. Relying on fellow villagers for help in bad times does little when a drought or flood broadsides an entire community, because you cannot borrow much when all the potential lenders are themselves suffering. And if loans are restricted to neighbors and relatives, then many creditworthy borrowers will go without credit, and many rewarding investments will remain unfunded.

That was one of the problems confronting American mortgage markets in the late nineteenth century. Lenders such as the local building associations could make loans in their own community, but they could not move capital long distances. Although they provided 24 percent of all the American mortgage funding furnished by intermediaries in 1890–1893, they could not shift capital west and thereby bring down the gap in interest rates that separated the East Coast from the Middle West and the Plains. Neither could another important mortgage provider, mutual savings banks, which like the building associations restricted their lending to local markets in which information flowed freely. The only organizations that could fund mortgages from afar were the mortgage companies and insurance firms, whose loan agents' misbehavior caused them severe problems. As a result, borrowers in the West paid dearly, if they could get mortgages; eastern investors missed an opportunity for higher rates of return; and the interest rate in the West may have been as much as 2 percent higher than in the East.[30]

By comparison, bigger financial markets will often have enormous advantages. By tapping a broader set of investors, they can mobilize more capital than any small market can. And by giving investors a chance to diversify their portfolios—as financial specialists recommend—they spare them the risk of lending in a small market and thereby cut the cost of capital. But with these advantages comes asymmetric information, for in bigger markets, borrowers and lenders, or investors and entrepreneurs, are much less likely to know one another well. It is also less likely that they will be thoroughly familiar with all the new financial instruments that are traded and all the new investment projects that are funded when financial markets grow. The resulting asymmetric information is an inescapable byproduct of the impersonal trade that provides the gains in larger markets—the gains from having more investors and a more diversified set of borrowers too.

The informational asymmetries can then usher in crises, the inevitable companions of greater market size. They are the bad side of the enormous good that bigger markets can do. The larger financial markets have a wider variety of crises simply because the market participants—not just borrowers and lenders or investors and entrepreneurs, but financial intermediaries too—know less about one another and less about all the financial products they trade, leaving more room for people to take advantage of what others do not know. Crises also occur in small financial markets, but they usually have a common cause—lack of diversification. In a big market, the causes are more varied: ignorance, management double-dealing, and a host of other informational problems. With so many possible causes, the lessons will vary in a complicated way, depending on institutional details and historical accidents.

Crises in large capital markets can also be provoked by the sheer difficulty of getting accustomed to new financial instruments. The trouble here may simply be the time it takes investors to revise mistaken beliefs about a new situation even when they all have access to the same information.[31] For example, although all the investors may have the same unpromising information about the fundamental value of a new financial asset, each may believe that fellow investors overvalue it and is therefore likely to bid its price up. The result can be a rise in the asset's price, followed by a resounding crash when investors realize that the process can no longer be sustained.

That in large part is what happened during the famous South Sea Bubble, which swelled and then burst on the London Stock Exchange in 1720, when shares of the South Sea Company jumped from a price of 130.50 at the end of January to 950 on July 1, and then fell to 300 in late September, leaving scores of investors ruined.[32] The origin of the bubble was an ambitious scheme to swap public debt for shares in the South Sea Company, a government-established trading firm that in the process became the early modern equivalent of a modern mutual fund. The attraction for the owners of the government debt was that they would be getting rid of annuities and other government loans that were hard to sell if they needed cash. In exchange, they would receive South Sea Company shares that would be traded on the London Exchange and thus far easier to liquidate than their government loans. They also had the promise of dividends and of possible appreciation in the company's stock.

The plan interested the government as well, which saw in it a way to reduce mountains of debt accumulated during years of war. The reason was simply that owners of public debt would demand the payment of less interest once they held shares that could easily be sold. Moreover, a similar scheme had been launched in France, England's great military rival in the eighteenth century. If it succeeded, the French would have an easier time financing future wars, and England would then face a grave military threat. If this was not enough to win the government's assent, the company did what was typical at the time and bribed officials and members of Parliament in order to get legislation authorizing issuance of the new shares that made the whole operation possible.

The scheme of course also appealed to the South Sea Company's directors, who could make a huge profit on the transaction, much like the modern management in one of the scandal-ridden American corporations. The size of their profits depended on the terms they offered holders of government debt and on the price that the company's shares fetched on the London Stock Exchange. Their profits would increase if the company's share price was high, for they would then need to offer government debtholders fewer of the new shares that they were authorized to issue. And they might be able to get by with offering even fewer shares if the price was rising, because the debtholders might then count on future capital gains.

The company therefore encouraged an increase in the South Sea share price. Its chief means of doing so was financing the acquisition of new shares on favorable terms. If an owner of older shares wanted to buy additional new ones, all he had to do was to put up his old shares as collateral, and the company would lend him the money to buy new ones. The company also allowed purchasers of new shares to buy on margin, and it released exaggerated reports about the firm's prospects in the financial press. It succeeded in boosting the share price, and to the extent that the company's directors were misleading investors, the bubble was caused by asymmetric information—information that the directors held but investors lacked. But statistical evidence from the bubble is also consistent with investors' all getting essentially the same information when they entered the market and then simply taking time to revise their beliefs about what the scheme was worth—in particular, their beliefs about what their fellow investors would pay for shares. During much of the bubble, many investors expected fellow market participants to continue to bid up the price of South Sea Company stock, and it therefore seemed worthwhile for them to pay more for it too. During this time they were also trading new financial instruments—not only South Sea stock but shares of scores of new companies formed to raise money during the bubble as well—and it took them several months to learn what all these financial assets were truly worth.[33]

In the South Sea Bubble, the financial instruments were new, but the investors had at least had some previous experience with the South Sea Company and with previous conversions of government debt into traded shares of other companies. Informational problems become much worse when investors begin financing projects with which they have no experience—investments in completely new technologies, for instance, or in enterprises in countries that are opening their doors to financial markets for the first time. That sort of market expansion magnifies the informational problems greatly, for alongside the difficulties of revising mistaken beliefs there is suddenly much more room for yawning asymmetries to open up.

Only a century after the South Sea Bubble, for instance, British savers rushed to invest in Latin America, now freed from Spanish restrictions on foreign capital. They lent money to the newly independent states and funded a host of seemingly promising enterprises. Mining projects generated particular enthusiasm, for Latin America was widely believed (as one prospectus put it) "to abound in . . . Gold, Silver, Copper, and other metals." British technological expertise, it was assumed, would easily make up for generations of incompetent Spanish mining management. The British investors confidently expected that their machinery and mining engineers would swiftly make the mines profitable and that British know-how would work similar miracles in agriculture and commerce as well.[34]

On the wings of such enthusiasm, the shares of mining companies founded in 1824 soared, rising twofold or far more by early 1825. Drawn by the elevated stock prices, promoters quickly formed new mining companies and offered their shares to the public. Unlike the existing companies, many of the new ones did not even bother to have specific Latin American mines under contract before selling shares. They would simply raise money first and then presumably locate suitable mines in Latin America. Although such promises seem dubious in hindsight, they readily convinced many British investors and did so for a simple reason: the investors lacked up-to-date information about what was happening in distant Latin America. Their only sources for Latin American mining were accounts of explorations conducted some twenty years earlier by the German explorer and naturalist Alexander von Humboldt and, more recently, letters sent by ship, which took months to reach London. The investors thus put up their money willingly, unaware that many mines were flooded or in disrepair, that mining regions lacked roads for bringing in machinery or taking out ore, and that much British technology simply did not work in Latin America. The lack of information also left investors vulnerable to London promoters and company managers who stole shareholders' money and to Latin American mine owners who kept their best sites for themselves and sold only their worst pits to the British. The rise in stock prices then encouraged even more outlandish proposals for Latin American investment, from a deranged plan to have Scottish milkmaids churn butter in Argentina to a fraudulent scheme to colonize a malarial Honduran swamp—the latter organized by a swindler who lacked any title to the land he proposed to settle.[35]

As 1825 wore on, the bubble burst as investors began to have misgivings about the mining companies and also about the loans to Latin American governments. Prices of mining shares and of Latin American government bonds plummeted, and the collapse was worsened by a monetary contraction as banks grew leery of taking the Latin American bonds as collateral for loans and the Bank of England (the government's bank and the only incorporated bank at the time) tightened credit. The number of bankruptcies skyrocketed, and an ensuing financial panic toppled numerous banks. In the end, most Latin American bond issues went into default, and more than half of the mining companies failed too.[36]

The market's expansion had opened the door to all sorts of informational problems. Beliefs about investments that were appearing for the first time proved far too optimistic, and the problem was compounded by the difficulty of learning about new enterprises in far-off lands. The lack of information then allowed ignorance, fraud, and misrepresentation to take their toll. Modern investors may of course protest that they would never be so naive, but the fact is that they too can easily fall into the same trap when markets expand, the

Internet bubble being but the most recent example.[37] Since the Internet was a technology that was going into operation for the first time, investors had trouble estimating what start-up companies would likely earn. And once again, asymmetric information worsened the situation. The lack of realistic earnings information and the run-up in stock prices encouraged blind investment and duplicitous behavior, particularly by intermediaries and information specialists. Financial advisers sold suspect advice, analysts publicly touted stock they privately derided, and investment firms eagerly peddled shares of dubious value for sake of the commissions and fees the sales earned.

There are, in short, simply more informational problems in bigger financial markets and thus more ways to trigger financial crises in them. Not that small markets are a safe refuge. Although some tiny markets may be immune to most of the informational problems, they severely limit possible financial transactions and may therefore leave market participants much worse off. The local building associations in the nineteenth-century American West created diminutive mortgage markets but could not meet the demand for loans. And small markets are themselves vulnerable to crises. With only a limited number of participants, they do not let borrowers or lenders diversify, and they are thus likely to collapse if a drought, a factory closure, or some other shock strikes the local economy. A small credit market in a Nigerian village can do little, for instance, if all the potential lenders have lost their own crops. Size, clearly, is an advantage, despite the different sorts of crises it can bring, and small markets are generally an extreme to be avoided.

Because a big financial market can be buffeted by so many informational problems, one often cannot tell, in the immediate aftermath of a crisis, what the precise cause was or what remedy would be best. And even if the cause is isolated in the days following a crisis, economic theory often cannot tell us what to do; and even when it can, its recommendations frequently fall on deaf ears, for the financial intermediaries or government officials who undertake most institutional reforms typically listen not to the dictates of economic theory, but to their personal interests.

Worst of all, even when an appropriate solution is adopted it can be designed only to ward off the crisis that has just passed. It typically cannot prevent the next crisis, which, in a large market, is likely to be provoked by a completely different cause. After the South Sea Bubble, Parliament investigated the South Sea Company, and the government defrayed some of the losses—enough, at least, that investors were not frightened away from markets. Legal decisions and government policy then made it more difficult to create the sort of new joint stock companies that had been floated alongside the South Sea Company. Yet none of these measures prevented crises from striking British capital markets repeatedly later in the eighteenth century.[38]

What then about the reforms adopted and lessons learned after the recent bout of corporate scandals in the United States? Will they shackle financial markets, impose an onerous burden on companies, and do little or nothing to prevent future crises? Or will they make dishonest accounting and management duplicity less likely in the future? It is, as yet, too early to tell, for the aftereffects of crises and reforms alike can take years to make themselves felt.

How Crises Alter the Value of Information

The information needed in financial markets does not simply materialize magically; market participants must seek it out. That is why lenders investigate collateral and scrutinize borrowers' financial health and why investors buy advice from information specialists. It is also why borrowers and entrepreneurs talk with bankers to learn about interest rates or loan terms. The interaction among market participants is what produces information; the information is in fact generated in the market.

Financial crises affect this process, chiefly by changing the value of different sorts of information. They do so in complex ways. On the one hand, a crisis can drastically reduce the value of some information, driving investors to pull back from certain tainted investments. What before the crisis seemed like a sign of glorious prospects will afterward lead investors to shun a whole category of entrepreneurs or borrowers, whatever their individual merits. That was the fate awaiting technology stocks after the Internet bubble in the United States: by the end of the third quarter of 2002, the technology-laden NASDAQ index, which contained most of the favorites of the Internet bubble, had dropped 90 percent from its early 2000 peak, while the broader Standard & Poor 500 had retreated only 42 percent.

Intermediaries whose information has proved wrong can meet the same fate. Yet while these unfortunates are burning in an informational hell, the crisis can make the reputation of firms that have managed to survive without breaking their financial commitments. It can do the same for financial intermediaries whose advice enables investors to escape disaster. Having ascended into the informational equivalent of heaven, they will lead the way for future market expansion. Their apotheosis may be nothing more than a lucky outcome that they have done nothing to earn, but their history of success will shape future market growth in ways that the principles of political economy alone will be unable to explain without taking this history into account.

The historical accidents and revised reputations in turn affect all the formal and informal rules that market participants impose on financial instruments and contracts. Stock markets, for example, have listing requirements, which firms must meet before their shares can be traded. Similarly, mortgage lenders in the United States have restrictions on the sort of real estate loans they will make, restrictions dictated by organizations such as the Federal National Mortgage Association, which purchase the loans, bundle them together, and then sell them off to investors. These rules amount to institutions, at least by our definition of what an institution is, and they vary from market to market, and from instrument to instrument, as does the information they demand.

The rules in fact help define the information that borrowers and entrepreneurs need to furnish in order to take out loans or to raise capital. In each case, they make clear what is an acceptable investment and what is not. Although the rules are not modified often, they do change under two circumstances. First, when markets are booming: then rules are relaxed. During the run-up in Internet and technology stocks in the United States, traditional assumptions about valuing equities went by the board, at least temporarily; so did beliefs about the reliability of companies' accounting data. Not surprisingly, after crises rules are revised and new regulations imposed. When the Internet and technology stocks plummeted and once-high-flying firms fell victim to corporate scandals, the NASDAQ and the New York Stock Exchange went to work to modify their listing requirements; investors grew cynical about accounting data and revised their opinions (albeit slowly) about equity valuation; and, last but not least, Congress passed the Sarbanes-Oxley bill, which imposed new requirements on accountants, investment banks, and corporations.[39]

The same pattern—of relaxing rules before a crisis and imposing new regulations after—has characterized scores of other disasters, from the South Sea Bubble in London to the 1929 stock market crash in New York. Thus it is worth spending a little time understanding why such a pattern persists. The reason, at bottom, has to do with the costs involved in changing regulations and in seeking the sort of information about investments that will protect investors against double-dealing and their own ignorance. Before a crisis, markets are booming, and returns from investments are temporarily high. Lulled into complacency, investors (or at least some of them) mistakenly expect that the high returns will continue into the future, with little risk.[40] They therefore relax their watch over investment projects, because seeking out information about bad projects does not seem worth the expense. Entrepreneurs react accordingly and take advantage of investors, by sneaking in inferior investment projects. Borrowers, financial intermediaries, and information specialists do the same. Eventually it is not worthwhile for any of them to uphold rigorous standards, for unscrupulous competitors will simply snatch away their business by dangling unrealistic claims in front of temporarily gullible investors. The door is then open to all sorts of blind or duplicitous behavior, and ultimately to a crisis—the scenario played out in the Latin American bubble in 1824–25, in the mortgage market in the late nineteenth-century American West, and, more recently, in the Internet bubble.

Afterward investors want new rules, but they are often expensive to put in place. If the new rules are formal ones, such as laws or regulations, the government will have to be lobbied to make the necessary changes. Even new informal rules of private behavior may require spending time and money to convince other market participants to coordinate their behavior. It will usually make no sense for an individual to undertake this sort of costly lobbying campaign, because the benefits will be shared by scores of other market participants. Only large organizations can lead such campaigns, and their efforts are often subject to what economists call economies of scale—in other words, initiating a campaign may not be worth their while unless the expected gains (reduced risk, higher returns from investment) are large. In the aftermath of a crisis, investors revise their beliefs about these gains, which now seem large. Only then do their organizations push for reforms.

What then are the new rules that are imposed after crises? By and large, they fall into three categories. First come stricter requirements for loan collateral. When real estate prices tumbled in southern California in the early 1990s, mortgage lenders who had once gleefully financed nearly 100 percent of a home's purchase price suddenly demanded that buyers have a 20 percent stake in their property that could be used as collateral. Such stringent collateral requirements, however, are among the fastest rules to fade. They reveal far too little about a borrower's behavior and cannot protect against many problems that investors face. Furthermore, heightened collateral requirements are hard to enforce outside areas such as real estate lending, for lenders do not know how to value the assets that guarantee repayment of the loan, and they cannot easily evaluate the claims that other creditors might make in case of default.

A second common set of rules warns lenders and investors to avoid particular geographic regions or economic sectors—rules such as "don't touch Internet stocks" or "avoid Argentina like the plague." Such admonishments are common, because financial crises frequently single out individual industries. They also strike particular countries or regions, either for environmental or political reasons (drought, flood, invasion, predatory behavior by a government) or because the area harbors a sector of the economy laid low by the crisis. When drought ravaged farms in the western United States at the end of the nineteenth century, investors on the East Coast who had put money into western mortgages ended up losing heavily. Thereafter they shunned the market, leaving it to larger insurance firms that had more diversified portfolios.[41] British investors who had funded a booming land market in Australia did the same when it collapsed in 1889. Banks and land companies that had taken charge of the investors' money failed, and thereafter "any sane British investor would have rather buried his money under the floor-boards than entrust it to an Australian bank."[42]

A third set of rules singles out financial intermediaries. After a crisis, investors will ask which intermediaries helped their clients escape disaster. Some intermediaries, who have pushed investments that were too risky, may have failed to see the hazards involved, or they may even have withheld information about the dangers of a particular project. After the crisis their reputations will suffer, with investors adopting the implicit rule of thumb that they are not to be trusted or used in the future.

Other intermediaries, by contrast, may have warned clients about the risks even if doing so meant a loss of fees in the short run. Or, if they have failed to foresee the crisis, they may have quickly learned from it and swiftly taken steps to safeguard their clients or to help them avoid similar trouble in the future. The crisis will then forge their reputation, or enhance it if they have already won investors' trust. That outcome in fact did much to foster the rise of famed financiers like the Rothschilds and J. Pierpont Morgan.

True, there are other ways for a financier to gain a sterling reputation. He may, like J. Pierpont Morgan, be able to mobilize capital from distant lands or funnel it to new industries. He may, again like Morgan, be able to reorganize industries or even create cartels. Or he may, like Morgan's father, Junius, have made a winning financial bet that thereafter attracted customers—in Junius's case, helping the government of France raise money in 1870 even while victorious Prussia was besieging the city of Paris.[43] Still, even J. Pierpont Morgan's reputation was in large part earned in crises.

Trust in Morgan and his bank was more than just trust in the famous banker himself.[44] It could be traced at least in part way back to George Peabody, an American who ran a London bank from which Morgan and Company would emerge, and to the actions he took to protect British investors after nine American states defaulted on their bonds in the early 1840s. Peabody had sold British investors a number of the bonds that were in default, and although he had not anticipated this crisis, he worked to get the states to resume payments on their debts. He was particularly effective in Maryland, the state in which he had first succeeded in business. There he helped launch a successful campaign to sway public opinion and to elect legislators who would support resumption of payments. Although he was not the only banker involved, he emerged from the crisis having earned British investors' trust, because it was widely believed that he was responsible for the states' decisions to begin making payments on their bonds again in the mid-1840s.

The British investors' trust was then magnified in subsequent crises by Junius Morgan, whom Peabody had taken on as a partner, and later by Junius's son, J. Pierpont, who would defend foreign investors in American railroads. After railroad bankruptcies in the early 1870s had cost foreigners heavily, J. Pierpont Morgan took a number of steps to safeguard their interests in the future. Initially he and his bank took steps to screen investments carefully. Screening was only modestly successful, but another tactic proved far more effective— his insistence on having more and more control over the companies that he recommended to investors. Trust in the Morgan bank had put so much money at its disposal (particularly during downturns, when other financial intermediaries were short of funds) that it could easily get away with such demands, which allowed Morgan and Company to monitor investments more closely than their competitors.

The companies approved by Morgan and Company had thus not only been carefully screened; they were also closely monitored after investments were made. In return for this supervision, they had the advantage of access to abundant funding, even during recessions. By the 1880s J. Pierpont Morgan could add yet another device to shield his investors—the controversial "combinations." These were mergers of competing companies that both rationalized management and reduced competition, thereby boosting investors' profits. Investors who entrusted their money to Morgan in fact did rather well—so recent scholarship suggests—although it is not clear whether their high returns resulted from his skills as a manager, his choice of good investments, or the market power of his combinations.[45]

At some point, in fact, foreign investors could simply decide that the only information they needed was whether a particular investment had been recommended by J. Pierpont Morgan. A similar story could be told for the great bankers of the Rothschild family and for many other successful financial intermediaries. Each burnished its reputation by protecting clients during or after crises. For Morgan and Company, protection consisted in repeatedly defending foreign investors in the boisterous American market. For the Rothschilds it involved rescuing the Bank of England and persuading weak states like Spain and Brazil to resume their debt payments after a crisis. A reputation of this sort could, of course, generate extraordinary expectations: in a crisis, investors might expect a fabled intermediary to step in and solve the problem. And such expectations are still with us. When the investment bank Salomon Brothers was jolted in 1991 by a bidding scandal in the market for government debt, Warren E. Buffett took over as interim CEO to salvage the firm's reputation—a sign that such matters are still important, particularly after a crisis.

A crisis forces investors to revise opinions and to reconsider what information would be most useful in the future. The result is a shift in the demand for information, a shift that in most cases gives rise to a host of new rules. These new rules will replace the slackened regulations that, in the booming days before the crisis, helped usher in the disaster. Ideally, of course, investors would modify regulations continuously and not lower their guard when markets boom. Yet typically, it is in the aftermath of crises that investors push for new standards of acceptable behavior, which may be embodied in laws or contracts or may simply be informal understandings or patterns of behavior. Whatever form they take, the new rules will make the reputation and the fortune of financial intermediaries such as the Morgans and Rothschilds, whose advice has saved investors from disaster.

Historical events—and financial crises in particular—will therefore shape the evolution of financial markets in ways that political economy alone cannot account for unless it is joined to historical analysis. Crises will be the turning points in financial development, the moments when rules and the reputations of financiers are remade. And because asymmetric information and predatory governments will never go away, neither will the crises. They will always redirect financial development.

CHAPTER 3

Crises and the Middle Class

In THE EARLY 1980S, prosperous farmers in Iowa and neighboring states suddenly found themselves caught between sky-rocketing interest rates and falling commodity prices. Many had borrowed to buy land and machinery in the booming 1970s, when export sales of corn and soybeans boosted farming profits. But when interest rates jumped and prices collapsed, they could no longer pay off their debts. Loan foreclosure rates tripled, and by 1985 a spokesman for Iowa's governor claimed that 40 percent of the state's farmers were in trouble.[1]

As farmers defaulted, they dumped their land and implements at fire-sale prices. The value of farm land plunged 69 percent in real terms (Figure 3.1). Lenders who had made too many farm loans began to founder themselves when their borrowers fell into arrears and collateral plummeted in value. The distressed lenders ranged from local banks (including Hawkeye Bancorporation, Iowa's largest bank holding company and its biggest agricultural lender) to older farmers who had personally financed the sale of their own farms back when prices were high. Although these investors of the middling sort all had some assets, they lacked the huge diversified portfolios that

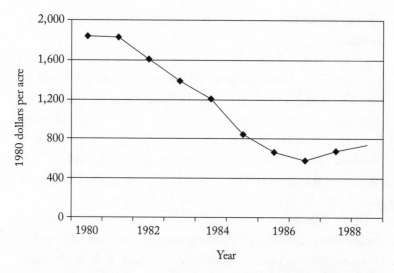

FIGURE 3.1 Value of Iowa farm real estate, 1980–1989, in 1980 dollars per acre. The consumer price index for midwestern urban consumers is used to correct for inflation. (*Sources:* "Value of Farm Real Estate" 2006; "Consumer Price Index, All Midwest Urban Consumers" 2006.)

could easily have ridden out the Iowa crisis, and in the end they suffered as much from the crisis as the bankrupted farmers or the ruined merchants in small towns. Neither they nor the farmers were rich enough to be diversified, and like the farmers, they could go out of business or lose their jobs. Poorer Iowans, who left to seek work in other states, were of course out of work too. But unlike the farmers, merchants, and middling lenders, they at least had no lost savings to lament.[2]

The events in Iowa are emblematic of what happens in many financial crises. The rich may end up enduring some losses, but diversification will usually protect them from disaster. At the other end of the social spectrum, the poor may face the specter of unemployment and have to move or change occupations, but they have little in the way of savings that can be erased, and if they can find work elsewhere, they will be no worse off than they were before. The damage will be more severe for individuals and organizations in the middle.

Yet it is the middling organizations and individuals who sustain most thriving financial markets and who will seek new financial institutions during and after a crisis. In Iowa this group included entrepreneurial farmers and medium-sized lenders like Hawkeye Bancorporation. So it is hardly surprising that the president of Hawkeye called for nationwide restructuring of the agricultural debt system and that farmers throughout the Midwest pushed for government loan subsidies and a moratorium on foreclosures.[3]

To see why support from individuals in the middle of the economic scale is critical for healthy financial markets and why they are also most likely to push for reforms after a financial debacle requires a look at how crises, inequality, and institutions interact. Typically, crises redistribute wealth and inflate the ranks of the poor. Yet precisely who bears most of the risk depends on financial institutions, which in turn affect how individuals react after the crisis. The demand for financial reorganization afterward is also related to inequality. That the poor rarely clamor for financial innovation is hardly surprising, but what has not been appreciated is how sensitive reform is to the size of the group in the middle—the borrowers, lenders, investors, and entrepreneurs who are neither rich nor poor. If this group is big, it will be a powerful force for vigorous capital markets and for financial innovation, and it will be larger in societies in which there are alternatives to being either rich or poor.

Admittedly there are some exceptions to this rule: in the former Soviet Union, for instance, disparities in wealth were minimal, but the group of borrowers, lenders, investors, and entrepreneurs in the middle was practically nonexistent. Usually, however, a substantial group in the middle goes hand in hand with less variation in wealth. When this group is small because of enduring inequality or when it has been drastically shrunk by a crisis, then capital markets lose one of their greatest allies in both the political and economic arenas, because there is less demand for financial innovation.

How Inequality Affects Financial Markets: A Simple Model

The easiest way to grasp how crises and inequality interact is to focus on a straightforward example or model—a make-believe market in which the only financial contracts are loans. Imagine then a world without more complicated financial dealings—a world without stocks, derivatives, financial exchanges, or venture capitalists. Such a world may seem oversimplified, but the insights it affords will generalize to a more complicated and realistic universe.

Let us suppose that someone in this imaginary world wishes to raise some money. It may be a young woman eager to expand her business raising chickens. Or perhaps it is a young man who wants to buy a truck in order to start a delivery service. In either case, the young entrepreneur has to borrow, but potential lenders or investors will naturally worry about her or his willingness to repay.

Broadly speaking, there are two ways to reduce their anxiety: via collateral or via a reputation for creditworthiness. When our borrower pledges collateral, she offers lenders her wealth as a hostage; they can seize it if she fails to repay the loan on schedule. If the borrower relies on her reputation instead, she puts her future access to credit at risk. Failure to keep up with the loan payments will make it hard—if not impossible—to borrow in the future.

Whether the borrower uses collateral or reputation will depend on several factors. One is the nature of the loan. Suppose that surging orders for poultry lead our imaginary young woman to hire some temporary workers. She may have to pay the workers before the chickens are sold and may have to borrow to do so. Yet it may be impossible to use the chickens as collateral because they could easily be stolen or removed from the farm. Offering her home or land as collateral—another possibility—may take too long and impose prohibitive legal costs on what needs to be a quick and inexpensive transaction. If so, she may be forced to rely on her reputation in order to borrow. If she has repaid loans in the past, potential creditors may conclude that she values her reputation highly, and may therefore grant her a new loan. But if she has never borrowed, she may be out of luck. Ideally she will have arranged sources of credit that can be tapped when she opens her business, such as a line of credit from her bank. Whatever the source of her loan, she will usually be able to borrow more and at a lower interest rate if she has some collateral that she can pledge, provided the associated legal costs are not too high. To get the lower interest rate or larger loan, she will of course need property that can serve as collateral, such as business assets or a house.

Collateral thus implies that our borrower has some resources. Her resources—her wealth—are valuable not only because they can be used or consumed but because they give access to credit. Our poultry farmer's house, for instance, not only provides shelter; it can also be mortgaged. Possession of tangible property like this is therefore appealing to nearly everyone, because it makes it easier to borrow.

In the long run, one might assume that wealth would distribute itself in an "efficient" way, with talented and eager entrepreneurs like our poultry farmer stinting and saving enough collateral to be able to borrow and thereby finance their own businesses. As their businesses grew profitable, they would acquire assets and thereby help to even out the distribution of wealth. With credit available for anyone willing to endure a little self-denial, the distribution of wealth and the financial system itself would eventually look the same everywhere, at least in our imaginary world.

In reality, however, we observe little such convergence. One reason is that it may be impossible to run a business small enough to be financed out of one entrepreneur's savings, particularly if the entrepreneur starts off with no wealth. Consider our imaginary young man who aims to start a delivery business. He has to come up with enough money—either by borrowing or by saving—to buy a truck. The truck itself can of course serve as collateral, but it may still be impossible for him to take out a loan, even in a country with an advanced financial system like the United States, if he has no other wealth and has not yet earned a reputation as a trustworthy borrower.[4] Without a loan, it may in fact take him so long to save enough money to buy a truck that he decides not to become an entrepreneur.

Moreover, in the real world, societies with puny financial sectors and huge disparities of wealth tend never to escape inequality and financial frailty. Latin America is a prime example; inequality there is greater than on any other continent, and most Latin American countries have never developed the financial institutions that would help their citizens start businesses and amass wealth. By contrast, societies lucky enough to enjoy both equality and an advanced financial system—western Europe is a good example—usually retain both advantages over time. They are likely to benefit from having more collateral lending, more financial intermediation of all sorts, and more credit overall. The only cost they face is a greater vulnerability to crises, because they depend on intermediaries, who do sometimes fail. Inequality is thus an extreme to avoid if financial markets are to prosper.

Key Groups: The Poor, the Rich, and the Middle Class

To see why inequality and financial frailty go hand in hand, suppose there are three types of actors in our imaginary world of lending: the poor, the rich, and what we will call the middle class. These actors can be individuals or firms. In our model, the label "middle class" carries none of the connotations derived from classical sociology; like the other labels, it describes only the amount of wealth and kinds of assets that our actors possess. Here we ignore other important characteristics—such as family ties, political associations, and connections to particular trades or industries—in order to keep things simple.

Our first group, the poor, often accounts for more than half the population. They have little wealth and no tangible assets that can be used for collateral. They might be workers in developed countries, whose only "savings" are the rights they have to government-sponsored social insurance programs and who must rely on their credit cards if the government cannot help them during a crisis. Or they might be farmers in less-developed economies, who borrow from their landlords in times of dearth. Lacking collateral, the only way the poor can borrow is via their reputations. Yet many of them want to take out loans to tide themselves over when they get sick, lose their jobs, or fall victim to some other economic shock.

Members of the second group, the middle class, possess tangible assets, in addition to having more human capital (in the form of skills and education) than the poor. Today their ranks include the Iowa farmers, local manufacturers, and home owners.[5] Similar individuals belonged to the middle class in the past, as did merchants and small-scale savers in early modern European cities. The size of the group varies greatly from society to society. In some cases it encompasses more than half the population (as was the case in the nineteenth-century countryside both in France and in the United States), while in others (nineteenth-century Paris, much of current-day Latin America) it accounts for less than a fifth. Whether it is big or small, many members of the middle class will want to carry out some project requiring money, such as starting a business or purchasing a house. The amount they need will not be enormous, but it will usually exceed what they can fund out of their own savings. These middle-class actors will therefore want to borrow. Others, in turn, will have savings to invest. In both cases they will usually turn to local capital markets, for the sums involved will not be big enough to justify taking out a loan or making an investment in a foreign country or in some other distant market. The costs of scouting out investments or of finding an inexpensive lender or reliable financial intermediaries will loom so large relative to the size of the transaction that it will simply not be economical to go elsewhere. Because they depend on local capital markets, the middle class will therefore care deeply about the quality of those markets.

Dependence on local capital markets will leave many middle-class investors undiversified, with too much of their savings sunk into their homes, their businesses, and local financial intermediaries. Clearly, the failure of local businesses and local banks will be a major worry.[6]

Borrowers in the middle class will have certain common characteristics. Although they may use reputational credit to fund their projects, they will typically resort to loans backed (either implicitly or explicitly) by collateral. One reason is that purely reputational loans will usually be too small the fund their projects. Today, for example, credit card debt is usually reputational, for although credit card companies can go to court to seize assets, they typically depend on the threat of cutting off future credit to get borrowers to repay. The card limits are too small, though, to enable borrowers to purchase a home or to start most businesses. Middle-class borrowers, however, have tangible assets that can serve as collateral, and they will often prefer to keep their reputational credit in reserve for use in case of an economic shock. When they borrow, their loans may be secured by a specific asset—a home mortgage may provide start-up capital for a business—or they may be backed by all of an individual's wealth.

Our third group, the rich, has human capital and far more tangible assets than the middle class. These are the people featured in most financial histories or lists of the wealthiest people and biggest corporations. Although they never make up more than 1 percent of the population, they may own up to half of an economy's material goods in parts of Latin America, and they have owned even more in past societies. In 1911–1913, for instance, the richest 1 percent of the English population held 69 percent of the country's wealth.[7] Today they possess less in most Western democracies. In the United States, for instance, the richest 1 percent of all households held some 34 percent of the country's net worth in 1998—a bigger share than in the 1970s. Europe is even more egalitarian, with the wealthiest 1 percent's portion ranging from perhaps 25 percent in Denmark to 10 percent in Ireland.[8]

Wealth opens doors for the rich that are closed to the middle class. The rich can usually start a business or buy a home without taking out a loan, because their enormous fortunes allow them to finance most of their projects out of their own pockets. Their wealth also has implications for the markets in which they participate. The rich are not deterred by the costs of scouting out foreign or distant markets, for the costs of doing so are small relative to huge sums they will invest. The rich can therefore spread their portfolios over multiple markets and benefit from diversification.

They will consequently worry less about any particular local market's short-term performance and need less insurance too. But they will be the ideal group to offer insurance to the poor and middle class if the state does not do so: all they need do is move resources from prosperous markets to one laid low by a crisis. That is what happened in France when wealthy landlords such as the La Rochefoucault family let their tenants fall behind in the rent during an agricultural crisis in 1870–71. Arrears, which had been averaging 20 percent of the rent due, jumped to 76 percent in 1870 and 60 percent in 1871—in effect, loans that the family was making to tenant farmers.[9]

With enormous fortunes, the rich can also afford to keep financial intermediaries on retainer or to hire advisers who will improve the performance of their investments. The fixed costs of hiring such experts shrink to insignificance relative to the size of their portfolios, and they can therefore invest heavily in financial intermediation. (Fixed costs refer to expenses that do not rise with the scale of transactions; here they refer to the cost of hiring, say, a fulltime banker or investment adviser to manage a portfolio.) The rich do not even have to take financial institutions as given; indeed, they can go so far as to open a bank if they think it worthwhile.

The affluent Brown family took just this step in late eighteenth-century Providence, Rhode Island. Having succeeded as merchants in the colonial era, they wanted to shift into manufacturing after the American Revolution. Their commercial success gave them enough money to fund any single manufacturing project, such as a textile mill. But their ambitions went well beyond one lone enterprise. To expand rapidly, they needed additional capital. Banks, however, were almost nonexistent in the new republic. The Browns and their kin therefore decided to establish their own bank, the Providence Bank, in 1791. Drawing its capital and deposits from the community, the bank invested most of its resources, at least initially, in the highly successful businesses that the Browns and their associates controlled.[10]

Founding a bank is not the only option for the rich. They can develop special relationships with financial intermediaries, and if their fortunes are truly immense they can even employ financiers fulltime. Take for example the Orléans, close relatives to the king and one of the wealthiest families in eighteenth-century France. The Orléans owned huge tracts of real estate, along with a major canal. To manage their extensive holdings, they employed a large staff, including a fulltime financial specialist, Etienne de Silhouette, who later took charge of the government's finances. But their capacity to deal with financial markets on favorable terms did not stop there, for they were also the principal clients of two of Paris's major loan brokers (notaries). Most Parisian notaries had to make do with a diversified clientele. The Orléans' two notaries, however, were among a dozen or so who owed their prosperity to the continued business of the very rich; and they also benefited from work for the Orléans' business partners, political allies, and artistic clients.[11]

There was one final benefit to the Orléans' gargantuan wealth. When they needed to borrow (say, to meet a temporary need for cash or to engage in real estate development without having to sell too many other assets), they could choose among a variety of exotic financial instruments. Consider, for example, the Duke of Chartres, the heir to the Orléans title and the family fortune. Both he and his wife stood to inherit enormous wealth, but he spent so heavily in anticipation of the legacy that he found himself squeezed for cash. He therefore decided to develop some of his family's property in Paris to increase its commercial value. He convinced his father, the Duke of Orléans, to turn the property over to him in 1780, and the result was the Palais Royal—a grand colonnade that for the next several decades would be one of the entertainment centers of Paris, complete with theater, drinking, dining, gambling, and prostitution. Since he was short of cash, he did have to borrow, but the financing for this eighteenth-century Las Vegas was not arranged via reputational loans or even the usual land-backed mortgages that funded most real estate development. Rather, Chartres chose the innovative route of selling life annuities, a popular (and presumably cheap) way of raising money at a time when government pensions did not exist and individuals were consequently eager to buy anything like an annuity in order to provide for their old age. He also borrowed from bankers in Genoa. He mobilized millions of livres at a time when a typical loan in France amounted to only 841 livres.[12] Because he sold so many annuities, he could protect himself against the likelihood that all the purchasers would live to a ripe old age, a form of diversification that was beyond the reach of most other private borrowers. Furthermore, the scale of his operation reduced fixed costs to small change and thereby made it possible for him to utilize other sources of funding such as the Genoese bankers.

Today large firms engage in similar behavior. Many—Berkshire Hathaway and General Electric are ideal examples—have finance arms, large reserves of cash, and the ability to tap multiple markets. When a new project comes up, they can invest their own funds or turn to capital markets. When they borrow, their options are vast; they can sell convertible bonds and other complicated contracts that are beyond the reach of smaller firms. On a more mundane level, an entire industry has long catered to the needs of rich private investors, with private bankers offering them individualized service provided they maintain balances of a million dollars or more. The middle class typically does not qualify.[13]

Collateral and Reputational Lending

The rich, the poor, and the middle class all behave differently in the credit market. They do not have the same demand for credit, and they do not take out the same kind of loans, if they borrow at all. What they use loans for differs too—in particular, whether they borrow to start businesses or to protect themselves when economic shocks strike. If the goal is protection, the borrowing is a form of insurance. The poor have an enormous demand for such insurance, a demand that they can satisfy only by taking out reputational loans, since they lack collateral. The middle class will seek less insurance of this kind than the poor, because they have more tangible assets that can serve as collateral and also offer some protection and diversification. The middle class can thus take out both reputational and collateral loans, and they will turn to the collateral market when they want to start businesses and finance investments. Finally, although the rich can obviously borrow in both the reputational and collateral markets, they do not need to do so to start businesses. They do not need insurance either, because they have large diversified portfolios and can invest in foreign countries and distant markets. Overall then, the demand for insurance loans in the reputational market declines with wealth, so long as an economic shock is not big enough to wipe out the middle class and make them as desperate for reputational loans as the poor. The demand for collateral loans has a different shape. Absent among the poor, who have no collateral, it peaks among the middle class and then drops again among the rich.

So far we have not really asked what kind of wealth can serve as collateral. We do know that human capital (one's skill as a cook or accountant, for example) cannot secure loans. Other assets such as real estate can, but their effectiveness as collateral will depend on several institutions. First of all, there must be a legal system that can enforce loan contracts and titles to property at low cost and give lenders effective rights to collateral when borrowers default. It is particularly difficult to do this with movable property (such as livestock, vehicles, commodities, and most manufactured goods), because a borrower can often sneak the collateral away. But problems can keep even real estate from securing loans. The cost of foreclosing on a home mortgage is much higher in Italy, for instance, than it is in Great Britain. The situation is even worse in many developing countries. In Vietnam and Mexico, legal restrictions limit the use of land as collateral, and in Cameroon establishing title to land takes years.[14] In Brazil, slum residents lack any title to the homes they occupy, a barrier that keeps fledgling entrepreneurs from borrowing. As one of them (a widow who sells toys and school supplies) recently explained, "If I could just get some credit, I could expand my shop . . . [but] I don't have the means to do that because nothing I have is recognized as valid by the legal system."[15]

It is also necessary to have some sort of low-cost lien or mortgage registry that records whether an asset has already been pledged as collateral and, if so, to whom. Such a registry will make it easier for lenders to see whether an asset has already been mortgaged to the hilt when they are deciding to make a loan. And a third key institution is a market in which collateral can be sold off. Assets that can be easily liquidated will obviously be more appealing as collateral than wealth that trades in thin markets. Collateral will thus depend on institutions, which are themselves the result of decisions made by current and past members of the society.

Digging deeper reveals another characteristic of wealth that affects its utility as collateral—the ease with which it can be divided. One might assume that divisibility is purely mechanical (after all, a truck that secures a loan cannot be split in half), but in fact it reflects a host of legal constraints and market innovations. Consider, for example, real estate in France. Land in France is divided into legally defined parcels, and until the middle of the nineteenth century, a parcel could not easily be split: each parcel, such as the plot of land beneath a building—had to have a single owner. In the countryside, this limitation posed no problem, for there were many small, inexpensive parcels that farmers could easily purchase and mortgage. In cities, however, land was valuable and parcels costly. Building single-family housing on such expensive land was out of the question, but the occupants of a larger building could not share ownership of the parcel, as in a modern American condominium. Owning real estate was consequently impossible for all but the richest city dwellers. Other urbanites rented, and if they saved, they had to acquire financial assets other than land or buildings. As a result, middle-class city dwellers did not benefit from all the money the French government spent in the nineteenth century to create mortgage registries that facilitated the use of real estate as collateral. Although the spending did help the middle class in the countryside, in cities it worked to the advantage only of the rich, because they alone owned real estate. That remained the case (not just in France but virtually everywhere else too) until the twentieth century, when legal and financial innovations finally allowed multiple owners to occupy a single building.[16]

In unequal societies, where the middle class is minuscule and the ranks of the poor large, more credit will be available for insurance than for investment. Demand for credit will be shaped by the mass of poor people, for the rich do not borrow and the middle class is too small. With no collateral, the poor will have to turn to reputational credit to borrow. Few of the loans they take out will go for investments (to start a business for instance), for they have too little human capital and will fear that such borrowing will limit the amount of debt they can take on if an economic shock hits. Their fears are not irrational. After all, with no savings, they are acutely vulnerable in economic downturns. Because what they can borrow in the reputational market is limited, they prefer to reserve the little credit they have for insurance in hard times. Furthermore, borrowing for investment may even convince a lender (whether he is a village usurer or a local banker skeptical of get-rich-quick schemes) that they are no longer concerned about being able to go into debt in tough times and thus no longer worried about preserving their reputations. After all, if the poor borrow for investment and succeed, they will not need insurance any more, and if they borrow for investment and fail, they will be so indebted that they will be unable to repay their reputational loans. Borrowing for investment may therefore tarnish their reputation, something many of the poor dare not risk, for fear of being left high and dry and without insurance in a crisis.

The poor will get insurance loans from the rich, usually in a way that builds upon existing bonds between the two groups. The existing links, which may connect landlords and tenants or the mighty and their clients, will supply the detailed information required by reputational credit—information that helps a rich lender distinguish whether a poor borrower is truly needy, whether he has contributed to his own dilemma, and whether he is likely to pay back his loan or not.[17]

Although the rich do not borrow at all in our model, the outcome will remain by and large the same for an unequal society even if the rich do take on some debt. The picture will change only if institutions arise to facilitate collateral lending—if, say, wealthy heirs like the Duke of Chartres want to borrow in anticipation of their inheritance. The development of such institutions is in any case likely to be slow, because there will be few middle-class borrowers to create a market for collateral lending. Still, appropriate institutions may eventually emerge in unequal societies. They did, for instance, in late seventeenth- and eighteenth-century England, despite highly concentrated landownership, giving rise to mortgage credit that allowed wealthy landowners to borrow against their estates. Before the seventeenth century, the law made it hard for these landowners to employ their property as collateral. At best they could use the land to secure a six-month loan, but if they fell even one day behind in making payments, they would lose their property forever and still have to pay the lender the principal due on the loan. But both the law and financial habits began to change in the seventeenth century, in part because wealthy landowners who had backed the losing side in England's Civil War sought to mortgage land in order to pay fines or to repurchase property that had been confiscated. By the end of the century, the rich were regularly turning to mortgages to manage their finances.[18]

What will happen in more equal societies—in other words, ones with thinner ranks of rich and poor and a larger middle class? Demand for credit in general and for collateral lending in particular will increase with the size of the middle class. If all goes well and there are no institutional obstacles that restrict lending, then the total amount of debt will be larger, with the collateral lending favored by the middle class predominating over reputational credit. The poor will still continue to want insurance, but as their numbers diminish, overall demand for reputational loans will fall, and the supply of credit will accommodate the greater demand for collateral loans from the middle class. If the rich no longer fund all the collateral debt, financial intermediaries will arise to mobilize the savings of middle-class lenders and pass them on to borrowers in the same class. Again, our simplified description assumes that institutional obstacles do not keep intermediaries in check.

The resulting contrast in financial development comes into clear focus in the history of North and South America. In the United States, where wealth was distributed in a fairly egalitarian way even in colonial times, mortgage lending using land as collateral was widespread by the early 1700s. In Latin America, extreme inequality left few potential borrowers with property to secure loans. Competitive banking also developed earlier in the United States, as did securities exchanges. Differing institutions certainly played a role—in particular, the possibility of competition between states under the American constitution, which spurred the creation of banks—but acute inequality, it has been argued, was the ultimate cause, the prime mover behind even the institutional change. It is telling, for example, that it took until 1884 for mortgage credit legislation to be drafted in Mexico. Furthermore, in much of Latin America the banking system did not arise to serve middle-class borrowers and investors; rather, for a long time it remained a "reserve of the wealthy elite."[19]

A similar contrast emerges if we compare the dispersal of wealth in Latin America and in parts of western Europe. These relatively egalitarian portions of Europe quickly developed financial intermediaries to facilitate mortgage lending, just as our model suggests. The intermediaries varied from place to place—they might be notaries, credit cooperatives, or agricultural banks—but what is striking is their ubiquity, a stark difference from inegalitarian Latin America.[20]

The intermediaries in western Europe mobilized far more capital than in Latin America for mortgage loans to middle-class borrowers. A pair of examples can illustrate the enormous disparity—the cities of Mérida in Mexico and Limoges in France, both of which had about 40,000 people in 1850. Only 70 mortgage loans were arranged each year in Mérida, whereas in Limoges the number was twenty times higher: nearly 1,400. One might be tempted to attribute the difference to higher per-capita incomes in Limoges, but in fact the average loan size there was much smaller than in Mérida: under 1,000 francs, versus over 5,000 francs in the Mexican city.

The difference was just as pronounced in larger cities, such as Lyons and Rio de Janeiro, which had roughly comparable populations in 1870 (318,800 for Lyons and 228,743 for Rio).[21] In Rio only 400 loans were arranged in 1870—a mere 1.75 per 1,000 inhabitants. In Lyons at about the same time (1865), the number was nearly four times higher: 2,032 a year, or 6.37 per 1,000. Again, the average loan size was smaller in Lyons: 9,094 francs, versus 44,650 in Rio. Essentially, Rio and Mérida had only a small number of huge loans, a result that the puny middle class would lead one to expect for Latin America. In such societies, the rich are the only ones left to borrow, and although our model does not allow them to do so, in reality they will occasionally take out loans—for instance, to finance extravagant consumption before inheriting a fortune. Their rare but sizable indebtedness is likely to dominate the credit markets in Mérida and Rio, and in any other society without a large middle class.

The most insidious effect of extreme inequality in places like Brazil and Mexico is that it slows the development of institutions that support a thriving capital market. With so few people having savings to invest or projects that require external financing, the credit market shrivels up. The tiny minority who do participate in it—essentially the rich—can rely on personal information to arrange loans. They have no need for financial intermediaries, and even if they do, they can always secure the services of specialists in other countries. Intermediaries in the local credit market will develop slowly, particularly if the rich seek to choke them off in order to limit competition in providing lucrative insurance loans to the poor. Mérida seems to have gone through just such a process. Sisal production fueled a boom there in the 1880s and 1890s, but, far from leading the economic growth, local banks arose only a decade later.

Extreme inequality and a small middle class are thus two major obstacles to flourishing financial markets. That is why the size of the middle class (along with information and the level of government debt) is one of the three factors that shape the development of financial markets. Many social scientists—political scientists in particular—see institutions as ultimate causes that shape social structure. But institutions can change, and this is an instance (and not the only one) in which social structure—here, the size of the middle class—influences institutions.[22]

So inequality and the size of the middle class affect financial institutions. But behind this simple truth lurks a hidden cost. Equality is likely to nurture financial development, but it may also leave societies vulnerable to financial crises. Crises can strike because indebtedness is higher, especially among individuals with limited wealth and little diversification—in other words, our middle class. When an economic shock hits, it will batter most middle-class entrepreneurs. Many will be unable to pay their debts and will go bankrupt, just like the farmers in Iowa. Their creditors may then be dragged down—in particular, financial intermediaries, like Hawkeye Bancorporation, which was forced to sell assets and give its own lenders a share of ownership.[23] If a large number of intermediaries go belly up, the result is a financial crisis. The virtues of equality and a large middle class go hand in hand with this risk—another way in which financial markets mix good and bad.

More Sophisticated Financial Transactions

Our simple model of a debt market with three groups stresses collateral rather than reputational credit. One might worry that the emphasis is misplaced. Modern entrepreneurs, the argument might go, have many ways to raise funds besides pledging collateral, from partnership agreements and unsecured debt (borrowing not tied to specific collateral) to venture capital and public stock offerings. At first glance, all these mechanisms seem to resemble reputational credit and to differ from collateral lending, at least as we have defined it.

Yet the resemblance to reputational credit is more apparent than real, and in the end many of these more sophisticated mechanisms turn out to resemble the collateral lending of our model. To begin with, most of them are really not reputational in the sense that they build upon repeated interaction between the entrepreneur and investors. Entrepreneurs who rely on venture capital, for example, rarely start up a sequence of firms to build up a reputation. The few who have done so, such as Thomas Edison, are clearly an exception. Most start up a single firm, and it is thus not their reputation that matters, as would be the case in reputational lending, because they will not be starting new companies in the future. Indeed, if any reputation is at stake, it is in fact the venture capitalist's, for the entrepreneurs may fear that he will steal their ideas, and their defense against him is his interest in preserving his reputation for future funding ventures.

Venture capital is thus not what we called reputational lending, in which the borrower's reputation is paramount. Furthermore, it actually embodies key features of collateral lending. The venture capitalist does not just supply investment funds and shoulder a greater part of the risk than in a debt contract; he also exercises control over the firms he finances. He screens entrepreneurs carefully before investing, monitors their progress as he progressively provides funds, and steps in to advise or take charge of firms when things go wrong. These are all steps that help resolve familiar problems of asymmetric information in capital markets, by protecting the venture capitalist against incompetent or dishonest entrepreneurs. But meanwhile the entrepreneurs retain a share of the ownership, and their retained equity helps too. It in fact acts much like the collateral in our simple debt market. It offers a valued prize if the entrepreneurs' firm succeeds, but as in the case of collateral, the entrepreneurs will lose it if they fail. Their equity share thus creates similar incentives to those associated with collateral—incentives that the venture capitalist can only applaud, since they increase the chances of success.

Partnerships and equity financing in general have similar features, with ownership shares playing the role of collateral. Moreover, with any of these methods of financing, the entrepreneurs will often put up some of their personal wealth—collateral in the sense of our model. The one source of capital that may in fact be reputational is unsecured debt, but start-up entrepreneurs have only limited access to it. Except for established businesses with rock-solid earnings, raising money usually requires pledging either the firms' assets or the owners'.

Not that innovations such as venture capital or equity financing are unimportant.[24] They all allow the process of raising money to move beyond the realm of tangible assets and thereby make financing easier for middle-class entrepreneurs who have abundant human capital but only limited collateral. Venture capital and partnerships can provide start-up funding. Securities markets and novel contracts can offer the prospect of valuable equity stakes in the future. All these advances in financial intermediation will benefit the middle class. The direct benefits, however, should not be exaggerated, at least as far as most middle-class entrepreneurs are concerned. After all, the venture capitalists and the investment bankers who prepare initial stock offerings are not going to help the usual small business. Rather, they will limit themselves to large projects, particularly those with a potential for a huge payoff. The venture capitalists, for instance, seek firms that can grow fast enough to make a rapid stock offering possible, and apart from the occasional biologist with a promising patent, most entrepreneurs will be starting businesses that are too small for equity markets. Unlike the rich, who can simply reach into their pockets to start a business, most middle-class entrepreneurs will therefore have to rely upon more pedestrian sources of funds such as commercial banks.

Financial innovation works to the advantage of middle-class investors too. Securities markets, new financial instruments, and the establishment of mutual funds make it possible for investors to diversify and thereby cut the cost of the capital, which further assists entrepreneurs. Middle-class investors will be particularly appreciative, since their portfolios are too small to be diversified. The middle class as a whole will favor these improvements in financial intermediation, just as in our simple model, and where the middle class is large, innovations of this sort will be more likely. Our model may thus gloss over complexities, but the insights it affords hold true in a more complicated and creative world. Whether our concern is lending secured by collateral or more sophisticated transactions, the relevant financial markets will all stand a better chance of thriving if the middle class is not small and inequality is not extreme.

How Shocks Can Damage the Middle Class

The enormous good that equality does inevitably brings with it some poisonous risks. Economic shocks can do more damage to capital markets in equal societies than to those in inegalitarian ones. The shocks can twist both financial institutions and the distribution of wealth in a way that compresses the middle class and, along with it, the demand for credit and for financial intermediation.

Consider what a shock does to the distribution of income (what people earn every year) and to the distribution of wealth (the total amount of property they have amassed). Normally, income inequality is assumed to increase in good times and to decrease in bad. The reason is that most income derives from wages and from returns to financial assets, such as interest payments. During bad times, the earnings from financial assets will fall more than wages. Since the rich depend heavily on such earnings, their income will suffer heavily. Those in the middle class, by contrast, get much more of their income from wages, even though they do earn a bit from the assets they own. As a result, their income will fall less than that of the rich, narrowing the difference between the incomes of the two groups. In good times, however, the reverse will be true, as the rich will find their incomes buoyed up by the high returns on financial assets. Income gaps will thus widen in good times and shrink in bad.

Income, however, is not the critical issue for credit markets, at least according to our model. What matters is wealth—especially collateral wealth. What does it do?

Wealth inequality may also rise in good times and fall in bad times in societies if individuals cannot invest outside their local economy. The reason is that the rich are more willing to bear risk than the poor. They will therefore own more assets such as speculative ventures, whose value will fluctuate widely; the middle class, by contrast, will fill their portfolios with more secure investments such as bonds or rental housing. When a shock hits, the rich will lose more, narrowing the gap in wealth between them and the middle class. This phenomenon, though, will disappear once the shock passes.

More relevant is the case in which the rich need not keep all their investments in a particular locality. This is the case our model envisages—the rich being able to afford the fixed costs of investing in distant markets—and it is a realistic one: capital does flow from one part of the world to another. These flows are largely financed by capital exports from the rich. The middle class, by contrast, tend to invest closer to home, and they suffer greatly from this home-country bias. The tendency of the rich to invest abroad is even more marked in parts of the world that are regularly battered by crises.

In most Latin American countries, for instance, private investment abroad is of similar magnitude to foreign debt.[25] In other words, for every dollar that enters one of the countries as a loan to the state or to private individuals, another dollar of private wealth seems to move out to be invested abroad. The distribution of this foreign investment is highly skewed, with the poor clearly owning none of it. As for the middle class, its wealth was for a long time strictly local, although some middle-class savers in Argentina did manage to diversify their portfolios a bit by opening bank accounts in Uruguay. The reason, again, was that the fixed costs of most foreign investments simply loomed too large.

The rich, by contrast, have long owned portfolios that are spatially diversified, portfolios with resources spread across regions and countries. Consider, for example, a family of aristocrats in eighteenth-century France, the Bourrée de Corberon. In the middle of the century, the head of the family was a judicial official living in Paris, but he maintained the family's estates in Burgundy's wine country. In Paris he lent money to private individuals and to the state; he made similar loans to private parties in the Burgundian capital of Dijon and in Nuits-Saint-Georges, a town near his estates. Although he apparently had little personal connection to his debtors in Paris or in Dijon, many of his loans in Nuits-Saint-Georges went to his tenants. After a bad harvest in 1770, he advanced them money and allowed them to reschedule their rent payments—precisely the kind of insurance only a wealthy and well-diversified investor could offer.[26]

Imagine now what happened to the distribution of wealth in Nuits-Saint-Georges after the bad harvest. The poor found that the bad grape harvest had depressed their income because there was less demand for their work, for although wages per day did not fall, the number of days worked did. The rich received lower incomes from local investments, but the impact on their income was small because of the offsetting effect of earnings from urban investments and from places unaffected by the bad harvest. The middle class endured a decline in income, and middle-class entrepreneurs faced the problem of making payments on loans and leases. Some would have had to draw down their savings; a few might even have had to sell a little land. Yet although middle-class wealth declined, and by more than the diversified fortunes of the rich, long-run change in the distribution of wealth would have been small, for in good times the whole process would be reversed: members of the middle class would rebuild savings and repurchase lost wealth; higher-income poor people would save enough to join the middle class, swelling its ranks. As long as shocks like the bad harvest were not large enough to bankrupt members of the middle class, inequality would change little.

A big shock, however, could threaten this stability. If middle-class entrepreneurs could no longer make payments on their leases or their loans, insolvency would force them to liquidate their businesses. But who could buy their land, tools, or animals? The poor surely could not, and other local middle-class entrepreneurs would also be unlikely candidates. So would middle-class investors, because their loans would have gone bad. The most likely purchasers would thus be the rich. They would have diversified portfolios and could bring in resources from Paris or Dijon to purchase assets at fire-sale prices. Inequality would then increase, as the rich acquired property. If the shock was bad enough, the middle class might even disappear, but even if it did not, its members would have less collateral and thus take out fewer loans.

This pattern is not peculiar to markets in the distant past, as the recent spate of corporate bankruptcies in the United States demonstrates. Each of the bankruptcies worked something like a local shock: though not large enough to paralyze the entire economy, it did hurt the firm's employees, management, creditors, and shareholders. To be sure, many of the share holders—even middle-class ones— owned very little of the bankrupt firm's stock: financial innovations such as mutual funds had diversified their portfolios. Their losses from any one bankruptcy were small, and their fate was thus quite different from that of, say, middle-class investors or entrepreneurs in eighteenth-century Nuits-Saint-Georges. The same would no doubt be true for commercial creditors such as large diversified banks or suppliers with many customers. But for the firms' employees and management, the situation was different. The poorest employees at the firms probably had few or no savings to forfeit, but they could certainly lose their jobs. For employees in the middle, the situation was even worse. Not only could they end up unemployed, but their savings could be devastated too, especially if, as was often the case, they had invested heavily in company stock through company retirement, share purchase, or stock option plans.[27]

They were our vulnerable middle class. The firms' management were our rich. One could of course find examples of managers who were ruined when their firms collapsed—managers who owned shares that could not be sold before the bubble burst or who spurned diversification in the hope of amassing even greater wealth. Yet unlike the middle class, most managers did have some chance to diversify. Indeed, even if they could not sell all of their company stock, they could usually sell some of it before prices collapsed, and thus diversify their holdings. No one yet knows precisely how much they lost from company shares they continued to own, but an investigation of the twenty-five largest American corporate bankruptcies in 2001 and early 2002 revealed that directors and top executives of the firms had been able carry away perhaps $3.3 billion in cash salary, bonuses, stock option profits, and gross revenue for stock sales before their firms went belly up. Although they may still have suffered huge absolute losses from company shares they continued to hold, the relative damage was likely much worse for middle-level employees, who lost both their jobs and their retirement savings. At Enron, for instance, 9 members of the upper management may have got out with $800 million before the firm's collapse. Meanwhile, some 24,000 employees lost an average of perhaps $85,000 each from Enron stock in employee savings plans.[28]

The dire effect that crises can have on the distribution of wealth is worth considering in greater detail, for it is the foundation for the rest of this chapter as well as the next. Crises, we shall argue, pose a serious threat to financial markets because of the long-run damage they can do to the middle class. If a crisis wipes out much of the middle class, the demand for financial intermediation will decline, and capital markets may take ages to recover.

The reason, at bottom, is that in a crisis the middle class will typically lose a greater fraction of their wealth than the rich, who are usually more diversified. The rich, it is true, may endure the greatest absolute losses in the local economy because they own so much. But if they hold assets outside the local economy—and they typically do—then the local losses will be offset by gains elsewhere, and the local crisis will not matter so much. Furthermore, their access to capital markets will not suffer if local financial intermediaries fail, for they can pay the fixed costs of seeking out and using distant intermediaries. The crisis may also lead them to shift resources into the local economy, just as in Nuits-Saint-Georges. They are likely to be making insurance loans to the poor, and since the crisis will cut demand from the middle class, they will be the obvious buyers when local markets are flooded with the collateral sold by distressed middle-class borrowers. The ultimate result may be that the rich gain control of local wealth at bargain-basement prices. The difference between what they pay during a crisis and the higher price at which the assets can later be resold is the cost paid by the poor and the middle class for the capital influx furnished by the rich. If the rich face little competition in local markets (either as buyers or as providers of insurance and loans), this cost can be large.[29]

While crises may generate opportunities for the rich, they can menace the middle class, whose investors will not be as diversified. Their portfolios as a whole will be more likely to plummet, and they can even lose safe investments like bank accounts if financial intermediaries fail.

The threat will be even greater for middle-class entrepreneurs who are likely to have borrowed to start their projects and to have placed a large fraction of their own wealth into their businesses as collateral to reassure investors. If their businesses fail, they will lose the collateral and fall into the ranks of the poor. True, they will retain their human capital, and they may have learned from their experience of failure. But they will not be able to start a business again—or at least not immediately—because they will no longer have the required collateral.

Crises thus have the potential to harm middle-class investors and to reduce the number of middle-class entrepreneurs. Yet crises will not always ruin the middle class, for their impact can be dampened by institutional innovation. To begin with, financial intermediaries can find ways to cut the cost of diversification for the middle class— for instance, via mutual funds, branch banks, or interregional mortgage funding. And they may be able to create new forms of insurance that can give the middle class partial protection against local crises.[30] The government can also step in, declaring debt moratoria, bailing out ruined middle-class entrepreneurs or reimbursing middle-class investors. Whether private or public, such innovations will be more likely when the middle class is large enough to generate enormous demand or powerful enough to interest politicians.

That crises can end up both wreaking havoc and at least sometimes stimulating financial innovations emerges clearly from events in France in the nineteenth and early twentieth centuries. Although wealth was far from equally distributed, France did have a large middle class. It was also buffeted by financial crises. Some were unleashed by environmental disasters, such as the phylloxera pest, which ravaged vineyards in the 1870s, reshuffling land ownership and ruining both farmers and financial intermediaries. Others were triggered by bouts of political instability, which caused bankruptcies to mushroom and financial intermediaries to fail. But the crises also sparked some beneficial institutional innovations alongside all the enormous harm they caused. Financial organizations arose in the aftermath of the crises to reduce the cost of saving and borrowing for the middle class. Savings banks allowed members of the middle class to accumulate enough to buy the smallest government bonds. Insurance companies helped them save and mitigated the financial consequences of death and of military service. Later the government created retirement funds. And although most of these innovations catered to city dwellers, the rise of a mutual agricultural bank (the Crédit Agricole) brought financial markets within reach of the rural middle class.[31]

The reason for all the innovation in France was that the middle class was big enough to surmount the crises and generate strong demand for new financial institutions and products. In Latin America, however, where the middle class was much smaller, the history of responses to crises took a very different route. In late nineteenth-century Mexico, for example, the financial institutions that developed were always aimed at large enterprises controlled by the very wealthy. During political crises the government might commandeer bank resources for the benefit of the ruling elite, but little or nothing was ever done for distressed members of the middle class. And in calmer times, rich bank owners limited their lending to bloated enterprises they themselves owned, and very little of the banks' scarce resources ended up funding middle-class entrepreneurs.[32]

Economic Shocks and Financial Intermediaries

What does a crisis do to financial intermediaries? And how is its impact on them affected by inequality? Obviously, a crisis can harm intermediaries, because it reveals that much of their advice was worthless, and demand for their service after the crisis will therefore diminish. Worse yet, in crises many intermediaries may go bankrupt, particularly if they have risked their own funds. Replacements will eventually spring up, but their development will be shaped by inequality and the size of the middle class. If the middle class is small and if a crisis further depletes its ranks, then the failed intermediaries may not be replaced, and the financial system will wither away.

To see why there may be no replacements for bankrupt intermediaries if the middle class is small, we have to consider an important cost that the intermediaries themselves have to bear in order to do their business—the cost of accumulating essential information about market participants. Like the expenses investors face if they want to invest abroad, this too is a fixed cost, which cannot easily be reduced or divided up, and it will keep individuals or companies from entering the business of financial intermediation unless demand from the middle class is sufficiently strong.

The information that intermediaries need concerns, first of all, the likely returns from a loan and the odds that a borrower will default. They will therefore want to know what other debts the borrower currently has or will take on in the future; whether other creditors will take priority in a default; how quickly the borrower has repaid loans in the past; what collateral he can offer and whether it is encumbered by other mortgages; what his income is and what the prospects for success are for his project, if he happens to be an entrepreneur. Intermediaries will also want information about investors—what sort of investments they prefer and what risks and returns they demand— and perhaps even about what competing intermediaries are offering.

For some kinds of loans—when the United States borrows by auctioning off Treasury bills, for instance—the task, at least nowadays, seems fairly simple. Since the bills themselves are practically riskless, the intermediaries who buy them for resale need not spend time collecting information about the creditworthiness of the U.S. government. But they still have to find investors who will purchase the bills—the ultimate lenders to the government—and they have to guess at the prices that other intermediaries will offer when bidding for the bills at the Treasury auctions.

All the simplicity here masks a number of institutions and financial innovations that have grown up over the years, from a government that can be trusted to repay its debts to sophisticated auctions and financial intermediaries who gather information to bid on the bills. Meanwhile, in other financial markets, information collection is much more complex. Credit card lenders may, for instance, want to follow consumption patterns for signs of financial trouble. If a habitual buyer of luxury goods suddenly makes all his charges at discount retailers, then not paying his bill may be next.

In a mortgage market, the requisite information is different still. Titles to property have to be searched, collateral appraised, and borrowers' credit histories and financial statements evaluated. Today the process is often standardized by government agencies or private intermediaries, which may even purchase mortgages from banks and mortgage brokers, group them together, and then sell the pooled assets as mortgage-backed securities on financial markets. In that case, the ultimate investors, who buy the mortgage-backed securities for their liquidity and low risk, are located by securities firms; the banks and mortgage brokers do not have to seek out that information. They are also spared having to hold on to the mortgages themselves, as was common in the past; thus they no longer need to know as much about the dangers of making too many loans in the same area.

In nearly all credit markets, though, the information has to be collected even before a transaction is proposed. It is not simply a matter of taking the cost of funds to be lent and tacking on a little profit, for deadbeats may well consent to any interest rate, but profits will be zero if they default. The expenses involved in gathering some of the necessary information will rise proportionally with the number of market participants: the fee for accumulating credit histories for 2,000 people, for example, is likely to be ten times what it is for 200. But before any credit histories can be amassed someone has to devise techniques to evaluate them, and the cost of devising (or of improving) these techniques is largely fixed. Because larger markets can bear these fixed charges more easily, they will typically enjoy more sophisticated information-gathering and more sophisticated intermediation as well. The same holds for other financial markets generally, albeit with one enormous caveat: the techniques are only partly transferable from one type of finance to another. Evaluating equity investment requires different tools from those used to evaluate bonds, and mortgages are not the same as credit card debt. If an innovative financier creates techniques that make possible one kind of financial intermediation—bank financing, for instance—then the market for bank credit may expand, but other forms of intermediation, such as equity financing, may remain stunted, because the market for bank credit will always have a size advantage. Potential intermediaries who might like to furnish equity funding will be deterred from doing so by the initial fixed costs. Equity markets will not arise, leaving bankers in control. This is one reason (there are of course others, such as anticompetitive lobbying by existing intermediaries) why financial systems differ so much from economy to economy.

The size of each individual financial market has an enormous effect on the costs that intermediaries face. The size of the market here reflects the number of people who invest or borrow: in other words, the number of people in the middle class. It is their absolute number that matters, not just their relative strength vis-à-vis the rich and the poor. The members of the middle class are the ones who rely on financial intermediaries, and as their numbers grow, the fixed costs of acquiring the information intermediaries need will fall. Meanwhile the demand for financial intermediation will rise too, making it all the more tempting for intermediaries to serve the middle class.

Both the relative size and the absolute size of the middle class are important factors. Overall, absolute size probably makes more of a difference. Ideally, the middle class will be both numerous and own a large fraction of the wealth; in that case, we would expect abundant, low-cost intermediation, assuming that the government is not predatory and that all the legal institutions are in place. If however, the middle class is small—both in absolute terms and as a proportion of society—the demand for intermediaries will be low, and intermediaries will not be able to overcome the relatively heavy fixed costs of information-gathering. These fixed costs and the lack of demand may discourage potential intermediaries from going into business, and the supply of financing for the middle class will suffer. The result will be a shrunken middle class. The outcome will be the same if the middle class is small in absolute terms, for the market will simply be too small for intermediaries to enter.

Crises thus do two sorts of harm: they reduce the size of the middle class, and then, once intermediaries fail, they cut the supply of credit that passes through the hands of financial intermediaries. If inequality is severe, then after a crisis the middle class will no longer be large enough to sustain financial intermediation. New intermediaries will not arise to replace those that disappeared during the crisis; the fixed costs involved will simply be prohibitive. Without new intermediaries, it will be difficult for members of the middle class whom the crisis has reduced to poverty to borrow or save and thereby regain middle-class status. The middle class will remain small, recovering too slowly from one crisis to avoid being further debilitated by the next one.

The capital markets we have in mind here are the collateral markets of our model. Again, however, the same arguments will apply to equity markets and other sophisticated financial transactions. They too require information, and demand for such transactions will come from the middle class. How big the middle class has to be for such markets to thrive is a question of both absolute numbers and relative size. If 99 percent of the population is mired in poverty, demand will remain too feeble for intermediation to take root and develop. On the other hand, a huge total population may make intermediation possible for a larger but still relatively small middle class by spreading out all the fixed costs.

Economic Shocks and Reputational Credit

What about the other form of lending in our model, reputational credit? Crises, it turns out, boost the demand for this form of financing because it is one way the rich can take advantage of attractive opportunities in a stricken economy. To begin with, they can buy up collateral sold by members of the middle class in distress. The rich will also make reputational loans to the poor to use as insurance, and they will do the same for members of the middle class who find themselves short of cash. Each lender making such loans will be betting that the borrowers will repay their debts in order not to risk their reputations and their future access to credit. To make such a bet, the lender must possess considerable information about his borrowers. He must be convinced that the borrowers will work hard once the economy recovers and that they will at least eventually have the income needed to repay the loan with interest. He must also make sure that they have no other source of reputational credit that might allow them to decamp and borrow in the future from someone else in another town. Reputational lending will thus require investment in information-gathering too, just like collateral lending. Once again, the investment will have to be in place before lending can begin.

The information needed for reputational loans will come from existing ties between borrowers and lenders, ties that make it possible for a lender to assess whether a borrower is likely to default. Often the link has nothing to do with credit, at least initially. That is why, in various parts of the world, we see landlords lending to their own tenants (whom they obviously know well), or wholesalers extending credit to small-scale manufacturers, or powerful political families making loans to clients. Such a relationship takes time to construct, but once in place, it allows borrowers to repay in a variety of ways: by paying higher rents, by accepting lower prices for products, or by performing political services.

Because reputational credit depends on ongoing relationships, it is often difficult for borrowers to switch lenders. Borrowers may therefore hesitate to move, take another job, or start a business because doing so will undermine their ties to lenders and imperil their access to credit. The problem will be especially severe for poor borrowers in underdeveloped countries. Even members of the middle class may prefer to preserve existing links to reputational lenders if they fear that shocks will overwhelm local collateral lending. If so, then the availability of reputational credit can block development of the collateral market and more sophisticated financial innovations.

Reputational credit is not confined to underdeveloped economies. Over the last half-century or so, credit cards have in fact offered a variety of reputational credit in the United States and in many other developed economies. Credit card debt is not secured by collateral, and access to credit is determined, at least in part, by a borrower's history of repayment. Credit histories are obviously necessary, and in the United States they are gathered not by the credit card companies but by credit reporting agencies.

At least in the United States, it is possible to have multiple credit cards and hence multiple lenders, in sharp contrast to most traditional reputational credit. It is also possible to switch credit card companies. But even in this case, there are limits to what a cardholder can do: in particular, it will not be easy for him to acquire a new credit card after losing his job, unless he is rich. Elsewhere, credit card debt bears a much closer resemblance to conventional reputational credit. Usually only one card is issued, and it is difficult to get another because the card issuers hold the information and refuse to release it to competitors.

Reputational lending is typically dwarfed by collateral lending and by innovations such as equity finance. Yet reputational lending often proves more resistant to crises. In a big crisis, the collateral market (and other advanced financial markets too) can shrivel up or collapse, leaving nothing but reputational lending behind. That will happen if the crisis slashes the size of the middle class. Inequality will then jump, demand for financial intermediation and financial institutions will fall, and potential intermediaries who might consider opening shop after the crisis will be frightened off by the reduced demand and by the higher fixed costs of serving a smaller middle class. In severe cases, the middle class will never recover, and the old-fashioned reputational lending that builds upon time-honored social ties may be all that remains.

Argentina may have recently come uncomfortably close to that extreme. The crisis there, as we saw in Chapter 1, began late in 2001, when the government froze bank accounts, defaulted on its debts, and then devalued the peso, which had previously been pegged to the dollar. The freeze and devaluation devastated the middle class, who were less diversified than the rich and had parked less of their fortunes abroad. Savings they had not deposited in foreign banks plummeted in value, and newspapers and radio broadcasts told stories of ruined savers and entrepreneurs and of thousands of other erstwhile members of the middle class who were reduced to scavenging through the trash. In Buenos Aires, the number of people living in poverty jumped from 20.8 percent in October 2000 to 42.3 percent in October 2002.[33]

Devaluation did eventually raise demand for Argentine exports, but the damage done to the country's financial intermediaries and the institutional chaos remained major obstacles to a robust economic recovery. It was bad enough that the government froze bank accounts and defaulted on bonds that banks owned. But it also managed to break away from the dollar in a way that left the banks with meager loan revenues relative to the size of their deposits. (It did this by using a different rate to convert dollar debt into pesos—a rate that left loans worth less than deposits of the same size.) Banks did not shut down, but they stopped making loans. Measured in dollars, bank credit dropped 72 percent between the end of 2001 and February 2003, leaving entrepreneurs or consumers who wanted to buy cars unable to get loans. Some shoppers even switched from supermarkets to neighborhood grocery stores because the local stores offered what we would call reputational credit.[34] It would seem like a ripe opportunity for banks to expand and new financial intermediaries to enter, but the shriveled middle class and continued institutional uncertainty hampered the whole process of recovery.

The lesson seems clear. A shrunken middle class slows financial development, while a large middle class does the reverse. But as we shall see, that is not the only link between financial markets and inequality.

CHAPTER 4

What Happens after Crises

USUALLY FINANCIAL CRISES are followed by change, in a pattern that has been repeated many times: first, the market shrinks, then reformers and everyone who has lost money cry out for something new. On the one hand, they may want to modify government regulations or to alter what the government does in financial markets. We are accustomed to that sort of public intervention in capital markets; the Sarbanes-Oxley Act, which was passed after the recent American corporate scandals, is only one of the more recent examples. But change can also be a purely private shift in behavior. In the 1860s and 1870s, for instance, New York was rocked by financial panic and major corporate scandals. When the government failed to act, investors adopted new rules of behavior on their own. Many put their money into local firms they knew well or (if they were wealthy enough) entrusted it to bankers with sterling reputations, such as J. P. Morgan. The bankers insisted on exercising considerable control over the companies whose securities they underwrote; their control and reputation in turn reassured the investors. The resulting standards of behavior characterized investment banking in the United States for twenty years.[1]

Sometimes the change provoked by crises works to the benefit of financial markets. The system of deposit insurance and banking regulation established in the United States during the Great Depression, for example, finally halted the bank panics that had long afflicted the American economy. But the adjustments after crises are not always advantageous, for while change can usher in wonderful financial innovations, it can also shield financial intermediaries from competition or from the dire consequences of their own incompetence. Often, in fact, it does both good and bad. The same Depression-era legislation that created deposit insurance and banking regulation, for instance, also stifled competition that would have helped depositors, borrowers, entrepreneurs, and investors.[2]

Whether the consequences are good or bad, though, only a subset of the changes proposed after a crisis is ever implemented. Crises make change more likely but not necessarily certain. Crises are not, of course, the only time when financial institutions are altered—far from it. Indeed, market expansion in good times also alters markets. But crises do increase opportunities for institutional change, because they teach key lessons about how risk is managed. Since the lessons will be most vivid immediately after a crisis, it is then that their impact on institutions will be greatest; later the crisis will have faded into irrelevance.

Several factors will determine whether a crisis initiates change and the kind of change it is likely to introduce, if any. The size of the middle class is one, for, as our simple model of credit markets suggests, a large middle class generates enormous demand for innovative financial services and for new institutions that can guard against the sort of crises that have struck in the past. Politics is another. Together with the size of the economic shock that triggers the crisis, they will tell us whether there is likely to be a great deal of change afterward, or only a little. They will also determine whether a crisis will lead to a type of change that can undermine financial markets (such as a seizure of property or the bailout of an inefficient borrower) or whether it will generate innovations that can improve them.

To understand how crises play out requires a look at both the demand for and the supply of new institutions, because the most important kind of change that crises bring about is institutional change. Here our concern is the demand for institutional change: demand from the poor, the rich, and the middle class, who are the actors in our simple model; but also from government officials and financial intermediaries, who are not only potential suppliers of financial change but sources of demand for it as well. Whether all this demand translates into new institutions will depend on politics, on the size of the middle class, and on the economic shocks that bring on crises. The way these three factors interact will determine whether a crisis is likely to unleash bailouts or property confiscations, or whether it will go beyond such potentially harmful measures and give birth to the kind of institutional innovation that can actually enhance markets (provided, of course, that it is not derailed by self-interested parties, such as intermediaries who fear competition). Institutional change of this sort is what allows markets to grow. The next two chapters will then examine whether the demand for such innovation, if it exists, will be met by private institutional entrepreneurs or by governmental action.

It turns out that we can predict what conditions will foster demand for this sort of change by using principles of political economy and our simple model of credit markets from Chapter 3. But political economy alone is not enough, for the process of change after crises is a complicated one, in which the accidents of history play an essential role. Historical contingencies acquire such a large role because they can have enormous long-term consequences. Legacies from the past can exercise a hold over politics, for instance, for years, and an institution adapted after one crisis can constrain future reforms for decades, often in an unintentional way. To understand institutional change in financial markets, we must therefore steer a course that combines predictions from political economy with long-run historical analysis. We need both if we are to understand how devastating crises can sometimes give rise to beneficial financial innovations.

Institutional Change

Institutional change after a financial crisis can take several forms. First of all, investors, entrepreneurs, and financial intermediaries may alter their behavior in order to protect themselves in future crises. One simple way to do so is to diversify their investments. Diversification may of course be impossible for middle-class entrepreneurs, who put nearly all that they have into their businesses, but it will certainly appeal to investors, and to intermediaries too if they worry about possible losses from future shocks. The idea is to add investments or assets that behave differently and do not all falter at the same time. Investors are generally interested in earning high returns and avoiding risk, but they will often be willing to make an investment that pays a low return if it acts differently from the other parts of their portfolio. That is why investors will put money into something like gold or real estate, which will reduce the risk of losses. An entrepreneur may try to do the same, by selling off shares in his company and then investing the money in other assets.

Simply rearranging an investment portfolio to diversify (by selling stocks and bonds, for example, in order to buy more real estate) does not necessarily entail any institutional change. But often the quest for diversification will fuel demand for new financial instruments. Financial intermediaries may then establish something like a mutual fund, which will help small-scale investors diversify their stock portfolios, or they may concoct something like a real estate investment trust to facilitate investment in real property. The mutual funds, real estate investment trusts, and other new financial instruments they create are only private contracts, but as contracts, and innovative ones at that, they constitute new institutions.

New financial instruments are not the only institutions that arise when individuals seek to shield themselves from future crises. A banker, for instance, may resolve to spend more time monitoring borrowers. A mortgage lender may refuse to lend in neighborhoods where property values have plummeted. Or investors and financial intermediaries may seek out information, creating demand that may be met by private firms such as R. G. Dun & Company, which reported on the credit rating of firms and individuals in nineteenth-century America. All these new rules of behavior constitute institutions, and the aim of all will of course be to reduce the risk and increase the returns for individual investors and financial intermediaries.

So far the institutions have not involved the government, except when it has to enforce the new contracts and adjudicate disputes that arise. But clearly the government itself can create new institutions. One obvious way to do so is to impose new laws or regulations. That has been an increasingly common reaction of governments around the world from the 1930s on: in the United States during the Great Depression, in Asia after 1997, and in both America and Europe after the recent bout of corporate scandals.

And sometimes after a crisis, the government goes beyond imposing regulations and takes on a new role as a borrower, lender, or financial intermediary. It may borrow heavily, something that states have long done. It may become a lender and channel investment to a particular sector of the economy, such as housing or transportation. Or it may provide financial services, such as old-age pensions or insurance against unemployment, at least some of which could otherwise be furnished by private entrepreneurs. The government's new role after the crisis may entail creating financial intermediaries or even nationalizing part of the market, either because the political rewards are high or because the crisis has made it impossible for private actors to do their job. After World War II drove European banks into insolvency, for example, governments nationalized them, both because it was politically popular and because the banks themselves were no longer able to make loans or protect their customers' deposits. Finally, the government's new role may entail abandoning responsibilities that the government had once assumed. After nationalizing the banking system at the end of World War II, for instance, the French government privatized it again starting in 1986. This sort of withdrawal from financial markets has in fact become the norm in much of Europe since the late 1980s.

The issue here, however, is not who supplies new financial institutions after a crisis. For our purposes in this chapter at least, it does not matter much whether the supplier is, say, a private company that sells workers insurance and helps them save for retirement or, alternatively, a political leader like the German Chancellor Bismarck, who created a government-mandated system of social insurance for workers in the 1880s. Our concern is instead with demand for institutional change after crises, for without the demand no private firm—or political leader either—will supply the new institutions.

The big question here is whether the demand for change translates into new institutions or whether it instead veers off into calls for a bailout or for seizing property. Such measures are an understandable reaction to financial crises, even in the most capitalist economies—what, after all, is more natural than helping the losers or confiscating the winners' ill-gotten gains?—and the political pressure for a bailout can become overwhelming, particularly in a democracy. In the long run, however, bailouts and property seizures can do considerable damage. It is true that they do not always do so: bailouts in particular can sometimes help achieve social peace, and they may be the political price that has to be paid to fashion a new formal institution. But bailouts and seizures of property do have the potential for harm.

Consider, for instance, what happened in Japan in the 1990s. When the Tokyo Stock Exchange and Japanese real estate markets were soaring in the late 1980s, many medium-sized companies in Japan borrowed heavily from banks, often using land as collateral. But when the bubble burst in 1990, the economy soured, leaving many of the borrowers unable to repay their loans. Banks themselves then began to founder, for they had a huge number of delinquent loans on their books and collateral—land in particular—that was now plummeting in value. Faced with a financial crisis, the Japanese government embarked upon a bailout program that had considerable political appeal. It obliged stronger banks to assist or take over weaker ones—a traditional practice that the government now pushed further than it had in the past—and it eventually provided insolvent banks with direct infusions of cash. At bottom, this policy involved taking money from taxpayers and from the owners of the stronger banks and using it to prop up the weaker ones so that they would not close down companies that were behind in their loans. The government's aim was to prevent politically unpopular layoffs and to protect influential companies, as on the island of Hokkaido, where the government offered money and also twisted arms in order to have the large and insolvent Hokkaido Takushoku Bank taken over by a smaller bank in a way that would protect bankrupt local employers and save a politically connected construction company.[3]

The trouble with this sort of bailout is that it removes the incentive to create institutions that can solve problems and actually improve financial markets. Calls for a bailout, which are virtually inevitable in the aftermath of crises, will conflict with the demand for innovation, for if the government is likely to bail out the victims of future crises, there will be little reason to establish any new institutions to ward off the crises or even to use any institutions that have already been created. In short, a bailout will undermine demand for institutional innovation.

This is hardly a theoretical problem. In Japan, the government's commitment to bailing out banks and insolvent employers delayed reform of the banking system and thereby helped slow economic growth through the 1990s. Because investors could foresee that taxes would eventually have to rise to pay for the bailout, they cut back on the projects they funded. Meanwhile, banks kept propping up inefficient companies with further loans, and they were slow to improve the sort of retail mortgage lending that might have helped the middle class.[4]

The consequences of seizing property after a crisis can be just as bad. Confiscating the winners' ill-gotten gains may be practically irresistible after a crisis, but in the long run it can discourage savers from investing their money and entrepreneurs from starting new firms. Why, after all, take risks if the profits will be taken away? And if the confiscated property will be used to assist the losers, there will again be less of an incentive to create new institutions that can protect against crises in the future.

Who Will Call for Institutional Change

Several actors are likely to call for institutional change and generate the demand for financial innovations that we are interested in. The middle class (so our model of financial markets suggests) are a prime candidate, but they will share the stage with the rich and poor, and with the government and financial intermediaries as well. If the financial intermediaries manage to survive a crisis, they will undoubtedly want to shape the path of institutional change, for new financial institutions will affect the business they do. As for the government, it has to be given an independent role, because its actions will not simply reflect the preferences of constituents or citizens. The reason is that creating an institution or intervening in financial markets gives political leaders an appealing way to reward constituents or attract new supporters. That was one of Bismarck's motives when he established the system of social insurance for workers in the 1880s. His hope (a vain one in the end) was to lure workers away from socialism and attract them to his own regime.

If, for the sake of simplicity, we temporarily set the government and financial intermediaries aside and consider just the three groups in our model—the poor, the rich, and the middle class—we can naturally ask which of them will desire innovation. Which ones, in other words, will generate the demand for new institutions that will help financial markets grow? What do our model and the principles of political economy model say?

Because the poor have no assets to secure loans, they will, as we know, be excluded from markets that require collateral for borrowing—the sort of markets that would allow them to become entrepreneurs by, for instance, mortgaging their homes. They will as a result have relatively little interest in innovation in these markets, for no matter what the new institutions are, their lack of collateral will still keep them out, at least as borrowers. Their participation in the collateral market as investors is also unlikely, for with little human capital and no financial assets, their income will remain too low for them to amass much in the way of savings. As a result they will not generate much demand for change in the collateral market, which is often the essential one for funding enterprises. They will remain dependent on reputational credit, which is always limited, and they will favor forming an alliance with the rich—the chief lenders in the reputational market—to ensure that reputational credit is protected. As we shall see, this alliance may undercut the natural desire they might have to support bailouts or property seizures, but it may also work against innovation.

What about the middle class's demand for innovation? On the one hand, they fear economic shocks, because, as our model suggests, their undiversified assets leave them vulnerable. There are two ways they can protect themselves. The first is insurance, or, in other words, a financial contract that, like auto insurance, pays off in case of disaster—in this case, whenever the economy is jolted. Unfortunately, this sort of insurance does not exist for all shocks, even in advanced economies.[5] But there is enough of it to protect members of the middle class against many calamities, at least in most developed countries. They can, for instance, buy life insurance from private companies, and they usually have some sort of unemployment or disability insurance, often from the government. But to defend against the numerous shocks for which they have no insurance, the middle class may well seek bailouts for those laid low by the crisis, such as investors who have lost money, or entrepreneurs whose projects have failed.

Members of the middle class, though, will seek more than just protection against crises. They also have a deep interest in nearly all institutional change that promotes the development of financial markets, particularly local ones. As we know, they invest their savings in such markets, and they borrow in them to start businesses, pursue careers, and buy houses or farms. If a crisis makes it costly or difficult for them to borrow, or if it casts doubt on the information they have about investment risks and returns, they will be eager to see new institutions put in place that can reassure both borrowers and investors. At the very least, the borrowers will want credit at lower cost; the lenders, higher returns, plus insurance against risk and the devastating effects of crises.

Our third group of actors, the rich, turn out to generate relatively little demand for institutional innovation. With their large, diversified portfolios, they have little need for insurance and hence little incentive to create institutions to ward off future crises. They can simply ride out most crises, knowing that a debacle in one market will usually be offset by gains elsewhere. Furthermore, if they want a different institution, they can often find it in another market or arrange to have it incorporated into a custom-made private contract that a financial intermediary can prepare. The fixed costs of doing so will deter other investors, but these fixed costs pale to insignificance relative to their large fortunes. Hence they are less dependent than the middle class on widely available innovations.

They do, however, want to avoid a bailout or a property confiscation, because they are the ones most likely to get stuck with the tab. Adding to the danger of such measures, from their perspective, is the damage a bailout can do to the sort of alliance they often have with the poor. Since the poor can borrow only from rich people who know them well—a landlord, employer, or local grandee—the rich can use the loans to build up clienteles, a practice that is particularly common in developing countries. But if the poor can benefit from a postcrisis bailout, the reputational loans become unnecessary, and the poor will abandon the loans and the clientage that goes with them. The potential threat of bailouts (and property confiscation too, if some of the proceeds go to the poor) is therefore a double one as far as the rich are concerned, for they risk both footing the bill and losing their hold over their clients.

The rich may admittedly care about improving a large national financial market, but even then their ability to shift resources abroad will dampen their desire for innovation, provided, of course, that there are foreign markets that have the institutions lacking at home. Obviously, if change is inevitable, they will seek institutions that reduce the likelihood of having their property seized or having to pay for bailouts in future crises. They will also avoid investing in markets where confiscations or bailouts are a threat.

Clearly, the size of these three groups and their political clout also matter for institutional change. If the rich possess a large share of a society's wealth, then the middle class will be tempted to seize their property or have them pay for a bailout. The rich will be able to retain their wealth provided they hold the reins of power, but otherwise their only recourse may be to diversify their portfolios geographically or to hold assets that are difficult to confiscate. That may mean highly liquid assets, such as checking-account balances that can easily be wired abroad. It may also mean almost the opposite—a large farm that the state would find difficult to manage if it were seized. Meanwhile the middle class, if it is large, will generate enormous demand for institutional change after crises, and innovation, as we shall see, will be even more likely if the middle class is a political power.

Why Institutional Change Occurs

If the middle class wants institutional change, while the rich simply want to avoid paying for bailouts or having their property confiscated, what will the outcome be? Under what circumstances will new institutions emerge, and when will there be bailouts and confiscations? The answer will clearly depend on the relative political might of the middle class and the rich, and of the poor as well, on their importance as constituencies and their effectiveness as lobbies. It will also depend on the goals of the government and of financial intermediaries, whom we have until now ignored. The whole process, obviously, can be quite complex, at the very least because of all the politics involved. The government will certainly worry about its ability to borrow and to raise resources, but politicians will also care about retaining power or getting reelected. Financial intermediaries will fret over competition, but their own effectiveness at lobbying may vary greatly from firm to firm.

Nonetheless, there are some general patterns that do not depend on who has political power or the specific structure of political institutions. First of all, the demand for institutional change waxes and wanes with crises. That is not to say that crises are the only moments of creativity in capital markets. Bismarck's retirement schemes were not proposed or enacted immediately after a financial crisis, and they are far from the only innovations that had nothing to do with crises.

But crises do shift the equilibrium of forces, and they therefore have enormous potential to alter institutions radically, particularly if the calls for a bailout or confiscation can be overcome. The clamor for a bailout or confiscation will be loudest during the crisis and in its immediate aftermath. Laid-off workers, unpaid creditors, bankrupt entrepreneurs, and insolvent financial intermediaries will pursue such remedies as a way to recoup their losses. Over time, however, their cries for help will subside as calls for new institutions grow louder.

There are a number of reasons why the demand for institutional change will peak shortly after a crisis and then fade away. Some are psychological. Individuals, experiments have shown, are extremely sensitive to financial losses (more sensitive, apparently, than they are to gains of the same magnitude), and the sort of reverses that a crisis typically causes (huge ones that come on suddenly at the end of a long buildup) are likely to seem particularly painful. They will affect even people who have not suffered any personal losses, for individuals tend to seize upon recent disasters when they form opinions about what they should do in the future. A crisis is the sort of striking event that gets their attention and even causes them to exaggerate the odds of similar troubles in the future; it will not have the same immediacy and effect years later, when memories are no longer fresh and people's concerns have abated. Realizing this, the political and economic entrepreneurs who can supply the new institutions will play upon the fears that a crisis spawns when they suggest institutional change. They will simply find it easier to promote a new institution or mobilize individuals in a political campaign to obtain it when the crisis is still in the news. And because people learn from one another, one individual's decision to support a new institution right after a crisis (by, say, buying a new financial instrument or joining a political campaign) is likely to convince others to join in too. Support for institutional change is therefore likely to grow so long as the crisis is still a salient issue.[6]

The demand for institutional change will also be affected by inequality, which will intensify the demand for confiscation or bailouts and muffle calls for innovation. If the rich own a large portion of a society's wealth, it will be tempting to tax them or even to seize their property and then use the proceeds to pay for a bailout. In an unequal society that tactic can easily divert the middle class from truly innovative institutional change. On the other hand, if a society is more egalitarian, it will have a larger middle class and hence more demand for innovation. Whether equality or inequality will have these effects, however, ultimately depends on political institutions.

Imagine, for example, what would happen in a democracy if voters cared only about how much they paid in taxes and how much they got back from the government. In such a democracy, a politician might win votes, in the aftermath of a crisis, if she proposed taxing the rich in order to relieve the poor and the middle class, who, she might argue, had suffered disproportionate harm during the crisis. Her proposal could appear quite evenhanded; for instance, it might involve taking a fixed fraction of everyone's wealth and dividing it up equally for every citizen. Such a proposal would be a bailout, but it could be quite popular. True, it would leave the rich worse off, because they would pay more in taxes than they would get back in return. The poor, however, would find their situation improved, and they would not be alone. A simple calculation shows that any voter with below-average wealth would favor this kind of bailout. Potentially there would be many such voters, because distributions of wealth are unequal and most people would have below-average wealth. The only problem would be getting all of them to the polls, for poorer voters are less likely to vote than rich ones. But if inequality were great enough, the bailout would be popular, and politicians who wanted to be elected would propose it.

Reality, of course, is more complicated, for opinions about bailouts or confiscations of property are affected by other issues besides one's being a net winner or loser under the proposed scheme.[7] But the insight this imaginary example affords is still important: great inequality is likely to bring about bailouts and property seizures in democracies. The same would be true in an unequal society as the franchise expands: if inequality is high enough and enough people can vote, then proposals for a bailout or confiscation will presumably carry the day.

Similar arguments, it should be stressed, apply to government-sponsored insurance programs such as unemployment insurance, assistance to the poor, and old-age pensions, which may figure among the new institutions proposed after crises. These programs provide a form of insurance and usually shift tax revenues from the well-off to those who are less fortunate. Support for this sort of redistribution is more likely when the franchise expands, and in democracies total spending on such programs rises when eligible voters go to the polls. It also increases when the gap between the poor and the middle class narrows and a chasm opens up between them and the rich. What actually happens in a democracy is complicated because it depends on lobbies, political parties, ethnic divisions, and the opinions of the median voter—the man or woman whose attitudes lie right in the center of opinion, at least among those who turn out to vote. If voters believe that their families could easily fall victim to the next economic shock, they will favor a redistributive insurance program that promises protection, particularly if it seems to benefit people like themselves.[8]

In short, while democracy can encourage calls for confiscation or bailouts, it can also promote government redistribution that blunts any postcrisis clamor for seizing the winners' ill-gotten gains or helping out those who have lost money. Unlike the bailouts and postcrisis confiscations, government redistribution has the virtue of being set up in advance and of not simply being a Band-Aid applied once a crisis strikes. It therefore does not do as much as bailouts or confiscations to dampen incentives for institutional change after crises, and although it is sometimes simply a substitute for private insurance, it does not seem to slow economic growth, at least in wealthy democracies—yet another contrast to the bailouts and property seizures.[9] Such redistribution is particularly likely when the middle class is large—since the median voter is then likely to be middle class—and when members of the middle class see themselves as the likely beneficiaries. It can then wean the middle class away from confiscation and bailouts, leaving them free to elicit real innovations from politicians and private entrepreneurs.

If, by contrast, the political regime is a plutocracy, in which wealth counts rather than votes and the rich end up controlling the government, it will block both confiscations and bailouts that tax the rich in order to aid the poor and middle class. Such a regime is also likely to obstruct the creation of government insurance programs that redistribute from rich to poor. Financial markets will thus be free to flourish, because there will be little risk of assets' being seized, and less of a danger that earnings will be taxed away, at least in peacetime, for, apart from the expenses of warfare, the government will not be spending heavily to fund bailouts or redistribution. If one of these plutocracies happens to have a large middle class, the latter will generate demand for innovation. Innovative institutions may follow, including insurance, but whatever insurance there is will in all likelihood be provided privately and not subsidized by the government, for such a step would require taxing the rich. Despite some differences, one can thus imagine financial markets in democracies and plutocracies developing in parallel, provided that neither one has too much inequality and provided too that shocks remain small. If a shock is too big, insurance, whether public or private, can easily fail, making confiscations and bailouts more attractive, and more likely under democracy.

If we look more closely at the interaction between inequality and

TABLE 4.1 Inequality and political structure: Their effect on financial markets and institutional change after crises

Political regime	Large middle class	Small middle class
Democratic	Financial markets	No financial markets
	Institutional change	No institutional change
	Bailouts likely	Bailouts unlikely
	Some redistribution or confiscation possible	Redistribution and confiscation likely
Plutocratic	Financial markets	Small financial markets
	Institutional change	Some institutional change possible
	No redistribution, bailouts, or confiscation	No redistribution, bailouts, or confiscation

Note: Both here and in the text, redistribution refers to government programs (such as welfare or progressive taxation) that are in place before crises and that shift tax revenues from one class of citizens to another. Bailouts and confiscation, by contrast, involve actions taken after crises either to help out the losers or to seize property from those who have emerged unscathed. The political regime (democratic or plutocratic) is independent of the social structure—here the size of the middle class—even though democracy and a small middle class cannot long coexist. For us there are three social classes (the rich, the poor, and the middle class), and by our definition the rich are always a tiny minority. Hence a small middle class goes hand in hand with a large number of paupers. Plutocracies here refer to governments controlled by a wealthy elite, as in many dictatorships, absolutist monarchies, and polities that restrict the franchise to the rich.

the political structure, the divergence between societies becomes striking. Table 4.1 summarizes the expected patterns in an idealized way, with each cell representing a combination of a political regime and a distribution of wealth. Equality here is gauged by the size of the middle class, the critical measure in our model of how financial markets operate. Plutocracy in the table includes a number of political regimes that some might consider democratic because they rely on voting. But when the franchise is limited to only the richest 1 percent of males (as in France in 1817–1830) or when vote-buying is prevalent (as in eighteenth-century England or twentieth-century Mexico, when the country was under the control of the Institutional Revolutionary Party, or PRI) the label "plutocracy" seems more appropriate. It also fits most dictatorships and monarchies. Countries in nineteenth-century Europe were by and large plutocracies, while we would consider the United States, Canada, and most western European nations after 1945 to be democracies, each with a large middle class. Developing countries in the late twentieth century have usually been democratic and unequal (such as Argentina or Brazil) or plutocratic and unequal (such as Zaire under the dictator Mobutu, or Guatemala when the military was in control in the 1970s and early 1980s).

Although there are four cells in the table, there are only three likely outcomes—three equilibria, if you will. By equilibrium we mean an arrangement of political institutions, financial markets, insurance organizations, and equality that persists through time. The reason there are only three equilibria is that an unequal democracy (the cell on the top right with a small middle class) is inherently unstable. In it the pressure to seize property or to arrange a bailout after a shock is so great that the rich will move their assets abroad or stage a coup to prevent the loss of their property.[10] If the coup fails, confiscation is likely to follow, making everyone equal. In any event, either inequality will diminish or the country will become a plutocracy.

The best example of such instability is Latin America, where countries have labored under such a mix of regimes for the last two centuries. Alternating between dictatorship and democracy, the countries of Latin America have experienced both frequent financial crises provoked by massive capital flight and a number of attempts to take property from the rich and give it to the poor, notably via land reform. From our perspective, the land reform would count as confiscation, but because such a measure would create a middle class and thereby nurture financial institutions, it would be one of the instances in which even confiscation could actually do good. In Latin America, however, land reform has by and large proved ineffective. Inequality has remained high, and financial innovation has been minimal, at least until recently. The reason, in part, is that the rich, knowing that confiscation is likely, have either subverted the efforts at land reform or acquired the means to transfer significant fractions of their wealth abroad. And at the same time, the tiny middle class has generated little demand for institutional change.

Let us now consider the other cells, each one an equilibrium that can persist. The oldest one is plutocracy, with an unequal wealth distribution (bottom lower right in Table 4.1). From Russia under the tsars to many developing countries today, this sort of regime has certain common characteristics. Local formal financial markets are small—in part because the middle class is tiny and in part because the rich find it advantageous to take their demand for financial services elsewhere. There are few bailouts and property seizures after crises (and little redistribution beforehand either), because the rich can block such measures, and by and large the only insurance that exists takes the form of reputational loans binding the rich and the poor. Financial innovation would normally be encouraged by the absence of any real threat of confiscation or heavy taxation (at least in peacetime—wars are of course another matter), but whatever institutional change there is will be limited by the small size of the middle class. Some institutional change may nonetheless take place if members of the middle class are politically powerful or if their numbers are growing.

Locating a perfect example of plutocracy with a large middle class is not easy, because most plutocracies are far from equal. Taiwan would perhaps come closest, when it was under the thumb of Chiang Kai-shek and his son, for although land reform had created what we could call a middle class, political power remained in the hands of a small number of nationalists from mainland China. Since the nationalists were not Taiwanese landlords, they were willing to undertake land reform in 1949–1953 to avoid unrest in the countryside. Once that was over and inflation had been controlled, the country experienced little of what we would call confiscation under Chiang and his son, and bailouts for inefficient firms were relatively limited too. Taiwan did spend a great deal on education, which could be considered a form of redistribution, but overall the tax system was not progressive. And although Taiwan did strictly regulate financial institutions, it quickly developed a dense network of banks and informal financial intermediaries.[11]

More significant examples can be found in eighteenth-century England and nineteenth-century western Europe as a whole. At first glance, the countries involved might seem to be a poor fit in the lower left-hand cell of the table, for although they were by and large plutocracies, some crude measures of inequality (in particular, the fraction of income going to the richest 20 percent of the population) would rank them down with Latin America. The trouble with a measure like this is that it does not get at what really matters here— namely, the absolute size of the middle class. To begin with, many of the people in the richest 20 percent of the population were themselves middle class. More important, the key factor in our model here is not so much the share of income (or even of wealth) owned by the rich. Rather, it is the absolute size of the middle class—the number of people in it. And by that standard Europe was not like Latin America.

Western Europe in fact had a sizable middle class even before it industrialized, and the middle class grew during industrialization, even though the rich were amassing more wealth. The middle class here were, once again, individuals who possessed some wealth, and there were far more of them than in Latin America. The most significant difference in western Europe was that far more people in the countryside had some land than in Latin America, although numerous city dwellers in western Europe would also count as middle class. In England, the most unequal country in western Europe, over 14 percent of household heads outside of London owned some real estate in 1873; in France, comparable figures in the years 1850–1873 are much higher, on the order of half the population. In Latin America, figures on land ownership today or in the past are hard to come by, but those that are available for the same period are much lower than the ones from western Europe. In the Mexican countryside in 1910, for example, only 2.4 percent of rural household heads owned land.[12] This sizable middle class in western Europe borrowed heavily to finance enterprises, and it also invested, creating considerable demand for institutional change. True, the middle class did not have political power, even though elections were held; the rich dominated governments until late in the nineteenth century. Meanwhile the political power of the rich made confiscations and bailouts impossible, and it kept governments from preying upon the capital markets that did exist—conditions that also encouraged financial innovation.

There were, however, some limits to institutional change in eighteenth-century England and nineteenth-century Europe. In particular, the government provided little insurance against unemployment or financial disaster, because plutocracy ruled out that sort of redistribution. Even deposit insurance did not exist, and when financial crises struck, central banks by and large did not intervene. Banks simply closed, and firms were allowed to fail. Although plutocracy could coexist with financial innovation in nineteenth-century Europe, it was one of the reasons (in addition to the prevailing laissez-faire ideology that discouraged intervention in the economy) why governments rarely interceded in capital markets to set up insurance or impose new regulations after crises.

Hence in western Europe at least the high share of wealth held by the rich was offset by the increasing absolute size of the middle class and by political regimes that reduced the threat of confiscation, bailouts, and government predation. The middle class had grown big enough to create enormous returns for financial innovation by private entrepreneurs. In addition, governments created new financial institutions even though they refused to create insurance or to impose new regulations after crises. England again led the way, beginning at the end of the seventeenth century. Not only did the government leave financial markets unmolested—a rarity, we know, in the eighteenth century—but Britain was one of the first European states to create a centralized exchange for state debt. This centralized exchange in turn facilitated private institutional change to meet the demand of the country's merchants and other members of the middle class.

The equilibrium in western Europe came to an end because of yet another crisis, this one after World War I. The war marked a turning point in the history of equality, suffrage, and taxation. To meet the enormous expense of the fighting, European countries had to abandon the gold standard and print money. The result was severe inflation everywhere, and in central Europe even worse—a bout of hyperinflation that in Germany saw prices jump by a factor of over a trillion. Except for Britain, none of the belligerents restored their currency to its prewar value in a way that would compensate creditors for their losses. Bondholders therefore lost heavily and in central Europe were ruined. Although some middle-class savers were ruined and those rich people who managed to hold on to real assets muddled through, the net effect was a reduction in the fraction of wealth held by the rich. In France the drop was rapid; in England, more gradual. What mattered most, though, was that the middle class in Europe survived and was no smaller than it had been before the war.[13]

Progressive taxation accelerated the redistribution of income and wealth wrought by the war, as did spending on social programs such as welfare, pensions, health care, and housing. Most European states expanded the franchise in the late nineteenth century or early twentieth century, in part because elites feared social upheaval: a broader franchise would help assure disfranchised citizens (particularly workers) that they would get a share of the pie. Widening the franchise was also a way to ensure that politicians would spend money on the sewer and water systems that Europe's burgeoning cities sorely needed.[14] But the war was still the prime moving factor behind all the redistribution. Nonetheless, progressive taxation did not exert much of a bite until the 1920s and 1930s, and the real giant step in redistributive social spending did not come until even later, after World War II. As a fraction of gross domestic product, the median western European country spent 0.4 percent on social programs in 1880 and about the same amount in 1910. By 1920 the median had risen to only 0.6 percent. By 1930 it was much larger—1.2 percent—but it was only after the war that it exploded, reaching 11.0 percent by 1960.[15]

By then the fourth equilibrium (the top left-hand box in Table 4.1) prevailed in most developed countries. Progressive taxation had reduced wealth inequality, and democratic governments had created social insurance programs, giving individuals considerable protection against financial shocks. Although these policies redistributed wealth, they did not stifle economic growth or financial innovation. Why did they not slow growth or the creation of pioneering financial institutions? In part it was because some of the government programs funded by the taxation—education is perhaps the best example—produced a high economic return for all of society. In part it was that governments adjusted the details of their tax policies to avoid reducing incentives for investment—for instance, by keeping a progressive tax system but cutting levies on capital gains. The incentive here, in many of the countries, may have been the fear of losing elections if economic growth faltered.[16] Finally, since members of the middle class were major beneficiaries of the government insurance programs, they could regard the progressive taxation as the price they had to pay to be protected against shocks. That protection in turn encouraged them to take risks—say, by borrowing to found a business or by investing their savings in the stock market.

According to Table 4.1, a large middle class is clearly a major impetus to financial development. Yet it is worth reminding ourselves that it is not the only factor at work. Information and government debt levels also play a role, as does the nature of the political regime, which is an independent force. It is true that a weak relationship exists between the size of the middle class and the political regime, for democracy cannot coexist for long with a small middle class. But the political regime has an effect on financial markets above and beyond the size of the middle class. Furthermore, crises clearly affect financial development too, either by destroying information and harming the middle class, or by triggering institutional changes that can be either good or bad. Whether the reforms prove to be beneficial will, to a great extent, depend on the political regime and the size of the middle class, as in Table 4.1. Even that, however, is not the full story.

Crucial Information from History

The story we have told so far—one based on the patterns of behavior in Table 4.1—applies to much of what has happened to financial markets over the last two centuries. But the story remains incomplete. To grasp fully what happens during crises and in their aftermath—whether they trigger confiscations, bailouts, beneficial innovations, or nothing at all—we also have to take into account historical contingencies and their long-run consequences.

The primary way for historical accidents to have enduring consequences is through the actions of the government and financial intermediaries, which our basic model and Table 4.1 gloss over. Both the government and financial intermediaries can unleash crises or generate demand for institutional change in their aftermath. But they can also supply the new institutions that others seek after a crisis has struck. Since the institutional change will inevitably depend upon the government (which, at the very least, will have to enforce new contracts and adjudicate disputes even when the new institutions are supplied by private financial intermediaries), the whole process of institutional change will be a political one, in which contingencies will play a huge role, whether the government is a democracy or not. Historical accidents can break or form political coalitions that support particular institutional arrangements and that endure for years. Other historical legacies can lock institutions in place.

Consider, for instance, what happened in the United States when a financial panic in 1837 and subsequent economic slowdown drove nine state governments (Arkansas, Illinois, Indiana, Louisiana, Maryland, Michigan, Mississippi, Pennsylvania, and the territory of Florida, which was about to achieve statehood) to default on their debts.[17] From the perspective of political economy, the sequence may appear quite simple: by borrowing too much, the nine had veered too close to their danger zone, to use the language of Chapter 1, and the economic downturn had pushed them over the brink. Default then became attractive, for the only alternative, a tax hike, would have been unpopular in states where most taxpayers (at least if they were white men) could vote. None of these states was the sort of plutocracy one found, in, say, Great Britain, where the government could run up huge debts (as it did during the wars of the French Revolution and the Napoleonic Empire) and then, to pay the bondholders back, raise taxes on the many poor and middle-class consumers who did not have the right to vote. The small number of bondholders in Britain benefited, as might be expected in a polity in which the franchise was limited and in which a government default would have been an unacceptable form of confiscation, seizing money from owners of government bonds and using it to bail out taxpayers. But the situation was different in the nine American states, which, even if they did not yet have universal suffrage, were far closer to fitting in the equal democracy box of Table 4.1. Property ownership in the nine states was fairly widespread and the franchise much broader than it had been in Great Britain after Napoleonic Wars. It is no wonder then that they defaulted on their debts in the early 1840s, unlike Great Britain a generation before.[18]

This simple story of political economy, which seems to fit the table so well, is persuasive; yet for all its appeal, it is incomplete. To begin with, it hides the reasons why the states were borrowing in the first place. What was the reason they were running up their debts? It was, quite simply, to build canals and railroads and to invest in local banks that would promote economic development of newly settled territory. Measures of this sort appealed to the numerous middle-class voters—particularly farmers, who made up the bulk of the population—and they would also attract more new settlers. The states thus had powerful political reasons for borrowing, all the more so because regional rivalries and the ideological legacy of Thomas Jefferson kept the federal government from funding similar efforts.[19]

Inheritances from the past and historical contingencies also explain why default was so attractive politically. The investors who bought the bulk of the state bonds happened to live in England or on the East Coast of the United States; most did not reside in the states that reneged on their obligations. The burden of default would thus be born by outsiders who did not vote. A tax increase, by contrast, would have fallen primarily on middle-class farmers who had mortgaged their land during the boom times before the slowdown. It could have easily driven them into bankruptcy, and it might also drive prospective settlers to move to states that had not increased taxes.[20] It is no surprise that the politicians running the state governments chose to stiff the bondholders.

Finally, and most important, political economy by itself cannot explain the innovations that this crisis gave rise to. The default by the nine states in the early 1840s was not an unmitigated disaster, for, alongside the investors' losses, it also gave rise to new institutions. The default did make it hard for Americans to raise money in Britain, but when enterprising bankers like George Peabody helped get many of the states to resume payment, it kept state governments from earning the sort of disastrous reputation for predatory behavior that could have paralyzed the market for state bonds; along the way, Peabody helped make the reputation of what eventually became the Morgan bank, which would fund much American industry. Also important here were measures adopted by states to limit their ability to borrow—measures that were not removed when state constitutions were revised. In the long run, having the states tie their own hands in this way improved their creditworthiness and helped preserve the market for state bonds.[21]

Like some other crises, the state default in the early 1840s thus mixed both good and bad. The good was that it gave rise to significant innovations—a private banker's reputation and restrictions on state debt—that had a lasting effect on the development of American capital markets. One could argue that innovations of this sort were likely in the United States because it had a large and politically powerful middle class and was fast approaching a position in the equal-and-democratic box of Table 4.1. But the innovations that followed this crisis would be hard to understand if one ignored the history, and the same would of course be true of the state defaults themselves.

CHAPTER 5

Financial Intermediaries and the Demand for Change

IN THE AFTERMATH of a financial crisis, the public will pillory bankers, brokers, and other financial intermediaries and hold them responsible for their losses. The outcry against stock analysts and investment bankers after the dot-com bubble burst in 2000 is only one recent example of this general pattern. Yet for all the diatribes and public lamentations directed against financial intermediaries, the fact is that they can actually be agents for good after a crisis, by creating the new institutions that people seek for the future. Despite the harm that intermediaries may sometimes do, they can reduce the risk involved in financial transactions by providing insurance, solving problems of asymmetric information, creating financial instruments that help investors diversify, and arranging the loans that entrepreneurs need to surmount economic shocks. History shows that they can also facilitate economic growth. In early modern Europe, bankers oiled the wheels of commerce by trading novel forms of short-term debt. Today venture capitalists help scientists commercialize their discoveries. The spur financial institutions give to economic growth—so the evidence suggests—is real, and not merely a response to a process already under way.[1]

What conditions will drive these private financial intermediaries to make the institutional innovations that can help ward off future crises and encourage economic growth? The answer, as is so often the case in financial markets, entails avoiding extremes, but it also depends on politics and on the chance outcome of crises themselves, which can never be eradicated, no matter how innovative intermediaries are. Political economy can tell us which extremes are likely to discourage innovation, but historical accidents and enduring institutional legacies also have a critical role to play.

Avoiding Extremes

What are the extremes that hamper financial innovation? One way to find out is to look at a region such as western Europe, where intermediaries have been devising novel financial instruments and building new institutions for centuries—not just the short-term debt and stock exchanges of the early modern period, but long-distance trade contracts in the Middle Ages, life insurance and fire insurance in the eighteenth century, and banks that operated branches and owned stock in companies in the nineteenth century.

Much of the innovation in western Europe has taken place in a small number of urban financial centers: Venice and Genoa in the Middle Ages; Antwerp and Amsterdam in the sixteenth and seventeenth centuries; and London, Paris, and Berlin in the 1700s and 1800s. The same is true today, with London and New York functioning as centers of financial ingenuity. Certainly there are financial innovations in other parts of the world—the Grameen Bank, for example, which made it possible for villagers in Bangladesh to borrow without collateral. Nevertheless, the innovations in these key cities deserve our attention because they have become models for much of what happens elsewhere.

One feature common to all these cities is the size of their financial markets: all were sites where an enormous number of valuable financial transactions took place, far more than in neighboring towns. In Paris in 1789, for example, the volume of lending per person was six times what it was in other sizable French cities such as Lyons or Rouen. The size of these financial centers demonstrates how important economies of scale are in financial dealings and especially in financial innovation. New financial institutions are expensive, and the costs of developing them can be more easily recouped when markets are vast. The legal cost of creating a new type of loan will be lower, for example, when it can be spread among many borrowers, or, in other words, when the loan market is big. The cost to each borrower will thus be lower and the return to the banker who offers the loans higher.

But if size encourages innovation, why do all financial innovation and all financial transactions not end up concentrated in a single center that dominates every other city? Why, in other words, can several financial centers exist at the same time—London and New York today, or London, Paris, and Berlin in the nineteenth century?

One reason is that while large size allows legal expenses and other fixed costs to be spread among more transactions, it also exacerbates problems of asymmetric information, which can be particularly serious for new financial instruments and other innovations. At some point it will not be worth trying to expand the market further, because it will be too costly for parties to learn enough about one another.

Precisely where this point lies depends on a number of factors, including the state of technology. Someday the costs of gathering financial information may fall enough that all financial dealings can be concentrated in a single electronic market. But such a market does not yet exist, and today, as in the past, financial innovation tends to be concentrated in large cities. In smaller cities the fixed costs of a new institution cannot be spread over a large enough number of transactions, and there may be too few parties who are willing to try something novel. On the other hand, if a market is too big, information costs loom too large, and attempts to expand the market further court disaster, as happened (so we saw) with East Coast and British investors who had difficulty funding mortgages in the American West in the late 1800s. The lesson seems to be that extremes of size work against innovation.

An extremely high level of government debt will also curb financial innovation, for all the reasons laid out in Chapter 1, because it boosts the odds that the government will prey on capital markets. As the history of the European financial centers demonstrates, intermediaries will simply not fashion new financial institutions if they or investors are threatened by the government. For instance, it was not until the 1690s, after the English monarchy had stopped imposing forced loans and itself become a good credit risk, that London intermediaries started to float rafts of new securities and the city's bankers began to extend loans beyond a limited circle of merchants and aristocrats.[2] Similarly, eighteenth-century Paris did not witness extensive private innovation until the French government had ceased manipulating the currency. And when the government of France resumed tampering with money during the French Revolution, the long-term capital market in Paris that had been the scene of the greatest financial creations ended up collapsing and took two generations to recover.

History suggests that the opposite extreme—a government that refuses to borrow at all—is equally likely to hinder innovation. That was clearly the case in China, where, as we saw, the government's failure to borrow slowed the development of banks and capital markets.

Extremes in the size of the middle class will also stifle innovation. We know that a large middle class will generate demand for financial innovation, and the demand should in turn incite private intermediaries to devise new financial institutions. An extremely small middle class, by contrast, will give them no incentive to do so. History agrees here too, for all the historical financial centers in Europe—from Venice and Genoa in the Middle Ages to Berlin, Paris, and London in the 1800s—served a sizable set of customers whom we would call middle class, and the same certainly holds for New York and London today.

From this analysis one might conclude that innovation will be greatest in a society in which the middle class is so large that there are no rich people left—a society of completely equal farmers, for example, each of whom has exactly the same amount of property and thus belongs to our middle class; or one of middle-management executives, each with the same house and an identical portfolio of mutual funds. Will innovation reach a maximum there?

The answer is no. Although a large middle class will generate enormous demand for innovation, its members will neither supply the new financial instruments and institutions nor provide the initial investments to test them. The reason is that they will capture too small a share of the benefits from new institutions, and if the new instruments and institutions initially entail a high fixed cost, that cost will loom too large relative to the amount of money they will borrow or invest. The rich, by contrast, can easily shoulder these fixed costs, which are small relative to their portfolios; indeed, they can easily afford to have intermediaries craft custom-made instruments or contracts that take the place of broader institutional innovations. Once a new instrument or even a new tailor-made contract is created, the costs of replicating it (particularly for items such as legal expenses) are likely to drop, making the innovations affordable for the middle class.

The rich will therefore help supply financial innovations, even though their diversification and their ability to invest elsewhere keep them from generating much demand. They will be pioneering investors, and because they already have diversified portfolios, they will often be willing to take on new and unknown risks that would initially scare off most middle-class investors. This pattern has prevailed in financial centers in the past, and it continues to hold in capital markets today.

The rich can play a particularly important role when the middle class is large but the government does not provide financial products such as insurance. Members of the middle class, we know, will want insurance to protect themselves against calamities, and if the government does not furnish it, as was the case in the plutocracies of nineteenth-century Europe, the rich can step into the breach and help financial intermediaries meet the demand. They will take on the risk, but as the new institution develops, middle-class investors will shoulder more and more of it themselves.

That is what happened with early insurance companies in nineteenth-century Paris, which offered middle-class policyholders life insurance and protection against the risks posed by fire, shipwrecks, bad harvests, or military service. Legally, the companies had to have capital in reserve to cope with unexpected losses. The companies raised the reserve capital by issuing a second class of equity; that is, in addition to issuing first-class shares, which were easily traded and used to raise working capital, they created a second class of shares that could not be traded without the approval of the company's board of directors. These second-class shares had a par value ten times that of the first-class shares, but, in contrast to the first-class shares, buyers did not have to hand over this large sum when they purchased the shares. Instead they had to stand ready to contribute to the company's reserve fund if necessary, up to the par value of their shares. In return for taking on this risk, they earned a handsome annual dividend even though they made no monetary contribution to the company for several decades.[3]

Arrangements of this sort are in fact still in use—in the insurance syndicates run by Lloyd's of London, and in the catastrophe bonds that insurance companies sell to protect themselves against huge damage claims from earthquakes, windstorms, and hurricanes. The purchasers of the catastrophe bonds lose their principal if the insurance companies suffer catastrophic losses, but if not, they earn a high return and also diversify their portfolios. Similarly, venture capitalists often raise a substantial amount of money from a small number of rich investors. The investors bear the risk of new ventures, and although many of the new companies inevitably fail, the small number that do succeed earn an immense return when the shares are released for sale to the public.

Private financial innovation will thus suffer at the extremes, whether it is an extreme of market size, government debt, or the magnitude of the middle class. A large middle class, for instance, will stimulate innovation, but not if it is so big that there are no rich people left, because the rich help supply financial innovations, particularly when the government will not intervene. Similarly, it helps if a market is large enough to spread the costs of creating new financial institutions yet not so vast that problems of asymmetric information rear their head.

Other Requirements for Financial Innovation

Still other conditions must prevail if private financial intermediaries are to create financial institutions. And some of these are contingent factors that turn on historical accidents, not just on the principles of political economy.

At the very least, intermediaries have to be able to make a profit, for otherwise they will have no reason to spend their time creating new financial institutions. Sometimes these profits can be gigantic, but they may still be dwarfed by the value of the intermediaries' innovations. (Of course, if a crisis strikes, the public will quickly come to see these profits as ill-gotten gains.)

Michael Milken, who created the market for the high-yield and high-risk corporate debt now known as "junk bonds," is but one example. Although Milken is usually held up as the poster boy for the financial excesses of the 1980s—he did, after all, plead guilty to six felonies—a more reasoned and dispassionate analysis suggests that the junk-bond market was an extraordinary invention. Junk bonds financed the expansion of numerous medium-sized firms that had been unable to raise money for expansion and thereby directed capital into productive sectors of the economy. Many of these firms offered consumers lower prices or new products, and a number of them (MCI and CNN, for example) grew to become major corporations.[4]

The junk bonds also made corporate takeovers possible, because corporate raiders such as Carl Icahn and T. Boone Pickens used the bonds to finance corporate buyouts. The takeovers did cost people their jobs and sometimes part of their pensions, but when they were successful, they also dislodged managers who were making disastrous business decisions and squandering corporate earnings. They helped trim bloated firms such as the Beatrice Companies down to a more efficient size. Even the threat of a buyout was often enough to force management to run things more effectively, as happened, for example, after Pickens failed in his try for the oil company Unocal. Overall, the takeovers obliged corporations to concentrate on shareholder value, and at least in some instances they saved firms that would not have survived competition without downsizing. The shareholders were clearly better off, and the evidence suggests that their gains were not always just transfers taken out of the employees' hides.

Milken's junk bonds made much of this activity possible, and the inspiration for the innovative market he established stemmed from his belief that investors were exaggerating the risks involved in owning this sort of low-quality corporate debt. The investors, he was convinced, could earn a high return at relatively low risk if they could assemble a large portfolio of these junk bonds, for diversification would protect them even if each individual bond was risky. The trouble was that investors could not easily put such a portfolio together. Most investors shunned the bonds, in part because they were hard to sell. (In the jargon of finance, they were "illiquid.") Because demand was limited, the supply was small too, making it even more difficult for anyone to amass a diversified portfolio.

If more companies could somehow be induced to issue this sort of debt, then investors would find it easier to diversify, making junk bonds more attractive to hold. As more investors bought them up, they would become easier to trade, and the growing demand and greater liquidity would in turn bring down the yields and boost the supply even more. In short, if some additional companies could be persuaded to issue junk bonds—and investors be convinced to buy them—then a whole new market could be created.

Milken believed that he could do this and along the way earn a high return for his firm, Drexel Burnham Lambert. He worked to get corporate raiders and entrepreneurs to use junk bonds to raise money, while at the same time persuading money managers to buy junk bonds for their portfolios. At first portfolio managers had to be offered very generous terms to buy the junk bonds, and Milken's personal involvement mattered a great deal, for he had to convince the managers that the companies issuing the bonds were not as risky as the staid bond-rating agencies assumed. Over time, as the market broadened, it became easier to trade the bonds and to assemble a diversified portfolio. Drexel Burnham Lambert prospered, and Milken himself earned roughly $1.1 billion between 1983 and 1987. Some of the profits derived from Drexel Burnham Lambert's temporary dominance over the market for junk bonds, but even so, his fortune was still a reward for innovation.[5]

Open and competitive financial markets are another condition that stimulates private financial innovation. If markets are competitive, intermediaries cannot set up a cartel or collude with one another. If they are open, new intermediaries can readily enter with new products or better terms; alternatively, investors or entrepreneurs can easily go elsewhere in search of a more attractive deal. Competition and openness will kill off intermediaries who fail to adopt innovations and reward those who create them. And they will keep intermediaries from taking advantage of investors, borrowers, or entrepreneurs.

Competition and openness are, however, difficult to foster and sustain; they depend on historical accidents and politics, a combination that makes financial innovation a tricky and contingent process. Sometimes the informational problems in financial markets give a small set of intermediaries a fortuitous advantage (as we saw in Chapter 2, investment bankers like J. P. Morgan had this edge in late nineteenth-century New York) that enables them to come close to exercising a monopoly.[6] And because intermediaries are often effective lobbyists, they can therefore simply get the government to close off markets or restrict competition.

Despite all these obstacles, most of our historically important financial centers did manage to keep their financial markets open or competitive. Thus in Antwerp and Amsterdam, if merchants were not satisfied with a banker, they could take their business to a local competitor or even conceivably to a banker in neighboring city. Similarly, London was open to foreign capital, and the chief financial intermediaries in eighteenth-century Paris could not take advantage of their clients for fear of losing them to one of their counterparts. It is true that there have always been relatively few investment banks in New York, and at times they may have tended toward collusion. But political hostility to large banks has usually kept the Wall Street firms from getting too powerful, and the way has never been completely barred to newcomers with bright ideas. Milken was in fact one of them. He and Drexel Burnham Lambert thrived precisely because established investment banks would not use the junk bonds to finance takeovers for fear of alienating clients whose firms happened to be the corporate raiders' targets.[7] Although Milken did admittedly gain a near-monopoly over the junk-bond market, it was only temporary.

Probably even more important than competition, though, is a third condition that has to be in place if private intermediaries are to create new financial institutions: support from the government. Simply having a government that refrains from preying on financial markets is rarely enough for private innovation. Governments can also do good, and they often have to lend intermediaries a hand if innovation is to occur. But because government help inevitably brings in politics, it adds yet another dose of contingency to the process of financial innovation.

Government support begins with essential protection of property rights, enforcement of contracts, and adjudication of disputes, but it often goes well beyond this. Indeed, the state often has to step in and impose regulations when individuals cannot agree on a solution, or when intermediaries cannot capture the benefits of institutions they have devised. And sometimes the state is the only source of insurance against the largest shocks. Without such insurance, which private vendors usually cannot supply, it may be difficult to create financial instruments and other new institutions.

At the very least, governments have to be involved because the large markets needed for financial innovation feature numerous transactions between individuals who do not know each other well. They are therefore better off having the state enforce their contracts and their property rights, for with so many relatively anonymous people involved, it would be difficult for them to form expectations about one another's behavior and to punish misconduct on their own. Without state enforcement—the essential characteristic of what we called formal institutions—financial transactions could certainly continue, but markets would be restricted to dealings among those individuals who could watch over one another's actions; and that situation would bring us close to the extreme of small size, where innovation is virtually impossible.[8]

The parties in most financial transactions must therefore rely on state enforcement of contracts and property rights. They will also turn to the state to resolve disagreements—ideally, in a swift and predictable fashion. Individuals may also supplement state enforcement with private measures: the collateral that backs up a loan is the most obvious example. But ultimately, the state has to stand behind the private measures too. After all, if a lender defaults, it is the state that ensures that the lender gets the collateral.

What happens if property rights or contracts are not backed by the state? Consider the heartbreaking example of Mexico. There lenders have long found it extremely difficult to repossess collateral when loans go bad; the state and its judicial system will simply not enforce property rights to the collateral backing loans. Lenders have consequently been reluctant to take land as collateral—a major handicap, particularly where agriculture is a major sector of the economy—and as a result many loans that would have stimulated economic growth were never made. The problem persists even today, despite the privatization of the Mexican bank system in 1991 and the more recent arrival of foreign banks in Mexico. Banks still have trouble enforcing their contracts and property rights, and bank lending is still small relative to the size of the economy: in 2002 bank loans amounted to only 15 percent of Mexico's gross domestic product, versus 80 percent in Italy, 100 percent in Great Britain, and 150 percent in the United States.[9]

Since financial contracts and institutions depend on state enforcement, private innovation can falter when state enforcement becomes too costly. In the first half of the nineteenth century, a novel bank, the Société Générale, helped Belgium to become the first country in continental Europe to industrialize by providing funds for ironworks, coal mines, and industrial plants, accelerating Belgium's economic growth to a pace unrivaled elsewhere in Europe.[10] What set the Société Générale apart from other banks was its practice of holding shares in a number of manufacturing firms spread across the country.

Furthermore, it opened many branches and not only made the sort of short-term commercial loans that were the usual business of nineteenth-century bankers but also engaged in investment banking, by floating bond and stock issues. It was, in short, the first so-called universal bank, a bank that did everything. It had stumbled upon this way of doing business almost by accident, but its tactics proved so attractive (chiefly because they gave the bank a diversified and profitable portfolio of investments in the burgeoning manufacturing sector) that they were soon imitated through continental Europe.

Yet despite its profitability and the fact that its strategy was eventually copied in neighboring France and Germany, the Société Générale rarely dared to make loans in neighboring French or German cities such as Lille and Aachen, even though they were just outside the Belgian border. Demand in these nearby areas was huge, and by making loans over the border the Société Générale could have diversified its portfolio even more. But it rarely did so, even though it willingly accepted large infusions of capital from investors in France. The reason was the increased legal costs of getting contracts and property rights enforced in France and Germany.[11]

Government help for innovators is not limited to backing contracts and property rights. Sometimes innovation requires a new rule or regulation that private intermediaries cannot impose voluntarily. The trouble may be that each individual intermediary is reluctant to act, out of fear that he will have to bear the entire cost of creating and imposing the new rule but will receive only a meager portion of the benefits. Or it may be that only the state can get intermediaries to agree and accept a specific new rule.

That is what happened in sixteenth-century Antwerp, which was the home of the world's first real financial exchange, with trading in securities ranging from short-term debt to futures contracts. The new financial institutions in the Antwerp market served as models for other early influential financial exchanges (notably in Amsterdam and London), but to get the market going the traders in Antwerp first had to resolve an eternal informational problem of financial markets: How could purchasers of a financial instrument be protected when they might know little about the parties who had created it? The obstacle is one that has to be overcome before any financial market can function smoothly, for otherwise people who do not know one another will find it too risky and too costly to trade in financial instruments. When the chances of being defrauded loom too large, financial markets will remain stunted. The problem was particularly challenging in the realm of short-term debt that funded shipments of goods passing through Antwerp; trade in this short-term debt (technically, bills of exchange and promissory notes, which typically involved loans due in several months' time) was what got the financial market in Antwerp going. Yet how could a buyer of one of these short-term notes (such as someone who purchased it from the original lender) protect himself in case the borrower defaulted?

Initially the buyer had to get permission from the original lender before he could take a defaulting borrower to court. A legal decision in 1507 freed buyers from this burden, but they still faced the informational problem that frustrated easy and anonymous trade in short-term debt: How did the buyers know whether the original borrower was a good credit risk, particularly if they did not know him personally? The solution to this problem was to make all the previous owners of the debt instrument responsible for repayment along with the original debtor. Each sale would then actually make the debt more secure, for if the borrower defaulted, the buyer could go after the person who had sold him the debt instrument and anyone else who had owned it. By the early seventeenth century, the successive owners were writing their names on the back of the debt instrument when they sold it—essentially our modern practice of endorsement—and a buyer could therefore easily tell who the various owners were. A long list of endorsers—particularly if some were known to be wealthy—

would compensate a buyer for lack of information about the original debtor, and hence that debtor's creditworthiness did not matter any more.

The government played an important and beneficial role here in nurturing the efforts of innovative bankers and merchants in Antwerp. Customary law—itself a formal, state-enforced institution—had begun to recognize that buyers of short-term debt had the same rights as the original lenders, but it took the 1507 legal decision (from an official group of town citizens who could declare what the legal custom was) and a 1537 law to clarify the legal situation. It also took further legislation—a 1541 edict—before buyers had the right to go after all the previous owners when there was a default. And behind the laws lay successful lobbying: Antwerp merchants and bankers had in fact asked their city government to push for change.[12]

These bankers and merchants might conceivably have been able to reach such a solution without any government help. One could imagine them drawing up debt contracts specifying that each successive owner would bear responsibility for repayment. But such a process might have required costly legal amendments every time a short-term debt contract was sold, and at least initially buyers would have hesitated to accept such debt instruments without consulting their own attorneys. The result would be added costs and further obstacles to swift and low-cost trading. And if the new contracts caught on, the individuals who first devised them would have no way of preventing others from simply copying the contracts and thereby profiting from their idea without bearing any of the legal costs. It is thus hardly surprising that the merchants and bankers sought the 1541 legislation, and their efforts to do so suggest that government intervention was in fact the best way to solve the informational problem that financial intermediaries and their clients faced.

True, intermediaries or their clients can sometimes adopt new rules voluntarily, without much government help beyond enforcement of contracts. The recent corporate scandals in the United States have given rise to innovation of this sort. In order to ease investor misgivings about stock options and executive compensation plans, Microsoft declared its first dividend and shifted to a policy of giving its employees restricted stock rather than options. Companies that were undoubtedly far more suspect in investors' eyes (such as the erstwhile Internet high-flyer E*Trade or the bankrupt telecommunications company WorldCom) put independent directors on their boards and revised their rules of corporate governance.[13] But one can ask whether these companies (or intermediaries such as the New York Stock Exchange, which itself proposed rules of corporate governance for the firms it listed) would have favored these reforms had it not been for government prodding and the outraged public reaction provoked by the corporate scandals. WorldCom adopted the new rules only as it was emerging from bankruptcy, and apart from the New York Stock Exchange and some large pension funds, few intermediaries were urging companies to modify the way they were governed. There was simply no profit in changing it.

Government help can admittedly be a two-edged sword. Today, for instance, states commonly offer banks and other private intermediaries deposit insurance and loan guarantees, which were virtually unknown before the twentieth century. This sort of assistance has the great virtue of having practically eliminated bank runs in most developed countries, thereby removing a hurdle that had tripped up many private intermediaries in the past, even the most inventive ones, such as the Société Générale in Belgium. Time and time again in the past, private intermediaries had stumbled when shocks triggered bank runs. This same obstacle had caused nineteenth-century banks to falter, and it also brought innovation to a halt in medieval Venice, where banks that had devised an ingenious way to economize on coin (by simply arranging paper transfers between accounts) stood powerless when their depositors rushed to withdraw their cash.

But as is so often the case with financial markets, a government presence can also bring disadvantages. Deposit insurance and loan guarantees may stop bank runs, but they also can encourage private intermediaries to make risky loans, since they know that the government will pick up the tab. The prospect of government bailouts for banks that are in difficulty has the same effect. Worst of all, if combined with lax regulation, deposit insurance and loan guarantees can even attract swindlers, who can plunder financial intermediaries and leave the government holding the bag.

That, essentially, is what transpired during the 1980s savings-and-loan scandal in the United States. Owners and managers of the savings and loans, which had traditionally funded housing mortgages, began to take huge risks with government-insured deposits, and some of the more dishonest ones actually looted their businesses by paying themselves huge dividends or by making loans to cronies that they knew would never be repaid. Their savings-and-loans institutions folded, but the unscrupulous operators were confident that the government would pay off the depositors (it did, at a cost of at least $150 billion) and that they themselves faced little risk of criminal prosecution or personal liability.[14]

Whether the government provides the necessary support for innovation and whether that support will have beneficial consequences depends on politics and historical accidents. We could never really comprehend the savings-and-loan debacle, for instance, if we did not know one essential bit of historical background: state and federal authorities had responded to an earlier bout of losses in the savings-and-loan industry by relaxing the regulations and strict accounting rules that seemed to be keeping the savings and loans from earning a profit. Without this slackening of the rules, the savings-and-loan crisis would never have occurred.[15] The greatest source of contingency in financial innovation, however, comes from crises themselves, which will never disappear, despite all the ingenuity private intermediaries have shown.

Why Financial Intermediaries Cannot Prevent Crises

Private financial intermediaries have been extraordinarily creative, particularly in Europe, Japan, and North America, where the pace of change has often been astounding. And it is not just intermediaries who have been inventive, for they have been assisted by entrepreneurs and by accountants, lawyers, and other information specialists, who have helped fashion scores of new institutions and financial instruments. Yet for all this ingenuity, financial crises have not come to an end. The United States had the savings-and-loan meltdown of the 1980s and, more recently, the dot-com bubble and the rash of bankruptcies tied to corporate scandals. Europe endured its own technological bubble, with a number of new companies going belly up and one exchange—the German Neuer Markt—shutting up shop. And after the 1980s bubble burst in Japan, the economy lapsed into a coma from which it took fifteen years to emerge.

Why, with all the innovation displayed by private intermediaries and entrepreneurs, is it impossible to banish crises in financial markets for good?

In large part, the answer lies with the widespread problems of government predation and asymmetric information that we have already discussed. But it also stems from the lack of insurance against certain shocks. While an ideal market would provide shelter from all possible risks so that unexpected and uninsured troubles could never arise, the real world is quite different, for some risks cannot be insured against. You cannot buy protection against a sudden drop in demand for your job skills, even though plunging demand has damaged the livelihood of typewriter repairmen and scores of other skilled workers. Nor can you shield yourself against plummeting home values if a major local industry goes bust.[16] And even if you obtain insurance, you have little recourse against another risk—the chance that the insurance company will itself default and leave you uncovered.

Beyond the difficulties of getting insurance loom patterns of investor behavior that exacerbate informational problems. Often, when there is asymmetric information, investors take their cues from one another's behavior, and when this happens, they can drive prices up and create speculative bubbles. The sudden corrections that this herdlike behavior precipitates can then cause investors and intermediaries to fail. The same thing can happen if investors form erroneous beliefs about what will happen to market prices. It may take them time to correct these beliefs, or they may make mistakes in what they choose to do—deciding, for instance, to put their money into stocks because they are convinced that a recent increase in share prices must be part of a long-term trend. More rational investors may of course want to take advantage of their mistakes, but they may be temporarily unable to drive prices back to their true value. The result again will be a bubble followed by defaults.[17]

There is one way for financial intermediaries to contend with bubbles and economic shocks of any sort, even when they have no insurance. All they have to do is to hold some cash in reserve. Individual investors can do the same when they have no insurance. Holding reserves, however, clearly imposes costs. The money kept in an intermediary's reserve is money that cannot be lent out at interest, and cash that an individual investor keeps in a checking account earns little or no interest either. Just as with an insurance policy, when it is available, the costs necessitate calculating how much money must be put in reserve. That means determining which shocks are likely to occur and what the likely losses will be and then not wasting too much money on shocks that pose little danger.

In short, both investors and intermediaries have to forecast the likelihood of all possible shocks and their probable consequences; they then must try to shield themselves, either by holding the right amount of reserves, buying insurance (if it exists), or seeking out financial instruments that will do well when shocks strike. Yet when they make these calculations and forecasts, they have only one real source of information to turn to—the past. Almost inevitably, they will turn to historical data to forecast the future.

Historical data, though, can easily be misused. If the advertising employed by mutual funds—which usually tout their past returns rather than their strategy for the future—is any indication, many investors apparently extrapolate from past experience. And even knowledgeable investors and intermediaries may make the same mistake, albeit in a far more sophisticated way.

An error of this sort contributed to the collapse of Long Term Capital Management (LTCM), the hedge fund that in September 1998 was saved from what would have been a catastrophic bankruptcy. LTCM had borrowed heavily to finance securities trades: at the beginning of 1998, it apparently had over $125 billion in loans outstanding. Its trades, however, did not go as expected, and its net worth plummeted. As it teetered on the edge of bankruptcy, the New York Federal Reserve Bank orchestrated a bailout to keep LTCM from defaulting on its loans and on billions of dollars' worth of contracts that it had entered into. (Many of these contracts were so-called derivatives, which simply means that they depended on the value of other financial assets.) Had it defaulted, the banks and securities firms that had entered into the contracts with LTCM would have hastily tried to liquidate any of the hedge fund's assets that they held as collateral. The result could well have been a market meltdown and widespread failures among financial firms—in short, a crisis.[18]

What had got LTCM into this predicament? In essence, the hedge fund was wagering that the difference in prices between various securities would diminish or that the volatility of prices in certain securities markets would decline. To make such bets, it might enter into a transaction with a bank in which the bank would pay LTCM money if the gap narrowed between the interest rates on a safe U.S. Treasury bond and the interest rate on riskier government debt from some emerging-market country; LTCM would pay the bank if the reverse occurred. Or it might make a similar deal that would reward LTCM if the volatility of U.S. stock prices returned to historical levels. Economic theory showed how to assemble a diversified portfolio of these wagers that would presumably entail little risk, and LTCM used borrowed money to make many of them. But to put the theoretical model into practice, and to forecast the likely risks, gains, and losses, LTCM relied on historical data. Implicitly, it was assuming that certain key relationships observed in the past would eventually prevail again in the future.

Such historical assumptions carry a number of risks. First of all, even if the historical relationships do re-emerge, there is no telling how long it will take them to assert themselves. The statistical theory behind the models, if correct, implies only that the old relationships are virtually certain to revive, but the wait may be long, and in the interval one's reserves may sink and disappear beneath the waters (as happened to LTCM). Worse yet, the statistical theory may simply not apply; the relationships observed in the past may not be valid in the future. In the jargon of statistics, the prices and other data series may be "nonstationary." In that case, the historical evidence used to prime the economic model will not help to forecast the future or assess the likely consequences, and the model may be particularly likely to fail (as LTCM's did) in the midst of a shock, when the historical assumptions will break down.

For LTCM, the shock that wrecked the historical assumptions was Russia's surprising default on its government debt. When panicked investors tried to dump their risky bonds from Russia and other emerging-market countries in order to buy safer U.S. government debt, the interest rate gaps that LTCM was betting on widened to unprecedented levels—the very opposite of what historical data had led the hedge firm to expect.[19] LTCM had assumed that bond prices in emerging markets would not all move together, that it could offset any exposure to an event like a Russian default by betting on bond prices in other developing countries. But when Russia defaulted, bond prices in nearly all emerging markets collapsed, and LTCM's capital evaporated.

Historical data can prove misleading if economic relationships shift as economies develop, political regimes change, and competition drives out older firms and technologies. Further complicating the task of estimating how bad an economic shock will be are unanticipated contingencies such as the terrorist attack of September 11, 2001, which killed thousands, changed foreign policy, and devastated the travel industry. Investors and intermediaries rarely take events of that sort into account in their planning and so do nothing to insure themselves against the resultant risks, even if they happen to be low.

Unforeseen events are hardly peculiar to our own day. In the eighteenth century, for instance, the French monarchy raised money by selling life annuities, which quickly became popular because they allowed purchasers to assure themselves of a guaranteed income for life—a great attraction in an era before there was any sort of private or public old-age pension.[20] The problem was that the annuities could be manipulated by clever buyers and financial intermediaries in a scheme that earned them a great deal of money—at least until something completely unexpected happened.

Initially the typical buyer of a government annuity was a fifty-year-old man who wanted an income for the rest of his life. He ended up getting a market rate of return of, say, 5 percent on his investment (which was in effect a loan to the monarchy) and made no extraordinary profits. But other lenders could boost the return on their investment by taking advantage of the terms on which the annuities were offered. It was possible for a buyer of the annuity to make the annuity payments depend not on his own life span, but on that of some other person. The buyer might seek such an arrangement for innocuous reasons. A father could specify, for example, that the annuity payments would continue until his daughter died: that way she would be assured of a lifetime income. This feature made the annuities even more desirable, but it also opened the door to manipulation, because typically the annual payments the French government made to the annuity buyer did not depend on the age of the person whose eventual death would bring the payments to a halt. This person did not even have to be related to the buyer, and it could be someone who might be expected to live for a long time—a ten-year-old girl, for instance. The payments would obviously go on longer than they would for a fifty-year-old, and the return on the sum invested would climb from the 5 percent that a fifty-year-old might expect to earn to 8 or even 10 percent—a rate well above what the market offered. The payments did not have to go to the ten-year-old girl. Instead the buyer could pocket them or could assign them to anyone he wished—his heirs, for example. Such flexibility for buyers had made these investments even more attractive.

There was of course a risk that the ten-year-old girl might die young. But that danger could be minimized by choosing healthy young women who had already survived major diseases like smallpox and whose relatives had lived to a ripe old age. They would normally be expected to live for a long time, and risk could be further reduced by finding a bunch of such girls and buying annuities on each of their lives. The death of two or three of the girls would reduce the total payments only slightly, and odds of more deaths would be slim.

That was precisely the scheme adopted by a number of Genevan bankers from the early 1770s on. They would select thirty appropriate girls in Geneva and then purchase thirty life annuities from the French government, one for each girl. The bankers would then lump the annuities together and sell shares in the resulting investment pool to their fellow Genevans, who earned a huge premium at what seemed to be very low risk. The investment was all the more attractive because the shares were easily sold: everyone in Geneva knew about the scheme and trusted the bankers to do a good job.

The Genevan bankers had thus designed an institution—an investment pool in life annuities—that reduced the risks investors faced and increased the return on their investment and its liquidity too. Yet although their institution did protect investors against the premature demise of one of the girls, the bankers had overlooked one potential disaster: they themselves would be taking on an enormous liability if the French monarchy defaulted or if the French currency was devalued. Their oversight was understandable: when they were pooling large numbers of annuities together, the French currency had been stable for two generations, and another state bankruptcy (the most recent one had been in 1770) now seemed unlikely.[21] Unfortunately for them, however, the French Revolution broke out in 1789. The revolutionary government fell behind on its annuity payments and was soon paying the bankers in nearly worthless paper money. While the bankers took in the nearly worthless paper payments from the French government, they owed the shareholders in their annuity pools hard Swiss currency. Not surprisingly, most of the Genevan bankers went bankrupt. So too did a number of investors, for in some of the investment pools, the bankers let the investors buy their shares on credit with only a small down payment in return for the investors' assuming the liability that the pool would remain solvent. In the end, nearly all the investors suffered, for when the banks failed, even investors who had not taken on any liability lost the annuity payments they had been expecting.

The sort of errors made by the Genevan bankers and LTCM are all too common, even among clever financial operators. They could perhaps have been avoided, though, had these intermediaries—and investors too—looked beyond the recent past. The Genevan bankers, after all, had generalized on the basis of what was happening in the 1770s; similarly, LTCM had relied on recent data to prime the model it used to forecast risks and expected gains. If either LTCM or the Genevans had examined a longer historical record, they might not have formed more accurate estimates of the likelihood of future crises, but they would certainly have understood that financial probabilities are not stationary, that shifting relationships and unexpected contingencies are the rule, and that initial beliefs may simply be wrong. That is the lesson history actually teaches, and it is a valuable one for anyone trying to analyze what is likely to happen in the future.

Beyond the difficulties of estimating how likely shocks are and what the probable consequences will be, there is another barrier to eradicating crises, a barrier that can confound any financial intermediary's efforts to help investors cope with economic shocks, whether it is by helping them hold reserves, by offering them insurance or some other new financial instrument, or by creating other novel institutions to dampen the effects of the shocks. The obstacle, which seems unavoidable, is the tendency of financial innovations to create new problems even as they solve old ones.

New institutions designed to ward off frequent small shocks often turn out to make matters worse when a big shock hits. New institutions may also cause investors and intermediaries to lower their guard and thereby encourage so much misbehavior and so many bad choices that new crises will strike.

In the nineteenth-century plutocracies of Europe, for example, many entrepreneurs wanted to take out long-term loans to fund large-scale expansions of their businesses, but they had trouble doing so. They sought the long-term loans because they did not want to be caught halfway through some lengthy project (such as constructing a building) and find themselves snared in a credit crunch and unable to roll over the sort of short-term loans that banks typically offered. Individual investors were hesitant to make the long-term loans on their own because they feared finding themselves short of cash if some personal misfortune struck. An obvious solution to this problem was to get banks to pool the investors' money in deposits and then use some of the money to make long-term loans. If the bank kept a reserve fund and mixed the duration of its loans, it could ensure that it had enough cash on hand to meet likely withdrawals by depositors who might suddenly encounter personal difficulties. As banks began to do this, they would reduce the risks of long-term lending, a feat that would be impossible for individual lenders, who would not have the banks' large portfolio of loans.

Not surprisingly, the innovation facilitated economic growth, but it also created a new danger: if a large shock struck the economy, many or all of the bank's depositors might suddenly want to withdraw their funds. Banks would not have enough cash on hand to cover all the withdrawals, and depositors would quickly realize that their best hope was to withdraw all their money at the first sign of trouble. Such a step would be better than waiting until there was a actually bank run, for then they would lose most of their money. But rushing to empty their accounts would then trigger the very bank run they feared, and the result would be a rash of bank failures, even though a new institution had made long-term lending possible and reduced the risks associated with it.

Not that the innovation was a mistake. The risks of long-term lending had dropped, and with banks now making long-term loans, economic growth would pick up as entrepreneurs who had been starved for financial capital got the money to fund their investment. But the newfound growth could now be interrupted by bank runs—a new sort of crisis.

Private financial innovation therefore has an Achilles' heel: it certainly improves matters, but it can sometimes bring on new crises or exacerbate downturns when events depart from historical patterns. That is one of the reasons crises do not disappear. So too is the tendency investors and intermediaries have of naively extrapolating from recent history when they decide how to protect themselves against future shocks, whether by diversifying their portfolios, creating new financial instruments, or designing new financial institutions. Reliance on history provides a familiar set of readily available examples, but extrapolating from the recent past is a poor guide to what will happen in the future, because financial markets evolve over time and do not repeat themselves. A real understanding of history—one that goes beyond the simple extrapolations from the recent past that investors and intermediaries rely on—would not leave people overprepared for the shock just past but underequipped for the crisis in the offing. Saying all this does not mean we deny the enormous value of private financial innovation. It is undeniably worthwhile, even if it cannot eliminate crises, for if capital markets did not adapt to changed circumstances—and to crises in particular—the economy would simply stagnate.

Because crises are inevitable, we cannot foresee how financial markets will evolve, for each crisis will create new institutions and redirect the path of financial development in ways that are unpredictable, at least from the principles of political economy. We can see as much by looking at one last example of striking and unexpected institutional change—the aftermath of the John Law crisis in early eighteenth-century France. It began when France found itself crushed by debt after decades of war. An enterprising Scottish banker, John Law, proposed a radical solution, and the French government took him up on his proposal, which he had earlier tried to peddle to other European monarchs. What it involved was creating a bank that would take over the French government's debts in return for rights to collect most taxes and exploit France's overseas possessions. To finance its operations, the bank would also issue banknotes, which would serve as paper money, and sell shares of stock to be traded on the Paris stock exchange. The idea was that the banknotes would help fuel economic growth, while the easily traded shares would prove so attractive to the government's creditors (chiefly because they could be quickly sold on the Paris stock exchange, unlike government debt) that they would readily trade their government notes for shares in the bank.[22]

To make the operation succeed, Law, who became the French finance minister, encouraged speculation in bank shares, leading to a stock market bubble that burst in 1720. One way he did so was to touch off rapid inflation by having the bank issue reams of banknotes. As the inflation raged, borrowers in Paris rushed to pay off their own debts with the legal tender of cheapened banknotes. Many a lender lost a fortune, and other investors were ruined in the collapse of the bank share bubble.

The curious and unexpected effect of this crisis was that it did not cripple French financial markets. Instead, it helped launch the new institution that would make the Paris mortgage market boom later in the 1700s. The new institution, as we saw in Chapter 1, was a pattern of self-reinforcing behavior among the city's notaries, the legal officials who had long drawn up contracts and mortgage documents; now, in addition to their legal functions, they began to arrange thousands of mortgages every year, because they knew who had money to lend and who had good collateral and was therefore a good credit risk. For them, the Law crisis was the turning point. Because they drafted most of the repayment documents when old loans were repaid in worthless paper, they knew who had been ruined by the Law affair and who had emerged unscathed. Having made their information about creditworthiness and collateral more valuable than ever, the Law affair propelled the notaries on to new and astonishing careers as mortgage brokers for the rest of the century—all because of the unanticipated effects of the crisis and a historical accident that made them the ones to draw up contracts and preserve legal documents.

The history of financial markets is one of both innovation and crises. Although investors and entrepreneurs are certainly responsible for some of the innovation, most of it has been the work of private financial intermediaries, who have developed an extraordinary mix of contracts that offer a wide range of risks and returns for investors and entrepreneurs alike. Today the banks, insurance companies, mutual funds, and other organizations established by the intermediaries make it possible even for small investors to enjoy a wide range of investment options, at least in developed countries. (In poorer countries, of course, nothing of the sort is yet available.) Yet despite all the innovation, crises are still (and will always be) with us, even in Europe, Japan, and the United States.

Intermediaries do not work this miracle alone. The government has to lend a helping hand by enforcing contracts and property rights and by imposing regulations and common solutions when no private party can. And sometimes, as we shall see, it must do more than this.

CHAPTER 6

Governments and the Demand
for Reform

ALTHOUGH STATES IN THE WEST have intervened in financial markets for more than half a millennium, government involvement has grown far more common in the twentieth century, even in countries that have gone through waves of privatization or deregulation, such as Britain and the United States. Even in these bastions of free-market ideology, the state plays a far greater role in financial markets than it did 100 years ago and does far more to deliver the institutions that are called for after crises. In at least some instances, governments have created extraordinary financial institutions and had great success. But in others they have triggered some of the worst financial crises the world has ever witnessed.

To set up a new institution, a government can intervene in capital markets in a variety of ways. It may simply pass necessary laws or impose regulations while leaving the actual task of financial intermediation to the private sector. But it may also shoulder private intermediaries aside and become an intermediary itself, by offering loans to strategic industries or by providing financial products such as pensions or insurance against unemployment and disability. Government intervention of any sort is particularly likely during and shortly after crises, when the demand for action peaks. It is then that the state is most likely to confiscate ill-gotten gains or to bail out weakened banks and firms so they do not go under.

When the state intervenes, it has one advantage (beyond its enormous power) that is not available to private intermediaries when they create new institutions. The advantage is that the government does not face a tight budget constraint, at least in the short run. (In the long run, it of course does have a budget constraint, but the short run of several years is what matters for most political decisions.) When a private intermediary devises a new institution, he has to earn enough from his innovation to pay his costs. By contrast, when the state intervenes, it can push a portion of the cost off on to taxpayers, including those in future generations, who do not have any direct voice in political decisions. Suppose, for example, that the government wants to encourage savings among the poor. To do so, it can offer them an above-market rate of interest because taxpayers will foot the bill. Private intermediaries who try to act in this way will lose money and swiftly be driven out of business.

A government can thus do things that private intermediaries would never touch with a ten-foot pole. This possibility has sparked a fierce, long-running debate that divides along traditional lines of left versus right, with the left promoting government intervention to improve markets and the right bewailing the failings of such intervention and championing private innovation. But it is time to ask whether it is possible to go beyond this traditional left-right debate and determine what has made government intervention in financial markets successful in some instances and disastrous in others. Is it a matter of avoiding extremes, as with innovation by private intermediaries? Can the principles of political economy alone account for what seems to work best, or does history too play a role? And what explains why governments have intervened so much in the twentieth century?

Traditional Left-Right Views of Government Intervention

Because a state is not hemmed in by a short-term budget constraint, it can resolve problems in capital markets without worrying as much as a private intermediary would about costs. For champions of government intervention, that is a great advantage, for governments can intercede much more easily than private intermediaries when a financial market fails. This same virtue, however, becomes a vice for those worried that lack of a budget constraint may allow expensive programs to survive even when they provide little in the way of benefits. For the right, government intervention is often sought by what are termed "rent seekers": individuals who will receive large benefits from government programs but bear little of the cost. (These lucky individuals are called rent seekers because they receive advantages that exceed what they would have got without the government programs—what economists call "rents.")

It turns out that both sides in this debate have important insights, despite the yawning gap that separates them. Consider, for instance, the argument from the left that state intervention in capital markets is desirable or necessary because of market failures. As an argument, it is an ancient one, reflecting long-standing fears that unfettered markets may violate fundamental political or moral principles. One need only recall the long history of prohibitions against lending money at interest in Christianity, Judaism, and Islam. In China, moneylending may not have sparked religious concern, but it was subject to administrative regulation.[1] In the West, government authorities began to take over most of the task of regulating capital markets by the end of the Middle Ages, imposing rules such as usury ceilings and licenses for foreign bankers and limiting the way financial contracts could be drafted. Governments even began to operate as financial intermediaries, though it was on the level of the municipality or the small city-state rather than the large centralized monarchies. Many Italian cities, for example, created municipal pawnshops out of a widespread conviction (both religious and political) that the poor deserved help. Private pawnbrokers, it was widely believed, charged interest rates so high that they could leave poorer borrowers destitute and provoke social unrest. In the eyes of city leaders, the private credit market failed to produce the socially desirable outcome they wanted: poor people who would remain docile in economic downturns because they could borrow as a form of insurance.

What sorts of market failures are most likely to invite state intervention? One involves private parties' inability to enforce financial contracts. How can a borrower be forced to surrender collateral if he defaults on a loan? Although enforcement can sometimes be arranged privately, it often requires state intervention, particularly in large markets, where it may be costly or difficult even to inform other potential lenders that a deadbeat has refused to hand over his collateral. State intervention is the solution, usually in the form of state-enforced laws or regulations that govern financial contracts. The laws may dictate what happens when a borrower in default refuses to turn over collateral, and ideally the state will also provide courts to resolve disputes over collateral and unpaid loans.

Private markets may also invite government action when the initial demand for capital is too anemic to pay for the fixed costs of setting up new institutions. If the demand were larger, the fixed costs could be spread over a large number of financial transactions and would shrink to insignificance. Here the state may be able to intervene by absorbing the fixed costs. It can be the first to sell government bonds in a centralized market, for example, and thereby defray part of the cost of creating an exchange that can later be used for trading other financial assets. Once the market is in place, investors, borrowers, and entrepreneurs can rely on it to trade private stocks and bonds, and the cost of financing and of diversifying portfolios will fall.

Even when financial markets have surmounted these initial hurdles, they face other problems that may justify government intervention. In particular, they may be battered by economic shocks that defy most efforts to diversify—a worldwide shock like the Great Depression, for instance, or even the smaller shocks that often trip up investors or intermediaries who rely too heavily on recent history when assessing the risk of their portfolios. Shocks of this sort can sink banks and other financial intermediaries by making them run short of cash. The banks and other intermediaries may collapse or be forced to cut back their lending in order to rebuild their reserves. Investors, fearing the worst, may launch bank runs or sell off their assets in a panic. Entrepreneurs will then find that credit has dried up, and individuals who borrow will cut back spending to avoid losing a home or an automobile pledged as collateral. The result may be a huge economic downturn triggered by a temporary shortage of cash. Recovery may take a long time if the crisis destroys the intermediaries' skills and organizational capital. Here the left would argue that the state should jump in and bail out bankrupt firms, intermediaries, and individuals. Better that than a severe depression.

And then there are the problems facing borrowers who lack collateral or have no past dealings to establish a reputation for creditworthiness. Borrowers of this sort abound, even in highly developed capital markets: young adults, for example, particularly those who have few possessions and no track record of previous lending. Without collateral or an established reputation, they cannot get loans to open businesses or to get an education even if they are talented. That at least is what our model of credit markets suggests, and its implications are unfortunately all too realistic, even in the wealthy economies of western Europe and North America. The reason is simple: a lender may simply have no way to determine whether potential borrowers are likely to pay back their loans and no way to recover their losses in case they do default. The government, however, can make the loans possible, either by insuring them (so that lenders have no risk of losses) or by providing them directly. In the long run, the borrowers' increased earnings may suffice to pay off the loans, and if the state can tax these earnings, it will not end up losing money. The whole program may bring large benefits for the economy as a whole that private markets simply cannot capture because private lenders cannot easily take increased future earnings as collateral.

These are the sorts of market failures that government intervention can repair, at least for the advocates of government intervention on the left. Even critics of government intervention on the right may well acknowledge the market failures and admit that the government can improve matters, at least at the outset. Their greatest worry, however, is what will happen in the long run, because in their view government intervention, even if it is well-meaning, inevitably opens the door to the waste of valuable resources when individuals seek to take advantage of the government's programs. This waste, or rent seeking, comes in many guises. Financial intermediaries can ask for regulations that shield them from competition. They can disguise what should be their operating expenses as the sort of fixed costs that the government should bear, or make risky investments and then plead for an undeserved government bailout if the investments fail. Borrowers and lenders can benefit too, by getting unjustified loan subsidies and loan insurance.

Rent seeking is what frightens the critics the most. The danger is greatest when the state takes over for private intermediaries, but it is still a threat even when the state is only imposing regulations. And it is hardly peculiar to the modern age. Before the municipal pawnshops were established in late medieval Italy, the poor borrowed from Jewish pawnbrokers, who could lend to gentiles without being subject to the restrictions imposed on Christian lenders. The interest rate they charged was high because the loans were risky, but it would have dropped had the city governments allowed the pawnbrokers to compete with one another. But instead of permitting competition, which would have reduced interest rates to a minimum, many cities sold lending licenses to a small number of Jewish families, who could then collude to raise interest rates even higher. The cities then used the licenses to siphon off the profits the Jewish pawnbrokers made, leaving the poor the ultimate losers, because they ended up paying for the cost of the licenses and the high interest rates, all at a time when they were strapped for funds. The villains were local elites who controlled the municipal governments: they spared themselves taxation and foisted the costs onto borrowers.[2]

Objections to this sort of rent seeking did not appear until the eighteenth century, but in the hands of the critics on the right they have grown into a potent, three-pronged attack against government intervention not just in financial markets, but in markets in general. The first prong of the attack begins with the observation that because firms and individuals will inevitably pursue rents, government intervention should always be suspect. Even seemingly benevolent actions, such as the creation of municipal pawnshops, may disguise efforts to create and siphon off rents. At the very least, then, one should be skeptical of any claim that government intervention improves welfare.

The second prong of the attack from the right is harsher. It notes that government intervention will always create beneficiaries, even when it is well intentioned. The beneficiaries may be recipients of government subsidies, bureaucrats who administer the plans, or lenders who enjoy government loan guarantees. They may be the politicians themselves, as in Italy in the 1990s, when state-owned banks with ties to particular political parties granted loans at below-market interest rates in regions where the bank's political party was strong.[3] Whoever they are, though, they will all want to protect the largesse they receive regardless of the costs the government program imposes on taxpayers and regardless of its value to society as a whole. At the same time, the bureaucrats who run the programs will try to hide problems that arise, and they may engage in cozy deals with a small number of beneficiaries instead of extending the program to everyone who is eligible.

Thus even if the government intervention is designed to fix a real market failure, it will create groups of beneficiaries who will agitate to keep the program running and if possible expand it. The pathology is not limited to developing economies or to notoriously corrupt political regimes. In the United States, for example, government-run student loan programs have allowed young people to finance a college education and thereby solved a market failure. But they also have permitted universities to expand their enrollments and raise tuition, giving the universities an incentive to lobby so that the loan programs grow despite their cost.[4]

Similarly, two financial intermediaries established by the federal government—the Federal National Mortgage Association (FNMA) and the Federal Home Loan Mortgage Corporation (FHLMC)—can rightly take pride in having created a market in which mortgages can easily be traded by buying new mortgages from banks and savings and loans, grouping them together, and then selling the pooled assets as mortgage-backed securities. This market has the great virtue of allowing banks and savings and loans to diversify their portfolios, and it has solved a problem that had long bedeviled mortgage lenders in the United States. But now that the market for mortgages is up and running, one can make a strong case that there is no longer a need for either organization. If the FNMA and FHLMC were privatized, the market for mortgages would continue to function without a government guarantee, just as it already does for large mortgages, which are bundled and sold by private entrepreneurs. Privatization would have the advantage of eliminating the implicit backing for the securities that both organizations issue, which allows them to raise money at lower rates. This unstated government guarantee constitutes a huge subsidy for both organizations, and it carries an enormous risk, for if either organization defaulted, taxpayers would have to bail out the debtholders, at a cost that could easily dwarf the savings-and-loan debacle of the 1980s. The risk of such a default cannot simply be ignored, for increasingly both organizations have been holding on to mortgages instead of selling them off. That trend leaves both the FNMA and the FHLMC open to potential heavy losses when interest rates change.[5]

What has for a long time made privatization unthinkable—something of a surprise in the promarket United States—is the fact that the FNMA and the FHLMC are accomplished lobbyists. Their shareholders and management pocket a significant portion of the subsidy, and to retain this benefit they have spent money and made charitable donations in a way that has probably influenced congressional votes. Meanwhile the taxpayers, who take on all the risk, are of course unorganized and by and large unaware of the size of the subsidy. As a result, even conservative legislators have had little reason to consider privatizing the FNMA and the FHLMC. Nor, until recently, have they contemplated imposing new regulations that would reduce the risk of a bailout. Only when the recent bout of corporate accounting scandals touched the FNMA and the FHLMC—yet another mark of how a crisis can change the political atmosphere—did Congress and regulators suddenly wake up.[6]

The third prong of the attack on government intervention in financial markets is potentially the most damaging. When the government steps in to correct a market deficiency, critics on the right argue, it reduces the incentive for private innovation. Private intermediaries can solve market failures too, but their incentive is profit. Once the government has stepped in, demand for whatever private intermediaries can offer will drop, as will their profits; furthermore, any private intermediaries foolhardy enough to compete with the government will face opposition from the beneficiaries of state intervention, who will want to protect their rents. Private innovation will thus disappear, forcing the state to remain involved longer than if it had never stepped in. For the right, therefore, government intervention will bring only limited benefits because of rent seeking, and in a worst-case scenario, the rent seeking will undo whatever gains a government program yields.

The right and the left have sharply contrasting opinions of government intervention, and their different takes on what states should do have strikingly different implications for the development of financial markets. For the left, market failures keep financial markets from developing fully without significant state assistance. For the right, state intervention inevitably imposes huge costs. And the side that has predominated—whether among experts or among policymakers—has varied over time. In the United States, for example, the Great Depression fostered a widespread belief (among both politicians and economists) in the dangers of market failures; that belief in turn framed the creation of deposit insurance, the Securities and Exchange Commission, the Social Security system, and a host of other programs that had the federal government regulating financial markets and providing financial services on scale unknown in the past. In the late 1970s and 1980s, however, fears of rent seeking came to the fore, spurred on in part by the huge costs and political embarrassments of the savings-and-loan disaster.[7]

Rethinking Government Intervention

Government intervention in financial markets inevitably causes rent seeking and can also stifle private innovation. Yet as we have seen, market failures are endemic in financial markets, emerging when demand is anemic, when contracts cannot be enforced, when investors cannot insure themselves against shocks, and when people cannot borrow because they have not earned a reputation for creditworthiness or have no collateral. The difficulties discussed in previous chapters will only make market failures more common. Asymmetric information makes it difficult to enforce contracts or to provide investors with insurance against shocks. Inequality deprives deserving borrowers of collateral. And private intermediaries may be unable to solve the problem without politicians' help. They may simply adopt conflicting solutions to the problem, or they may hesitate to devise something new if their competitors can quickly copy their creation without bearing any of the costs.

There thus seems to be a case for public intervention in order to repair market failures, yet only if rent seeking can be restrained. Government action will inevitably involve trade-offs, and some rents will have to be doled out to beneficiaries when the state intercedes. But if these rents can be limited, reform can succeed without causing too much damage.

That at least is what history suggests. We can see how by looking at several examples. Consider, for example, the American federal government's 1933 Securities Act, which established standards for financial reporting and thereby solved a problem of asymmetric information bedeviling investors who bought stocks and bonds. Private reformers had been trying since the 1920s to make the financial reports of the companies issuing the stocks and bonds more reliable and informative, but they were unable to agree on what to do. The New York Stock Exchange (NYSE), which already had relatively stringent reporting requirements, did begin to impose new accounting rules on the firms it listed, but that move left out all the companies whose securities traded on other markets. Along with companion legislation in 1934, the Securities Act of 1933 settled matters by establishing standards for financial disclosure and making accountants, underwriters, and company directors liable for providing misleading information. The legislation created a common solution for the informational problems, and it imposed this solution on many smaller firms that could not afford to be listed on the NYSE. It also put the force of law behind the sort of rules that the NYSE had adopted voluntarily and thereby added to the credibility of financial information.

The effect of the legislation was considerable. By itself, the 1933 Securities Act helped investors to evaluate securities more accurately, whether the securities were traded on the NYSE or other exchanges. Its most important effect was off the NYSE, where it brought an end to persistent overpricing of initial public stock offerings. It may have even spurred the growth of the over-the-counter market—the ancestor of the NASDAQ—making it easier for new companies to raise money.[8]

Nonetheless, the act did generate rents, especially for investment bankers, who used it to restrict competition in underwriting securities.[9] But in all likelihood the benefits of the 1933 Securities Act more than outweighed the losses to rent seeking. After all, without something like it, we might not have the NASDAQ and all the new companies it has helped launch.

Even programs that by their very definition allocate rents because they channel low-cost capital to a specific sector of the economy can end up being fairly efficient if the rents they produce are not excessive. Western Europe's remarkable growth in the three decades that followed World War II, when living standards in Europe caught up with those in the United States, furnishes a striking illustration. This period of rapid growth was also a time when states had an extensive hold over financial institutions. In every country, the state intervened to allocate resources in ways it deemed efficient, and in some—notably France—government ownership or control of banks was common. Yet the rent seeking generated by having the government allocate capital for roads, housing, schools, and electrical grids was not enough to make Europe's economic growth lag behind that of the United States. The same was true of capital loaned to enterprises. On the contrary: the state-sponsored investment both created infrastructure and produced rapid growth.

The 1933 Securities Act in the United States and the direct state intervention in Europe were thus successes, in the sense that the benefits were large, while egregious rent seeking was kept in check. When rent seeking dominates, however, the economic losses from government intervention can be huge. When the Mexican government of Porfirio Díaz passed a general banking act in 1897, it codified a political agreement that conferred enormous rents upon a small number of politically connected banks in return for loans to the government. For the bankers, the major advantage was that few new banks could set up shop. The bankers could thus operate almost as if they were monopolists, without fear of competition from new firms. In return, the government got its loans. The cost for the Mexican economy, however, was huge, because the monopolists charged higher interest rates and made fewer loans than competitive bankers would have. In the textile industry—a significant sector of the economy in a developing country like Mexico—loans by and large went only to a small number of entrepreneurs who had close connections to the existing banks. Because these entrepreneurs ended up running huge, bloated businesses that were too large to operate efficiently, the banking system handicapped the entire textile sector.[10]

The three examples illustrate the dilemma of government intervention, a dilemma that neither the proponents on the left nor the critics on the right have managed to capture, since each side understands only part of the picture. The truth is that government intervention in financial markets is always driven, at least in part, by politicians' willingness to provide rents to favored clients or constituents. But even so, state involvement can solve market failures. Intervention is successful when the cost of the rents that are offered is small relative to the benefits of resolving the market failure. This standard for success may gloss over differences between distinct kinds of rent (a highway that is convenient for a political leader can be used by other people as well, but his subsidized apartment cannot); nonetheless, it does have the virtue of getting at the essentials—the net costs of rents versus the benefits of functioning markets.

One might think (particularly on the strength of the Mexican example) that competition would be the obvious answer here—a foolproof way of having the state intercede without unleashing packs of rent seekers. Yet the economics of a particular financial market may simply rule competition out. If demand for bank loans is anemic, for example, a local market may not be able to sustain more than one bank, and perhaps not even that. Allowing only one bank to operate (or even subsidizing it if necessary) may be the best policy, at least initially, even though that bank will be a monopolist. India had this sort of experience, for instance, when it required banks to open branches in rural areas. The new branches expanded savings and lending in the countryside, even though each one operated as a local monopolist.[11] Other banks would not have been willing to open competing branches because the profits would have been too low, and even if they had, it is not clear that the additional branches would have boosted lending appreciably. A local monopoly, in short, may have been the best that could be hoped for, at least in the short run.

And sometimes competition may simply be irrelevant. Consider the banks that the French government founded in the nineteenth century in order to encourage workers and members of the middle class to save. These savings banks invested all the funds they had on deposit in short-term government obligations, and in return the government provided the depositors with a subsidy in the form of an interest premium that boosted what they earned on their accounts. The government did not stop private bankers from offering similar accounts (although they did not do so, perhaps because of the government subsidy), but it did not have its own savings banks compete with one another. Such competition would have been pointless, because it would not have cut the savings banks' costs or changed what they were doing.

Although there was no competition between the savings banks, these public institutions did make it possible for individuals of limited means to invest for the first time. These small-scale savers could not have purchased government bonds directly, for the minimum investment required was too high. They could have deposited their savings with a private banker, but for many of them the risk of a bank failure was too high to stomach. With their accounts in the savings banks, they not only earned interest but also could withdraw money if their expenses suddenly shot up or their income dropped.

To be sure, competition is usually one of the elements of success when a government intervenes in financial markets, but it is not a cure-all that allows states to correct market failures easily and without any risk of rent seeking. Sometimes competition may be unattainable; on some occasions it may even make market failures worse. And it is worth stressing that persistent competition is the result of a complicated interaction between public and private institutions, and not some initial condition that can be imposed with the wave of a hand. It has to arise, and even in a favorable institutional setting, it may be only one of a number of possible outcomes, each of them dependent on the accidents of history.

When Is Government Intervention Successful?

Successful government intervention in financial markets may therefore be possible, but what conditions will make it more likely? In other words, what is likely to bring a government to correct market failures and yet stop it from lavishing rents on cosseted beneficiaries? What in particular can someone who makes policy look for and even hope to change in order to make success more likely?

The goal is creating public institutions that promote financial development. Many development economists have wrestled with this issue in seeking to discover why some governments veer toward rent seeking while others actually resolve market failures. For some development economists, the ultimate answer lies with institutions or social structures established long ago. In their view, the root of the problem may lie, for instance, with the legal system—in particular, whether it is based on a written code (as in the civil law countries of continental Europe) or on precedent (as in the common law countries of Great Britain and the United States). Or it may derive from ethnic fragmentation, from fundamental religious beliefs, or from the structure of the constitution and whether the state is a federal one or centralized. Some countries may simply be cursed with bad institutions and social conditions—in what sounds like the economic equivalent of original sin—while others are not, and their governments will act accordingly.

In emphasizing long-established institutions and social conditions, development economists may discover what sort of society is more likely to nurture a stable financial system. That information is important for understanding the ultimate causes of economic growth, but it does not necessarily help policymakers, who will want to direct (or even limit) government intervention in a way that will make financial markets thrive. The trouble is that even the best-intentioned policymakers will rarely be able to transform their constitution or the religious beliefs or ethnic identity of their constituents, and they will not be able to redraft the legal system either. Furthermore, even if they could carry out such revolutionary change, it might be so destabilizing that financial development and economic growth themselves would be undermined. Policymakers usually have to take these long-established institutions and conditions as given; all they can do is to propose policies for government intervention.

Yet modest efforts of this sort do not necessarily put a thriving financial market forever out of reach, for there are many societies that have experienced financial development (and economic growth too) despite having very different constitutions, legal systems, religions, and ethnic makeups. Both France and the United States, for instance, have developed advanced financial markets, even though France has had a centralized constitution and a civil law legal system ever since the French Revolution, while the United States has lived under a federal system and the common law for just as long. Financial markets in Japan have thrived with an ethnically homogeneous population that is predominantly Buddhist and Shintoist; France and the United States have done so with more heterogeneous populations, with Catholicism as the dominant religion in one and Protestantism in the other. None of these countries provides an example of what is undeniably the best financial system or the most efficient division of labor between public and private sectors.[12] Rather they suggest that a wide range of institutions and social conditions are compatible with thriving financial markets—a broad middle ground where capital markets work well. The real problem is whether it is possible to adopt policies that can bring countries into this range.

History suggests that in the long run, the answer is yes, but only under certain conditions. Although these conditions will certainly vary from place to place and over time, the principles of political economy suggest that there are a few general rules that can almost always boost the chances for success. The key is making sure that these rules are followed. That will happen only if politicians have an incentive to support the right sort of government intervention: government intervention that repairs market failures rather than damaging markets or generating rents. The politicians who determine what the government does are not naive. When they choose bad policies it is because they have an incentive to do so.

There are three conditions that significantly increase the likelihood of successful government intervention. First, the government must be able to deal with private credit markets without regard to public finance; it must not be starved for cash, for then it will be tempted to prey upon financial markets. Second, it must have both the information necessary to deter misbehavior by beneficiaries and the ability to act upon that information. Third, there must exist a large or politically powerful middle class.

These three conditions are based on the simple models of political economy used in the previous chapters and on a close reading of history. But they are not guarantees. They make it more likely that state intervention will be effective, but they cannot assure success. Italy, for example, has a large middle class, but that has not kept rich families in Italy from using the government's involvement in banking and financial regulation to protect the firms they own from competition.[13] Nor can these three conditions dictate exactly the role that the government will take, for there are too many different ways to overcome a market failure or meet the demand for new financial institutions. One might suppose, for example, that all countries with thriving financial markets would have to imitate the United States and restrict the government's role to providing the necessary legal infrastructure. Yet the example of Scandinavian countries, where governments have taken on a much larger role without hindering growth, suggests that the American solution is but one of many possible outcomes.[14] Our three conditions do not predict whether the government's role will be large or small; they simply make successful government intervention more likely.

One might object that our third condition—the presence of a large or politically powerful middle class—would be one of those things that policymakers are completely powerless to change. Like the existence of a legal system or of ethnic fragmentation, it may be important, but it cannot really be modified. This objection, however, overlooks all the ways in which a state can nurture the middle class, at least over the long run. It can adopt fiscal policies that encourage savings. It can help establish mortgage markets or markets where collateral can be traded, which will make it easier for private intermediaries to make loans to entrepreneurs and to other borrowers who are entering the middle class. And it can guarantee or fund educational loans so that young people without collateral can also join the middle class. None of these policies can create a large middle class overnight, and none of them will turn a Nicaragua into a Denmark, but they can all help the middle class grow. They can, in short, create the possibility of a virtuous circle, in which the right policies will not only promote financial development directly (by, say, establishing markets for collateral) but will also expand the middle class, whose growth will in turn generate further financial development. History in fact suggests that such a virtuous circle can be extended beyond government policies to institutions in general. The right financial institutions can further financial development and augment the middle class, leading to more financial development down the road.

Now one might also worry that these three conditions are innocuous, but they are actually quite severe. Breaching any one of them reduces the odds of a healthy division of labor between government intervention and private innovation by financial intermediaries. Nearly all countries have violated one of these conditions at some point in their history. The result has often been a financial crisis.

The First Condition for Success: Manageable Government Debt

We already know that if a state is not burdened by huge debts, politicians will not be tempted to prey upon financial markets. Furthermore, the government will also be able to afford the sort of legal infrastructure that financial markets need to thrive. It will have enough money to operate courts, support property rights, and enforce needed laws and regulations. The government can even get involved in financial markets when demand is anemic, when potential borrowers lack collateral, or when the government needs to provide deposit insurance or even bail out intermediaries who are in trouble. Politicians may still be tempted to intercede on behalf of powerful interest groups who are pursuing rents. But even then the burden imposed on financial markets will be less than it would if the government itself had extracted its own pint of blood.

If, however, a state is desperate for cash, then it cannot afford the support that markets need. That is a severe problem in many developing countries, which may have laws on the books but no funds to pay for courts or enforcement. Lack of funds can also prevent a state from acting as a lender of last resort or from boosting anemic demand or providing loans to borrowers without collateral. Chronic market failures may therefore remain untreated.

Worse yet, if this first condition is violated, the government will be tempted to intervene in financial markets in order to get the funds it does not have. Even if it does not prey on financial markets, it may create rents that it can confiscate or dole out to political supporters. That (as we know) is why the Mexican government of Porfirio Díaz ended up granting local monopolies to a small set of politically connected bankers in 1897. Diaz needed money to consolidate his hold on the Mexican presidency, but if he had tried to raise taxes, he would have run into opposition from powerful provincial leaders. Another source of funds—borrowing abroad—was also out of the question because of Mexico's miserable history as a borrower. Domestic lenders were also leery, because they too had been burned in previous state defaults. But if Díaz could find a way to reassure them and guarantee them a profit, they might be willing to lend the government money. The monopoly did this. It gave a small set of bankers monopoly profits, and since Díaz and his circle also shared in the rents, the bankers knew that Díaz would stand behind the arrangement. Indeed, Díaz could use the rents to win the provincial leaders over to his regime. The big loser, of course, was the Mexican economy.[15]

Alternatively, a cash-strapped government may simply prey upon financial markets, in way we described in Chapter 1. The consequences, we know, can be devastating. Recall, for instance, the divergent paths taken by England and France. By the end of the seventeenth century, England had become financially solvent, and it stopped plundering financial markets. In France, by contrast, the government's thirst for funds led it to default periodically on a portion of its debts. The sorry state of its finances kept the French state from creating the sort of centralized market for government debt that the English government helped establish in London. The reason was the fear that if such a market were established, with publicly quoted prices for government debt, it would immediately reveal how precarious the French government's finances were. The consequences were significant: private financial markets in Paris lagged behind those in London by more than a generation.

The Second Condition for Success: Adequate Information

If the government does intervene in capital markets, it will need information. Whether it changes laws or enters directly into financial transactions, it will have to know whether its laws are being broken or whether it is being taken advantage of by the other parties in its financial dealings. It will also want the means to act upon the information, in particular the means to sanction misbehavior. It will, in short, have to have an effective administration or bureaucracy, one that has adequate funding and enough power to resist political pressure. This bureaucracy must be able to keep up with firms and individuals who try to take advantage of the government and its regulations. It will in fact be engaged in something like an arms race with firms and individuals, with the latter exerting endless ingenuity to undermine the quality of the government's information and its ability to enforce its rules.

In this contest, states drawing up laws to ward off future crises will usually be handicapped by their habit of basing their legislation on information drawn from the recent past. In this situation historical experience can be a misleading guide, just as it is for private financial intermediaries. Recall, for example, what happened to Argentina, which tied its currency to the dollar in the early 1990s in order to halt hyperinflation. The reform did hold inflation in check, but by making it difficult to devalue the peso it tied the government's hands and thereby made it much more difficult for Argentina to ward off the next crisis, at the end of 2001. Like many private intermediaries, government officials had perhaps forgotten that the next crisis need not fully resemble the crisis that has just passed.

If a government goes beyond enacting laws and regulations and begins to do something like lending money, it will have to determine whether the borrowers are making good use of their loans and whether they are likely to default. One might imagine that a state would have so much more information about borrowers than private financial intermediaries and so much power over borrowers who do default (after all, it could conceivably throw deadbeats into prison) that it would not run into problems with unpaid loans. Indeed, one might even imagine that state ownership of banks would be a means of protecting against financial crises, for what lenders would dare default on debts owed to a state-owned bank? In reality, though, state ownership of banks confers no protection against financial crises. If anything, the reverse seems to be true, at least in developing countries.[16]

One reason is that the harsh penalties the state can impose may prove meaningless if influential borrowers and intermediaries can lobby to avoid them. Furthermore, the government's information is likely to be less extensive than it appears. If the government preserves official records of income, property ownership, and mortgages, then it may have more information than private intermediaries do about collateral and possibly credit histories too. All these records will come from the past, however, and they will often reveal little about new projects that borrowers are undertaking. Worse yet, the records will not capture all sorts of informal information that is critical in financial markets—the sort of information that bankers are experts at gathering. A nineteenth-century government might have known whether a farmer had mortgaged his property, for example, but it could not have told whether he was a good farmer or had a reputation for paying his debts. A local banker, by contrast, would have known such things. Government bureaucrats will simply not have the kind of contacts needed to elicit this sort of information from the business community, and as a group they are likely to be less well informed than, say, the set of all private financial intermediaries.

Even if a government program encounters no initial difficulties with information, they can still develop over time. In the early 1960s the government of South Korea began to subsidize firms that would build plants in strategic areas and export their output—the first step toward the country's development miracle. The government knew that it lacked information about the firms' ability to carry out their investment plans, and to ensure that its money was not wasted, it made more credit available to firms that had succeeded in the past. The incentives did push firms to succeed, and the firms that did thrive—the conglomerates known as *chaebols*—grew rapidly. Yet the program as a whole had an essential flaw: once the Korean conglomerates grew big enough, they could easily hide the performance of any one of their enterprises from the state simply by shifting costs from failed projects to successful ones. The government's own incentives encouraged them to do so, because revealing the failures would have jeopardized future subsidies. Only when earnings plummeted in 1997 did the truth finally come out, but by that time the *chaebols* had compromised Korea's entire financial system. If the government had possessed more information, it would not have been forced to structure the incentives in the way it did, and it might have been able to force the *chaebols* to trim losing projects and thereby avoid a financial crisis.

One final problem is the cost of acquiring the information that states like Korea need. Governments have to decide whether they will pay for it before they intervene. If not, they simply have to limit what they do, for without information, they will encourage potentially devastating strategic behavior by recipients, financial intermediaries, or government employees—strategic behavior that is often enough to bring on a financial crisis of its own.

The Third Condition for Success: A Large and Powerful Middle Class

For state intervention in financial markets to succeed, politicians have to be induced to do two things: intervene to correct market failures, and keep the costs of intervention low by minimizing rent seeking.

The members of the middle class are the individuals most likely to apply this pressure. How much pressure they can exert will depend on the size of the middle class, the extent of its political power, the ease with which its members can be mobilized by politicians or activists, and also on existing political institutions—in particular, the extent to which politicians must respond to their constituents. In a nondemocratic regime, the middle class can exert pressure only indirectly; in a democracy, politicians cannot ignore the middle class's worries if the middle class is large.

Why is the middle class likely to pressure the government? The reason is simple: as we know from our model of capital markets, members of the middle class have a higher demand for financial innovations than do the rich or the poor. They will therefore be eager for the government to intercede and repair market failures when private intermediaries are not up to the task. And they will reward politicians who overcome problems in financial markets. At the very minimum, they will want the government to provide the essential public goods that thriving financial markets require: protection of property rights, enforcement of contracts, and swift and predictable adjudication of disputes that private parties cannot resolve on their own. They will also want the government to step in when financial intermediaries cannot agree upon a common solution to a market failure. And they may well want the government to deal with other difficulties that can afflict financial markets: anemic demand, shocks that cannot be insured against, or the obstacles that borrowers like themselves face when they have skills or an education but lack enough assets that can be pledged as collateral.

The reason members of the middle class are likely to be sympathetic to such borrowers—and concerned with nearly all failures in financial markets—is that over the course of their lives they are likely to be both borrowers and savers, or entrepreneurs and investors. When they are young, they will want to borrow to finance an education, buy a home, or start a business, even though they may not yet have any collateral. As they age, they will save and invest, and they will want to tap their investments for support in old age. One might argue that there are likely to be sharp divisions between individuals in the middle class—that older members, for instance, no longer care about institutions affecting borrowers, because their borrowing days are over. But even though their own borrowing days may have passed, they are likely to have children or relatives who want to take out loans, and because they can easily see themselves or family members wanting to borrow or invest, they are likely to support nearly all public and private measures that make credit markets thrive. The same argument applies to financial markets broadly defined—for instance, to markets for insurance. Members of the middle class will turn to their own families' experience—and to readily available news reports about the difficulties that people like themselves face when insurance markets do not function—when deciding whether to support government intervention in insurance markets; and similar reasoning will bring them to back necessary government intercession more generally.

There will, however, be limits to their support for government intervention. In particular, members of the middle class will want to keep what they or their relatives have saved. In general, they will therefore oppose government plans to confiscate property. They may also balk if government redistribution does not bring the middle class benefits in return for the taxes they pay.

The middle class will also worry about the cost of government intervention in financial markets. The reason is that even if some members will benefit from government programs, many others will end up bearing the cost. It is simply too difficult for them to avoid taxation. Unlike the rich, they cannot afford the fixed costs of setting up tax shelters or shifting assets abroad, and in any case, most of them have to work or operate firms in local markets, where taxation is unavoidable. Since they will end up bearing much of the cost, they will want to limit rent seeking and restrict government intervention to cases in which it can improve upon the sort of innovations that private intermediaries are able to offer. They will therefore support government intervention when needed, but never to the point where it completely discourages innovation by private financial intermediaries. Ideally, they will have the state engaged in financial markets alongside private intermediaries and in a way that limits rent seeking.

Admittedly, there are nearly always some members of the middle class who siphon off rents for themselves, such as small businessmen in the United States who get cheap government loans, or farmers in nearly all Western democracies, who benefit from price supports. Typically the benefits derive from programs directed at small sectors of the economy or at activities that were once considered strategic. But if the middle class is large relative to the other groups in society, then there will be numerous other members of the middle class who do not receive rents from such programs. They will seek to keep the costs of the programs from spiraling out of hand because, given the size of the middle class, they will end up bearing the costs.

A big middle class will stand a better chance of getting politicians to adopt financial policies they favor, at least in a democracy. The only real obstacle will be small special-interest groups—primarily financial intermediaries and the rich—who are affected by financial legislation. These groups will be easier to organize as a lobby, and politicians may prefer to serve their interests, particularly if doing so brings in campaign contributions.

In nondemocracies, state intervention on behalf of the middle class is less likely, even if this group is sizable. Whether members of the middle class get the financial institutions they want will depend on whether they have political power. It is no surprise that the earliest financial centers (Venice and Genoa in the Middle Ages, Antwerp and Amsterdam in the sixteenth and seventeenth centuries) were cities in which members of what we would call the middle class—merchants—exercised considerable political influence. Financial intermediaries such as bankers were influential too, but their concern was serving the middle-class merchants.[17] The middle class in the early financial centers thus wielded enough power to get the government to support financial markets.

Crises and Changes in Government Intervention

There is great variation in the role that governments play in capital markets, and what is striking is that these differences from country to country tend to persist over time. They have even survived the recent spate of privatization in the financial sector. It is almost as if historical accidents (such as the specific institutions created in the past or the enduring political coalitions that put previous institutional reforms into place) freeze states into a role that only a large shock or crisis can alter.

The boundary between what the government does and what private intermediaries do is particularly slow to change. Take stock exchanges for example: the Paris Bourse has been government owned since the early nineteenth century, whereas the New York Stock Exchange was created as a private entity and has remained so despite the Great Depression and other moments of turmoil.

In another financial market—the one for capital raised by local utilities—the pattern is just the reverse but just as persistent. Utilities—which may provide water, electric power, or transportation—consume immense amounts of capital to construct reservoirs and water mains, set up power grids and generating plants, and build rail lines and viaducts. Despite some privatization in the late twentieth century, municipalities and other local government bodies in the United States have owned most water systems and many urban transit and electric power systems ever since the late nineteenth century. These government entities have borrowed large amounts of capital for services that the private market could furnish—all this in an ostensibly laissez-faire economy. In France, by contrast, municipalities and other local governments tended to contract with private companies to provide utilities; until World War II transportation and electric power generation were privately owned, and water delivery remains so today. The reason for this contrasting pattern rests with historical accident, which affected local governments' access to capital markets. In the United States, with its traditions of federalism and decentralized government, the individual states had long allowed local government bodies to impose taxes, subject to some regulation.[18] Cities could therefore borrow by mortgaging their future tax revenue and raise the capital needed to build public utilities. In France, by contrast, regimes before, during and after the Revolution had made it very difficult for cities and other local public entities to establish or increase taxes. Without tax revenues to borrow against, local governments in France could not issue bonds and thus could not establish utilities. A historical divergence in political institutions thus dictated persistently different roles for local government not just in providing utilities but also in access to the capital market.

Crises provide rare opportunities to set aside legacies from the past. In France, World War II left local utilities facing an enormous job of reconstruction, for their capital stock had been severely damaged by the war itself and by a decade and a half of minimal investment following the Great Depression. The central government believed that rebuilding the infrastructure in transport and power delivery would hasten economic recovery. Leaving the private sector to take charge of this investment would be inefficient, politicians believed, because French capital markets were in tatters, with banks largely insolvent and equity markets moribund. The French government, however, could and did borrow abroad, primarily from the United States. The central government thus took over a number of sectors, including railroads and electricity, and in addition it nationalized banks in December 1945. The government's intervention was immensely successful if we judge by growth in the French economy through the 1960s. The government's new role was also persistent: banks were not privatized until the 1980s, and the national electricity company is still in the government's hands.

Although change may also occur in calmer times, a crisis is the moment when politicians, lobbying groups, and citizens themselves are most likely to push a government to alter its traditional role. It may intercede directly in financial markets, as happened in France after World War II, or it may impose new regulations, as happened in the United States during the Great Depression, and more recently after the bout of corporate scandals and the collapse of the Internet bubble. Or it may even pull out of financial markets.

One reason states react in such varied ways is that crises provide critical information about the efficacy of public and private financial institutions. The information is of course valuable to politicians and government bureaucrats, but it is often worth even more to the public, who otherwise often remain uninformed about most details of public policy. Because the typical individual can usually do little to change public policy, even in a democracy, most people have little incentive to learn what the government is up to. A financial crisis, though, can make the arcane details of what the government is doing a salient public issue, for psychological and political reasons. Psychologically, the crisis gives individuals frightening and readily available examples of what might happen to them, even if they are not personally affected, and it may cause them to exaggerate the actual risks they face. Knowing this, politicians and political activists can take advantage of the situation and mobilize the public for political action.[19]

What sort of information can a crisis divulge? It may expose too little insurance or diversification or a weakness of private intermediaries and push the government to intervene in these areas. Alternatively, it may bring government intervention to a halt by demonstrating that the state itself bears responsibility for the crisis. Or it may reveal how inefficient certain public financial institutions are and prompt politicians to change those institutions, as happened in the 1980s savings-and-loan crisis in the United States. The combination of deposit insurance and deregulation had brought on the crisis by encouraging savings-and-loan operators to take excessive risks or even to loot their own banks. When the federal government finally interceded, it did not involve itself directly in the savings-and-loan business. Instead it closed and sold off the insolvent savings and loans and then changed the regulations to remove the incentive for misbehavior.

A new financial role for the government—such as leaving or entering a financial market or imposing regulations—is not always prompted by a crisis; witness the important reforms of financial institutions that are creating a unified market across Europe. But by making the issues of reform and intervention salient, crises often prompt a shift in direction, which may itself last for years. Understanding how governments treat financial markets thus continues to require steering a middle course between history and political economy.

Explaining Government Intervention

Most of the examples presented in this chapter come from the twentieth century. Certainly, there are instances of state intrusion into financial markets before 1900, but what is striking is the increasing extent of government involvement ever since. Governments even intrude in other countries' financial markets, via organizations such as the World Bank and the International Monetary Fund. Some of this state intervention has itself triggered or intensified financial disasters. But whether good or bad, government intervention in financial markets seems likely to grow, and it can be traced back to contingencies of history.

Governments' assumption of a greater role was, for the most part, the result of shocks. A shock might push a state to the brink of a fiscal crisis and drive it to prey upon financial markets. It might suddenly reveal market failures and bring calls for new government regulation. Or it might force a state to provide capital for a hard-hit sector of the economy. For political or economic reasons, politicians might decide that they could not afford to have private intermediaries rebuild the decimated sector of the economy. Instead, they had the government step in.

Motives of this sort have led governments to intercede in financial markets both in developed countries and in those that are still impoverished. While the pace of government intervention has been similar in both areas of the world, the results in rich and poor countries are not at all alike. The different consequences reflect our three conditions for successful government intervention. In the rich nations of Japan, Europe, and North America, the three conditions for success have usually held, despite the shocks. Many poorer countries have not been so lucky.

World War I brought a great expansion of the state sector, engulfing all the rich economies of the world and in particular the three countries (Britain, France, and Germany) that had been significant capital exporters in the nineteenth century. The expense of fighting forced states to increase taxes and to borrow on a large scale. Governments also went off the gold standard and printed more money, which was no longer backed by precious metal. The eventual result was inflation, which cost government creditors heavily.

The tax increases and inflation might be expected, but the intensity and duration of the war led states to intrude in financial markets in unheard-of ways. Even Britain, whose government was among the most restrained, imposed a special tax on British owners of American stocks and bonds. The tax aimed at inducing these investors to surrender their American securities to the crown in return for British government debt. The British government could then use the American securities to buy American goods needed for the war effort. In France, the state controlled investment as it struggled to fight a war despite having lost much of the country's industrial plant in the early months of battle. Governments also managed investment and capital flows in Germany, Austria, and Italy; and although the war had fewer effects on government intervention in the United States, the Treasury did make direct loans to allied states. The war showed that government intervention had proved quite effective in an emergency and that managing financial markets had been crucial to the war effort. Although all the belligerents wanted to return to private capital markets when the fighting stopped, the positive wartime experience of government intervention encouraged a public solution to the next big crisis.

That crisis came a decade later, with the Great Depression. It drove governments to intervene on a large scale again, once it seemed clear that private firms and individuals were unable to cope with the problems. Politicians and much of the public became convinced that markets in general—and capital markets in particular—were unstable and prone to massive failure. Governments, it was believed, could provide the solution, and people adhered to that belief even though state policy was often incoherent and even though governments actually made the crisis far worse by their stubborn adherence to the gold standard.

Among Western democracies, it was perhaps in the United States that the state response to the Great Depression was most intense, at least for financial markets. Congressional hearings delved into seemingly shady practices on Wall Street, and along with the rash of bank failures, the hearings helped the administration of Franklin Roosevelt to create new financial institutions. The Securities and Exchange Commission was established to supervise the stock and bond markets and to make dealings in them transparent—a novelty in a country in which securities regulation had previously been the responsibility of individual states. The federal government also created deposit insurance and tightened bank regulations, measures that, among other things, drastically reduced the rate of bank failures. But the Roosevelt administration did not limit itself to securities and banking legislation. It regulated industries in the hope of avoiding the instability associated with excess competition or excess capacity. It set up Social Security, a nearly universal government pension scheme. To varying degrees, the European democracies followed suit, and rapid economic growth in the Soviet Union seemed to make an even stronger case for government intervention, for the Soviet Union appeared to have escaped most of the Depression, at least to observers who overlooked the horrors of dictatorship and collectivization. Intervention, all the evidence seemed to suggest, was the way to reduce risk and promote economic growth.

World War II made the case for government intervention even

more persuasive, in large part because the troops now demanded a much larger stock of weapons and other capital goods. The need for intervention in financial markets grew even stronger after the war, at least in continental Europe, where most private financial intermediaries were insolvent. The Europeans had to rebuild not just their factories and infrastructure but also their financial systems—a task whose very magnitude argued in favor of their governments' taking a leading role. As part of a political bargain that slowed wage growth in the 1950s and early 1960s, most European states expanded government health insurance, unemployment benefits, and pension plans. The median amount European states devoted to such programs climbed from 1.2 percent of gross domestic product (GDP) in 1930 to 11 percent in 1960.[20] Spending on such government insurance and pension plans also grew after World War II in other wealthy democracies, such as Canada, Japan, and the United States. So did government money for education, as with the G.I. Bill and the student loan program in the United States. The educational spending, it could be argued, helped many young people accumulate human capital that private markets would have been reluctant to fund.

State intervention was not limited to the wealthier belligerents in the two world wars. Latin American governments, for instance, had long used tariff policies to promote industrial development, but with the advent of the Great Depression they founded development banks that aimed to foster growth by guaranteeing private loans or funneling capital directly into their economies. Governments in other developing countries established state-controlled financial sectors too, particularly after independence severed their links to colonial banks. Sometimes, as in parts of Asia, these countries also enjoyed competitive private banks and budding equity markets. Yet alongside this private sector lurked a large state finance apparatus, sometimes disguised as export promotion. In the aftermath of World War II, government intervention in financial markets had become part of the standard remedy for developing countries. It was what economic advisers recommended and what politicians pursued to catch up with the wealthier countries of Japan, Europe, and North America. And it was particularly appealing to the leaders of newly independent nations, who were naturally suspicious of free markets.

On the whole, the record of government involvement with financial markets has been mixed. On the one hand, in societies in which the middle class was large even before World War I, capital markets were already well developed. These societies already had innovative private intermediaries, and they already possessed the political and legal infrastructure on which financial transactions depend: courts, law codes, regulatory bodies, and political support for the enforcement of contracts and property rights. For them, greater state intervention has generally been beneficial, even though it has occasionally imposed heavy costs, as during the savings-and-loan debacle in the United States. That outcome does not mean that division of labor between the government and private intermediaries has always been optimal or that societies with a large middle class have escaped rent seeking. But they have experienced economic growth and financial innovation, and when a particular government policy in these countries has proved obstructive or too expensive, it has usually been reformed (as with the ban on interstate banking in the United States) or eliminated (as with state ownership of banks in Europe). Middle-class voters would not tolerate huge inefficiencies for long, and the demand for financial innovation that they generated kept governments responsive to and supportive of growth.

In impoverished countries, government intervention in financial markets has not been so successful. The governments of poorer nations have often been more intrusive than those of rich ones, but their efforts have not always produced growth, and even when they have, their policies have helped unleash a number of crises whose costs on a relative scale far exceed the losses from something like the

American savings-and-loan disaster. According to Charles Calomiris, there were ninety financial crises between 1982 and 1998, primarily in developing countries of Asia and Latin America. In some twenty of the crises, the losses surpassed 10 percent of the country's GDP. By comparison, losses from bank failures during the Great Depression in the United States amounted to only 4 percent of GDP, and the cost of the savings-and-loan bailout was "roughly the same."[21]

There are several reasons why poor countries have such a mixed record. First of all, government intervention there itself created perverse incentives: politically connected individuals could borrow on favorable terms, because the state furnished the capital directly or guaranteed the loans; the borrowers and the banks who made them guaranteed loans had no reason to behave prudently, for they knew the government would bail them out. In addition, most poorer states either had an extremely small middle class, or, if their middle class was large, it was politically feeble because the governments were not democratic. In the absence of a strong middle class, politicians had no reason to stop rent seeking and wasteful policies.

Worse yet, while these states were insuring loans or making them directly, they were not creating the sort of political and legal infrastructure that had long supported financial markets in rich countries. In some cases, they may have been unable to afford such an infrastructure, for they had never developed effective fiscal bureaucracies and therefore lacked the revenue needed to operate courts or to enforce regulations and property rights.[22] (The lack of revenue could also lead them to take on much more debt during economic shocks and tempt them to prey on financial markets, yet another handicap.) But even states that did have abundant revenues often refused to create the basic political and legal infrastructure and opted instead to get in the business of making or guaranteeing loans. Perhaps making or guaranteeing loans yielded an immediate political reward, a reward visible in, say, new factories in a politically sensitive part of the country. There would be no payoff for establishing a legal system or effective property rights for many years, until markets flourished. Many governments in poorer countries did not have such a long lease on life. True, politicians in wealthy democracies can be equally short-sighted: their horizons may not extend beyond the next election. But rich countries already had the infrastructure, which grew up in response to middle-class demand and electoral power. The challenge the poorer states now face is thus not one of driving the government out of financial markets, but rather of redirecting its energies toward productive goals.

Conclusion:
The Lessons of History

CRISES—so history demonstrates—are inevitable. They are not just a feature of the distant past or of pathological financial systems. Indeed, the complex capital markets that are crucial for economic growth today turn out to be even more vulnerable to financial disasters.

History teaches other lessons too. It shows that there is no one set of institutions that solves all financial problems. Reforms adopted after a crisis are never perfect; they inevitably involve trade-offs with rent seeking, and they almost always have unintended consequences, sometimes long after the crisis has passed. But when new financial institutions are created, some things do matter more than others—in particular, information, levels of government debt, and the size of the middle class. Extremely high levels of government debt or low levels of information work against successful reforms; a large middle class does the reverse. Finally, domestic financial markets that benefit the middle class prove to be more important than international ones. If these domestic markets are nurtured via the right policies and the right financial institutions (an outcome more likely in a democracy already blessed with a sizable middle class), then a virtuous circle may arise, with financial development swelling the middle class further and the bigger middle class in turn promoting even more financial development and economic growth.

We did not arrive at these claims by analyzing large sets of contemporary data. Research of that sort is certainly useful, but because it is limited to a narrow slice of time, it cannot say much about all the effects that crises and institutions have or about long-run financial development. Our method was quite different. We took tools from political economy and applied them to histories of financial crises and of long-term financial development. That exercise in analytical history produced our conclusions, which readers are invited to test further and apply on their own.

In any case, history does clearly have something useful to say to policymakers. It is relevant in large part because of the long time it takes financial institutions to develop. Some scholars, it is true, believe that financial institutions change very quickly and in ways that are independent of the past. For them, history is immaterial, because any nation or private organization is free to choose its institutions at any point in time; it can simply copy them from more successful competitors or create entirely new institutions if it so desires. To determine what institutions are best, one need only examine the recent past—a period so rich in data that it is possible to undertake a careful statistical analysis of how different rules affect financial transactions.

But this narrow approach has two crucial flaws. First, it ignores the grip that history has on any financial system: capital markets simply cannot break free from the hold of older institutions and other legacies, such as enduring political coalitions. Second, and even worse, it cannot explain why some nations or organizations are simply more successful than others over the long term. If it is obvious what financial institutions are best and if it is easy to copy them, then why do so many financial systems fail?

The polar opposite view—that history is everything—is just as unsound. For those who hold this opinion, countries and organizations labor under a version of predestination: some ancient event propelled them into trajectories that they cannot escape; their institutions were locked into place by political stalemate and by the high cost of changing long-established rules governing behavior.

In the preceding chapters we have offered an alternative to both the "free will" and the "predestination" camps. Our approach stakes out a middle ground by acknowledging that although institutional structures persist, they change as well, albeit slowly—over the length of a generation or two, or in other words, over a span of time that is longer than a decade but less than half a century. Crises that are not surmounted can drive a country into recession for a generation, and meanwhile it takes time to build up successful institutions that can foster financial development and stand up to shocks without plunging the country back into crisis. It takes time to learn whether financial institutions can endure a wide array of shocks. It also takes time to develop credit reporting systems or mortgage registries that provide necessary financial information; time to make sure that this information is resilient; and time for the middle class to accumulate wealth that can serve as collateral. And of course it also takes time to put in place the political institutions that can ensure sound public finance and a reasonable protection of property rights.

Why History Matters for Policy

That for financial development time is measured in generations has important consequences for public policy. Each country has a unique set of traits that influence its financial structure. These may be physical endowments like natural resources or weather that may shape its economy and the shocks that it must confront. They may be social characteristics such ethnic or religious tensions, or historical legacies, including colonialism and past bouts of inflation. Or they may be institutions that have helped secure financial transactions in the past. In promoting further financial development, politicians and entrepreneurs must consider whether to jettison the negative legacies, whether to improve institutions by altering those that have worked well in the past, or whether to promote an entirely new set of rules. But to make these decisions, they must have a careful appreciation of a country's specific history.

Yet in doing so, they should not rely solely on their own country's history, or on that of any single country. Although doing so may satisfy impulses of national exceptionalism, it will lead them to make terrible mistakes. There will be far too many lessons that can be drawn from a single country's history, and that abundance of detail will make it hard to come up with useful generalizations about which institutions are best. Instead they should use the historical experience of different countries in order to eliminate erroneous inferences and to build up a stock of useful generalizations.

Such a venture into comparative history requires taking into account as many different experiences as possible rather than simply relying on the recent past, as much of the literature on financial systems has done. History is the only laboratory that can reveal the long-term consequences of institutional change.

How History, Information, the Public Debt, and the Size of the Middle Class Interact

Financial experts often believe that they stand on the dawn of a new age. They will point to ongoing change that marks a fundamental break with the past—the rise of capitalism, the Industrial Revolution, or, more recently, the new economy of the Internet. Today they might single out three novel forces that are changing the economy and financial markets: sweeping globalization, startlingly effective computer technology, and the rising value of capital embodied not in huge smoking factories, but in the knowledge and skills that economists call human capital. Since these forces are all seemingly without parallel in the past, the experts might therefore conclude that the lessons of the past are no longer of any relevance for improving our future. Although history can perhaps help us understand where we are, one might think that it has little to say about where we are headed.

Nothing could be further from the truth. Although the future will be different, the factors we have emphasized in this volume—information, government debt, and the size of the middle class—will continue to weigh upon the process of financial development and continue to influence the scope and frequency of financial crises in the future. These factors will constrain what the new forces of globalization, computer technology, and increasingly valuable human capital can do and ensure that the change we see today will never be independent of the past. Change may be rapid or startling, but it is always tied to history.

We can see as much by looking at each of the factors we have highlighted, beginning with public debt. In contrast to the eighteenth and nineteenth centuries, most countries today are not faced with the difficulty of creating markets for government debt: these already exist, both at home and abroad. Rather, the major danger they confront is the temptation to rely on government debt as the easy solution to social and economic problems. This danger has bedeviled rich societies (Italy and Belgium, for instance) and poor ones (Argentina is a striking example, although the scale of the problem exceeds anything that Italy or Belgium has experienced) alike, and it threatens many other countries as well. Although the globalization of financial markets and the ubiquity of public debt have altered the political economy of public debt, governments will still find it hard to stay away from their danger zones. Indeed, with global markets there are simply more lenders competing to invest in public debt.

Domestic political groups will play a critical role in keeping states away from the temptations of debt and default. To begin with, local political actors can put far more pressure on politicians to respect the property rights of bondholders than foreign political actors ever can. After all, a country respects foreigners' property rights only when it cares about the terms it will face when it wants to borrow abroad. Second, because most assets in a country are owned by its citizens, they will be the ones who have the greatest stake in holding public finance in balance. Even in a world of global financial markets, keeping government debt from spiraling out of control will depend on the existence of a politically powerful group that owns government debt and relies on domestic financial markets—in other words, the middle class. International capital markets have perhaps made it easier for politicians to ignore the middle class in the short run. A government can often raise money abroad inexpensively and in short order, while developing a domestic market to serve the middle class takes time and costs money. But once we consider the fact that most of the problems in public finance come from decisions made by political actors, investments in developing domestic sources of funds take on greater importance. The dismal financial and economic performance of Latin America, which has long lacked a middle class, is a lesson of history that still applies today.

If we consider private financial markets, globalization again does not solve every problem. To be sure, there are more international substitutes for domestic markets than ever before, but nonetheless only a limited set of firms or individuals has access to the global markets. For most firms and most individuals, the only market in which they can raise capital is the domestic one. Domestic markets therefore continue to matter.[1] The principal link between sound public finance and private credit markets still applies: crises of public finance cause domestic capital markets to contract severely. After such a crisis, it may take a decade for capital markets to recover. Easy access to international markets is, if anything, likely to delay the recovery even more, because the local savers who have shipped funds abroad will no longer be clamoring to rebuild devastated domestic credit markets. So, when there is no large middle class to push for sound public finance, crises will continue to strike, since politicians have little incentive to avoid them. The only difference from the past is that the consequences of crises are likely to be more severe because capital flight is now much easier. Indeed, the fixed costs, which once kept everyone but the rich from moving money abroad, have now fallen so much that some members of the middle class can now do it too.

Public debt will thus continue to affect financial development and the likelihood of crises in a way that makes history relevant. What about financial information? A half-century ago, nearly all the information employed in financial transactions was inscribed manually onto registers, where it could be recovered only by experts at a high cost. As a result, it only paid to keep track of highly valuable and durable assets that could be used as collateral. Today, however, computers have cut the cost of collecting information and to an even greater extent the cost of retrieving information. Hence one might well imagine that new information institutions can be put in place quickly and that these new institutions will be more effective than the old ones.

While there is no denying that the new computer technology vastly improves our ability to accumulate information, it is not likely to eliminate the risk of crises or to change the pace of the growth of financial markets drastically. To begin with, financial markets will remain incomplete despite the better technology, for at least two reasons. First, individuals will simply never have the information needed to write contracts that will cover every contingency that can possibly arise. Second, as markets expand and come into existence, they will in turn create new and unanticipated problems of asymmetric information that will slow further financial development. So computer technology will not give us a radically new way of speeding up the pace of financial development.

There are still other reasons to think that the time scale of financial development will not change much, the most important being that as markets grow, government agents can take advantage of valuable financial information. If these problems are sufficiently severe, investors will refuse to participate in an information system, out of fear that the system will be captured by the state and used by politicians to increase taxes or expropriate property. And if investors refuse to participate, the information system will remain stunted or be too expensive to use, and financial development will be slow.

Even if that problem can be solved, there is a second and more vexing obstacle—the self-serving behavior of providers of information services, such as firm managers, outside accountants, financial advisors, securities analysts, credit rating firms, and government agencies that register liens and mortgages. Because these information specialists are playing an increasingly important role, the troubles here are not going to disappear—far from it, as we saw in Chapter 2. The recent corporate and stock-rating scandals, shenanigans by mutual fund managers, and extraordinarily lax regulation of mortgage markets in Western democracies all demonstrate that the problem is not confined to developing countries and is not going to disappear. Anyone naive enough to have blindly trusted an annual report or financial analyst's recommendation knows this full well.

Since better computer technology will not free us from the past, history will continue to have something useful to say about policy. But history will remain important for another reason as well—the long time it takes for the middle class to evolve. The middle class is, as we know, the group that is most dependent on domestic financial markets, and it will never double overnight.

Admittedly, there are some social processes now at work that may allow the middle class to grow more rapidly. An important one is the expansion of financial markets that let people borrow to amass human capital. At first glance, credit cards and other means of going into debt without collateral do seem to offer a possible avenue to membership in the middle class. The recipe seems simple: just use your credit card to finance your education and then pay off the loan once your income has risen.

But will credit cards really allow people to borrow enough so that they can enter the middle class? The answer is no, for credit cards simply do not allow individuals to acquire significant amounts of human capital. Even in the United States, where credit cards seem to rain down on people and where lending for education is highly developed, someone who wants to go to college (let alone high school) will find it difficult to borrow the entire cost with a credit card or with loans from purely private providers. It is true that private lenders finance professional education, but they extend this service only to people who already have considerable human capital and fairly certain prospects of a high income. Private lenders will also lend students a portion of the cost of an undergraduate education, but they usually do so with some sort of government loan guarantee for at least part of the sums advanced.

History in fact suggests that borrowing to join the middle class will remain difficult unless government helps out. The last two centuries have seen a gradual elimination of the chief nongovernmental approach to financing skill acquisition—apprenticeship. Nor is that the only problem with using private unsecured debt to acquire human capital, for this sort of borrowing is always terribly vulnerable to crises. It is no surprise then that the amount of credit card debt or other unsecured credit is typically limited to a fraction of an individual's annual earnings and an even tinier fraction of what he or she will earn over a lifetime. While unsecured debt is an important addition to the range of credit, it will thus always remain small relative to other types of credit. And while the middle class may be keen about using unsecured debt to finance a surprising range of activities—including starting businesses—it will always remain a marginal source of credit overall.

Acquiring human capital will therefore continue to depend on public policy and on parental resources. The children of the rich of course do not need financial markets to get an education. For the children of the middle class, however, financing education will remain important because their parents will have to save or borrow to pay the bills. For the children of the poor, public education will be essential because their parents cannot afford to give them high levels of human capital and cannot borrow much either. Given the negative correlation between wealth and fertility, the role of financial markets and public spending is unlikely to shrink, and financial crises that decimate parental savings or curtail public spending will continue to have long-term consequences, particularly for the middle class, who will remain dependent on financial markets and vulnerable to economic shocks.

With the right policies and appropriate government help, it may be possible to accelerate the growth of the middle class, but we should not delude ourselves into thinking that a large middle class can blossom overnight. It takes two decades to educate an individual, and if one starts with a poor society, constraints on the resources available for education will mean that two or three generations will have to pass before a large cohort of people acquire much in the way of skills. Moreover, the whole process can easily be delayed by limits to what can be spent on education.

Information, public debt, and the size of the middle class will thus remain deeply intertwined with the development of financial markets. Technical and social change has tightened rather than loosened these links.

How History Affects Policy Debates

Beyond the general argument about the persistence of financial institutions and the continuing relevance of the three factors we have highlighted, we can best show why history matters by examining specific issues in the current financial policy nexus. We begin with one of the more exciting innovations of the past quarter-century—microcredit. Because the poor lack both real and reputational collateral, they are shut out of credit markets. Microcredit surmounts this problem by using mechanisms of group or joint liability to ensure that loans get repaid. Following the example of the Grameen Bank in Bangladesh, microcredit lenders have sprung up nearly everywhere in the world and have by and large done very well at improving the lot of households and facilitating borrowing by very small firms.

Lenders of this sort rely intensely on low-cost information, and cheap computers allow them (and the financial firms and nongovernmental organizations that assist them) to create credit histories at very low cost. The use of group lending has led to default rates that are remarkably low for poor borrowers. Group lending does this in one of two ways. The first is joint liability, which is common in Latin America. Under group liability, the other members of the group of individuals who receive loans are required to make up the losses when anyone defaults, and they nearly always do so.[2] The alternative way to police borrowers is to adapt the policy employed by the first microcredit lender, the Grameen Bank. It does not force the other group members to pay back a defaulter's loan but instead simply refuses to make any more loans to the group. Both mechanisms work, and both give the poor an opportunity to borrow, build a payment history, and accumulate assets. In fact some might argue that the advent of microcredit allows even the poor to enter the middle class as we have defined it—to derive more benefits than costs from participating in financial markets.

Placed in a historical perspective, however, group-based micro-credit is no cure-all. The first problem is that the size of loans is quantitatively trivial. Even if all the loans were invested in productive capital, the contribution of microcredit to investment is likely to be quite small. Loans are short-term, and interest rates by Western standards are high (often several percentage points per month); hence the net gain in capital from operating microcredit operations will be small. And there is another reason not to exaggerate the capacity of microcredit. The borrowers themselves will limit the size of the loans that they take on because joint liability forces those who succeed to pay for those who default. They will not want to bear the risk of having to cover big loans if others default.

More recently, some microcredit lenders have been moving beyond or entirely out of group-based lending. Realizing that even among the very poor there seems to be a significant demand for convenient savings vehicles, some have expanded the role of their widely dispersed field offices to function not simply as lending stations but also as places where individuals can make investments. The move away from group lending altogether involves a more complicated change, one that seems more prevalent in Asia than in Latin America. This shift reflects the fact that after two decades of lending to the poor, there are now large populations with credit histories and small amounts of accumulated assets. But these savers no longer want to bear the added risk associated with group lending—namely, having to make up a defaulter's loan or being cut off from future credit. They want to borrow as individuals without having to round up other borrowers who can be trusted. As microcredit lenders abandon group liability and begin to make individual loans, will default rates jump?

Our conjectural answer is yes. The transition under way can still succeed, however, if loans are made contingent on an individual's past behavior, either as a successful saver or as a borrower who repays on time. But the resulting histories still have to be accumulated, which will take time, and that implies that loans from microcredit lenders will remain small as a share of GDP for the foreseeable future. Those who think that microcredit alone can create prosperity should therefore not expect miracles: three decades after the beginning of the most successful micro lending program, the Grameen Bank, Bangladesh remains one of the poorest places in the world.

Might it still be possible to salvage a larger role for microcredit as an incubator for a market in secured loans, one in which individual borrowers put up collateral and bore responsibility on for their own loans? The odds seem unlikely. Again, microcredit lenders do not learn much about their clients except for their repayment histories, and their clients have too little economic weight to put much pressure on the state to improve the collateral value of assets. Furthermore, the clients are most likely to be engaged in small businesses that have limited economies of scale. In fact there is a real technical chasm between what recipients of microcredit do and the operations that involve large numbers of workers. To develop larger enterprises will require a serious improvement in property rights so that individuals can accumulate real assets and use them as collateral. Doing so requires a major improvement in titling, in the capacity of the lender to repossess pledged collateral, and finally in the monetary and financial stability of many countries. One critical change will be controversial politically: privileging lenders at the expense of borrowers and making it worthwhile for lenders to learn about potential borrowers and their assets. Such a political economy is hard to put in place, and achieving it will take a long time. Microcredit is clearly valuable, but it would be foolhardy to neglect investment in asset-based lending and investments in the infrastructure that reduces the costs of asset-based lending. While the poor reap important benefits from direct access to credit, they would probably derive equally important benefits if employment opportunities increased and vaulted them into the middle class, because they would then have greater access to other forms of credit.

Our second policy question deals with another potentially promising development—financial globalization. Here we might compare financial services with the global market for cars. Many countries have opted not to have a domestic producer of automobiles. Instead they import cars or have plants where European, American, or more likely Asian firms produce cars. The reason is that the scale economies in automobile production are large and most countries are better off buying their cars from foreign producers. It will cost them less in terms of forgone resources, and they will reap the gains from trade. Does this same principle apply to finance? Perhaps it does. After all, why should a country like Mexico, where the banking capital has been destroyed over and over again, try one more time to develop a healthy domestic financial sector, when it can buy financial services from foreign banks? And foreign banks have a number of major advantages. They can access many of the world's markets and thus have the lowest cost of capital. They can expand the loan volume in Mexico quickly no matter what the local savings rate might be. They do not need to worry about what fraction of local savings is placed in financial investments, such as deposits in banks. And they have the technical expertise and administrative know-how to run banks efficiently because they already operate in highly competitive markets. Free entry of large foreign financial institutions thus seems highly attractive.

Such an argument seems persuasive, but it has a serious defect. The defect is that finance is actually an array of quite different products, not just the provision of a volume of loans. Large international banks will excel in market segments where economies of scale apply and where information costs are low. They will do well with individual savings and with the financial demands of large entities, such as public agencies and major private firms. They will do poorly, however, when it comes to local small and medium-sized enterprises or individual borrowers. Indeed, for small loans of this sort, the cost of the international banks' information is relatively high; informal information gathered by local lenders or embodied in a borrower's reputation will be much cheaper substitutes, particularly where creditor rights are weak. But that means the international banks have to be embedded in the local economy if they are to serve smaller firms and middling clients.

Can new computer technology remedy the problem that large international banks face? Evidence from countries that have liberalized their financial markets suggests that new technology can do little in the short run, particularly if property rights have not been reformed in a way that makes middle-class assets useful collateral. In most vibrant economies, the local financial intermediaries continue to dominate lending to small and medium-sized firms. While huge banks like Citicorp or Morgan Stanley hog the news, the persistent creation of small commercial banks all over the United States has gone unheralded, although it points to a type of unmet demand even in one of the most financially developed economies in the world.

Whereas microcredit is too small to boost investment significantly, large international banks are too big to do a good job of serving small and medium-sized firms in developing countries. Once again, avoiding the extremes of having nothing but microcredit on the one hand and nothing but gigantic international banks on the other is the key to long-run success.

The last issue that our approach encourages us to reconsider is the interaction between demography and the welfare state. Here we must break from the past, because the demographic regime of the future will be radically different from the one in which current welfare states have been built. This break must come very soon for the wealthy areas of the world (the European Union, North America, and the rich countries of Asia), but it will also come quickly in other places—notably in Central and South America and China, where the demographic transition is already well under way.

Let us begin with western Europe and the United States. From the 1870s to the 1950s, when most national welfare systems were developed, the population and, more important, the salaried labor force were growing rapidly, but life expectancy at age sixty was limited, as was the value of health care in prolonging life. Since the 1970s these demographic conditions have changed radically. Fertility has plummeted, first in rich countries and then in poorer ones, and in some places it is far below replacement levels. Meanwhile the growth of the labor force has slowed, because most adult men and women are now working. And life expectancy is rising, particularly for the elderly. In fact, in many countries those who reach sixty-five can expect to live at least another decade because of advances in medical technology. As a result of all these striking demographic changes, the cost of old-age security is soaring. Not only are people living longer once they retire, but the medical care that keeps them healthy is costing more and more.[3]

In these rich countries, some form of social insurance was adopted during the twentieth century that made the government responsible for health care for the elderly and for some fraction of retirement income (nearly all of it in France, for example, and far less in the United States). These programs were based largely on intergenerational transfers, with current workers' contributions paying retirees' benefits—a sensible policy given the demographics and low levels of savings that prevailed in the immediate aftermath of World War II. The intergenerational transfers allowed retirement programs to offer old-age insurance immediately, and they also had the political advantage of benefiting a constituency—older voters—who tended to turn out at election time. The programs proved very popular, and politicians expanded both coverage and benefits. The typical pension grew at roughly the same rate as the economy as a whole, but the programs did not run a deficit because retirees formed only a small fraction of the population.

Today, however, all these pension systems are in long-run disequilibrium because the growing number of old people makes it impossible to afford the benefits that retirees are scheduled to receive if current trends continue. The disequilibrium is getting worse, because the demand for health care is rising with income and nearly all the elderly receive both pensions and health care. Most politicians and citizens recognize that some change is essential; the debate is how to go about it. A good solution to the problem must do three things: limit the red ink, avoid excessive interference with the functioning of labor markets, and provide adequate insurance against both individual and aggregate shocks. There are two possible ways to do this, either privatization or reform. Will either work? Here the lessons of history are not reassuring. Indeed, a historical approach suggests that, on the one hand, privatization cannot work and, on the other, that reform of the public systems, though feasible, will severely interfere with global labor markets. In short, there is no simple solution for the problem of old-age security.

Privatization is appealing because it seems it will automatically satisfy our first and second conditions. Consider for an instant an imaginary world in which there is no inequality and no uncertainty—in other words, all events in an individual's life can be forecast. Then, as life spans increase and medical science advances, individuals can adapt by some mix of later retirement, greater savings, and lower consumption once retired. If we assume that individuals know best how to make the necessary adjustments, a private system will yield the optimal solution, so long as changes in life spans and medicine are slow. Indeed, individuals will simply adjust their savings and retirement decisions, and nothing unanticipated will trouble their plans. Because everyone will save appropriately, no one will expect government help in old age. And meanwhile, labor markets will continue to function efficiently because saving plans will be independent of a person's country or employer, leaving workers free to find jobs and retire anywhere they want.

This imaginary world has no risk, so there is no need for insurance. The world we actually live in, however, entails considerable risk—some of which few individuals are willing to face on their own. In fact we face many dangers and uncertainties in life, and only a few of them can be insured against. True, well-developed insurance markets exist for the risks of death, thefts, auto accidents, sickness and disability, and a few other dangers. But there is no insurance at all for many of the other risks individuals face that can devastate their income. An economic shock can send them to the unemployment office or wipe out the sector of the economy in which they work. There is not much call anymore for typewriter repairmen, who have gone the way of blacksmiths and hand-loom weavers. People can also be battered by natural or environmental disasters that destroy their homes or wipe out their businesses: think of all the people who would be out of work after a major earthquake in Japan or California. Even a sizable shift in asset prices can ruin people, such as a sudden drop in housing prices. And without government programs, none of these risks can be insured against.

In the case of old-age security, the major risks seem to be independent of average income. Concern about these risks subsides only at the highest incomes: in all likelihood, it is only billionaires who do not worry about old-age security, while millionaires probably do. In fact the demographic and economic changes that have occurred in the last half-century not only raise the possibility of a much longer life in retirement but also open the door to a number of new and troubling risks. Consider, for instance, a woman who begins work, knowing that she has to rely on savings in a private account for support in old age. She faces considerable uncertainty about her health throughout her life course. She also does not know what the returns to her human capital will be. Both of these risks will affect her earnings and standard of living in retirement and thus her retirement decisions. It may turn out that she has a high income, because the sector of the economy she works in expands or because she remains healthy throughout her working years. Alternatively, she may have a very low income because her sector collapses or because she falls ill repeatedly through no fault of her own. As a result, she may accumulate either a large or small retirement capital entirely as a result of chance, and the rising cost of medical care will limit the amount of medical insurance she can buy to help contend with the uncertainties she faces.

In short, a world of private incentive involves a lot of unpalatable risk. Full privatization is in the long run doomed to fail because it falls short of meeting our third condition of providing adequate insurance, particularly for medical care. In the case of the woman we considered above, she might reach retirement age rich and healthy, or poor and ill. Not knowing her fate, she wants an insurance program that gives her access to health care and the assurance of a minimum pension later in life. The private market, however, cannot deliver this.

Even if health benefits are not privatized, it might still be worthwhile to privatize retirement income. Doing so would have obvious benefits both for labor markets and for avoiding red ink. In fact some authors maintain that privatization would actually lead to higher levels of income because individuals could invest in stocks rather than bonds.[4] Historical trends tell us that a portfolio of stocks does yield a higher expected return. But it also carries higher risk—risk that can devastate people's retirement plans.

Consider the case of individuals fully invested in Internet stock who had planned to retire in 2002 or 2003. The bursting of the bubble reduced their wealth by two-thirds. Would that event oblige them to continue to work for another decade? Adding to the problem is the likelihood that individuals who saw their stocks rise rapidly in the 1990s probably reduced their savings rate or went into debt under the assumption that they would have great wealth when they retired. If so, they ended up worse off than if they had ignored the bubble altogether. To be sure, some individuals found the bubble unimportant: those who made most of their investments before 1997, those who were well diversified, and those who did not change their investment strategies during the bubble. They could have profited from markets that had done quite well over the previous decade. Yet younger individuals or those who lost their savings during the bubble ended up five years later with portfolios that were much smaller than they had expected.

Losses in the past have been even more severe. Anyone who would blithely accept privatization should contemplate the difference in value of a Japanese investor's stock portfolio in 1989, when the Nikkei was well above 30,000, and the same portfolio a decade and a half later, when the Nikkei was mired far below 15,000. With yields like that, even low-yield bonds look like a better strategy. Given these uncertainties, it is not clear what kinds of portfolios people will hold. It may well be that most individuals will return to the dominant middle-class savings strategy of the pre–World War II period—bonds. But then privatization will not increase returns, and although it will solve the red ink problem, it will do so only because it imposes a budget constraint.

Perhaps the state will want individuals to buy higher-return assets such as stocks so that it can appropriate part of what they contribute in order to pay the retirement benefits of all the people who are caught between the old and new scheme. Those caught would include both older workers and current retirees, who never established private accounts and whose contributions have already been spent under the current scheme. Yet such a policy has real dangers. In particular, if a crisis erupts, individuals will interpret the state's requirement that they invest their retirement savings in stocks as implying a government guarantee that they will earn a certain rate of return. If political pressure forces the state to bail out investors whose stock portfolios have collapsed, then it is in effect offering insurance against bad outcomes but gaining none of the return in good times.

One might downplay such fears and deny that a state would ever bail out investors after a drop in the stock market eroded their privatized retirement accounts. But the pressure for such assistance would be irresistible, particularly in rich democracies. In rich countries at least, privatization would thus mean making the gains private but socializing the losses. That outcome would entail further losses, for if individuals knew the government would bail them out, they would be tempted to put their savings in risky investments in the hope of earning spectacular gains, confident in the government's largesse if their plans turned sour. To avoid such perverse behavior the state would have to limit the kinds of investment people could make in the first place. Total privatization is thus unlikely.

Although proponents of privatization invoke historical returns to argue that financial markets can improve current public investment, they overlook the likelihood that historical returns exaggerate the returns on stocks. Demand for stocks from investors saving for retirement is currently lower than it would be under privatization, while the demand for public debt is higher (since some retirement resources are invested in public debt). With privatization, the demand for stocks will rise, while demand for public debt will fall, and the bonus for investing in stocks will diminish.

At the same time, the massive flow of resources through private financial intermediaries will exacerbate problems with knavishness in financial markets. Given the very imperfect fashion in which financial intermediaries and publicly traded firms are monitored, scandals are sure to happen, and the government will end up bearing responsibility. How great would the backlash against the financial community have been if individuals did not have the guaranteed benefits of Social Security and Medicare when the dot-com bubble burst? Perhaps financial systems will succeed in investing all the money flowing into private accounts without any self-serving behavior, but it is more likely that there will be scandals and even crises. The state will then end up having to reimburse investors for damage done to their pensions.

The demand for insurance (in particular, a minimum guaranteed income in old age) is rising with economic development; any reform must take this demand into account. This is the great failing of a completely privatized system, for it will eliminate existing insurance. Would it be possible to preserve the current system? Perhaps, provided future retirees are willing to accept some combination of higher taxes, a slower growth rate of benefits, and a later age of retirement. But it will not be enough simply to tweak the current system: we must break with the past in an important way.

The essential change here involves moving from intergenerational transfers to intragenerational transfers. Government pension programs relied on intergenerational transfers when they were originally established because at the time (in some countries during the Great Depression, and in others after World War II) people were not wealthy enough to start a retirement system that would depend on intragenerational transfers alone: the people who were about to retire simply had not saved enough. Today, however, generational cohorts are much wealthier: they have considerable human capital, plus physical and financial assets, and it would be possible to base the government pensions and government medical benefits too on intragenerational transfers alone so that the payments to the current generation of retirees would not threaten their descendents' welfare.

In rich democracies, a transition to an intragenerational system could be arranged in a way that would take advantage of all the wealth that people now have. To do so would require a host of compromises, but the wealthy democracies have the advantage of an enormous demand for financial innovation generated by democratic government and a large middle class. History suggests that they stand a good chance of making the transition, as do other nations that are joining their ranks, such as South Korea. Each country will have to make the transition in a way that reflects its own history, but the solutions are not out of reach.

The compromises these countries would have to confront to make the transition would include limiting current pensioners to a lower growth rate for their benefits and imposing higher taxes on today's workers because they must share the cost of transition *and* build their own generation's stock of pension wealth. That wealth would continue to be invested in government debt—precisely because that would offer a convenient mechanism for insurance across generations. By maintaining a reasonable rate of taxation and low inflation, the government would protect the value of retirees' benefits. The system would involve intragenerational transfers, because part of each individual's contributions would go toward a minimum benefit for everyone that would include health care. The rest of an individual's benefits would depend on how much he or she had contributed. Our young woman who was just starting work, for instance, would be assured of health insurance in old age and a minimum retirement income, no matter how much she earned as a worker. Both of these benefits would be financed (over the course of her working life) by people of roughly her own age, and not by future generations. But she could also look forward to a larger retirement income if she earned a lot of money when she worked.

It would also be important for any such intragenerational plan to free people from a mandatory retirement age. Individuals who wanted to continue working could do so without losing pension benefits, as is so often the case under government retirement plans today. Indeed, the older generations are an important potential reservoir of labor. Their continued participation in labor markets can only be a good thing.

The most sensitive part of any such scheme is settling the payments for health care. That will require grappling with a daunting problem that up until now has been swept under the rug: deciding what monetary value we place on life. Currently most societies maintain the fiction that anyone who can be maintained alive will be, no matter what the cost; but if that were so, no system of insurance, public or private, would survive for very long. Advances in medicine and the high cost of health care at the end of life are actually threatening health insurance systems because we have not decided at what public cost people's lives should be prolonged. Like other problems of finance, the question sounds cold-blooded, but it will have to be confronted if public old-age benefits are to survive. By moving from intergenerational to intragenerational transfers we can at least begin to confront questions about the trade-offs between income and length of life for current retirees in an honest way. Up until now such questions have been hidden from view, for under a system of intergenerational transfers the issue is essentially one of trading off a lower income for future generations in return for a longer life span for today's retirees, and the future generations are not around to complain that their benefits are being cut.

At this level both the problem and the solution we have sketched here apply in both rich countries and poor ones. But on another, geographic level, public pension and related health insurance programs have major drawbacks. Because benefits can differ greatly from country to country, these public programs conflict with labor markets and the large-scale migrations that are increasingly common in today's globalized economy. The problems are particularly severe in regions that are experiencing large-scale migration from low- to high-wage economies—from eastern Europe to western Europe, for instance, or from Latin America to the United States.

In Europe, for example, the minimum pension in France is slightly more than 7,000 Euros a year—a paltry sum in such a rich economy, but one that exceeds the annual per-capita income in Poland.[5] Hence the French and Polish systems cannot be joined. A minimum pension affordable by the Poles is too little insurance for the French. Establishing the French minimum throughout today's European Union would involve either unacceptably heavy taxes in Poland or unacceptably high redistribution from France to Poland.

There are several problems here. First of all, to be eligible for full benefits under most government pension and medical insurance programs, a person has to have some sort of legal status. An illegal alien from Mexico may be able to collect U.S. Social Security payments if he returns home, but then Medicare will be useless for him, no matter how long he has worked or contributed to Medicare in the United States. But he will not be eligible for the U.S. Social Security program if he stays in the United States. Second, someone who divides his or her time among multiple welfare systems may qualify for insurance in none. Finally, although pension benefits are portable (one is not required to reside in a country to get pension benefits from public or private pension systems in that country), health benefits are not. People who work in the United States and retire in Mexico cannot enjoy the full benefits of Medicare in Mexico. One might think that it would be more rational to design welfare systems to fit the global labor markets that exist today. But that is not feasible when differences in income are high.

Members of the European Union must confront these problems directly because European citizens are supposed to be free to work in any member state. Many worry that the European welfare systems will be undermined by unbridled migration. As a result, the debate over greater freedom of markets is inevitably bound up with the issue of welfare benefits. The flow of labor from Mexico to the United States and to Canada raises similar questions.

Nor is this a problem just in Europe or the Americas. In China, old-age benefits are provided locally under a system that has not been reformed despite rapid economic growth and demographic change.

Because fertility has plunged, the population is aging rapidly, and meanwhile, because of large differences in income from province to province, workers are migrating in search of a better life. Some of the migration is licit, through a system of internal passports, but the rest is illegal. In either case, however, the migrants are not eligible for retirement benefits because the high-income areas have jealously guarded their welfare benefits and put them off limits to newcomers. As in Europe, integration of these welfare systems is stymied by differences in benefit levels.

Everywhere that we have considered, old-age security poses difficult policy questions. The elderly are the most rapidly growing part of the population, their needs are also growing, and the existing old-age security systems are proving unable to offer an appropriate mix of incentives and insurance. As we have shown, full privatization is unappealing. While partial privatization might be a solution, it would require such heavy government involvement that it would carry with it implicit public insurance. A better solution is for governments to admit the importance of their role in old-age security, alert the public to the need for sharing the costs of adjustments, and undertake reforms by shifting to a sustainable intragenerational retirement system.

Whether we consider financial institutions that benefit the middle class or those that provide for old-age benefits, one thing is clear: success is measured over decades, or so history suggests. Policymaking is thus a challenge, for although most politicians have short time horizons, it is the long-term consequences of their decisions that matter most for financial markets. In democracies few leaders last more than a decade, and they all face reelection at much shorter intervals. Hence they have a powerful reason to maximize the short-term gains rather than long-term benefits. But their myopia can be surmounted if citizens understand the importance of long-term success.

A historical perspective can also help poor countries. To promote economic growth, for instance, it would be worthwhile if the poorer countries learned from the experience of developed nations. Rather than trying to establish a complete financial system (long-term debt; short-term debt; equity markets; banks with consumer, commercial, and investment functions; and so on) they would be better off creating financial institutions that will sustain a political coalition in favor of further financial development. Unfortunately, political coalitions that support better financial institutions are usually tiny in such countries. No group with political muscle is willing to bear the painful costs of reducing government debt or of investing in institutions that can protect against crises in the future. But doing so is essential for further economic growth.

It is not that the denizens of poorer countries fear or hate financial markets. On the contrary, they lament the burden that the lack of functioning financial markets imposes on their lives. They may have no safe place to save for old age or be unable to borrow to buy a home or expand a business. Yet although the inhabitants of poor countries may want financial markets to work well, their desires rarely end up being translated into effective financial institutions— institutions that can keep financial markets working through thick and thin and in particular soften the effect of crises when they occur.

To a large extent this state of affairs is the product of a vicious circle, which begins with a small middle class—the only group that would want to rein in public spending in booms and thereby keeps shocks from turning into crises. The poor, as our model suggests, are shut out of capital markets and so care little about any damage the markets would suffer. And the rich, as we have said before, are not concerned either, because much of their wealth has been shipped abroad. Nor are foreign investors much interested, even though they are ripe targets for predatory governments if there is a crisis. And the middle class is too tiny to play an important role.

Many of the wealthy nations that possess highly developed financial markets today faced the very same problem in the past. Before 1700, for instance, the British crown defaulted on loans it owed both foreign and domestic lenders. Furthermore, these wealthy nations once had a relatively small middle class. Yet over time they developed financial markets. For some countries such as France and Britain the process took centuries because financial development was disturbed by warfare and predatory monarchical governments. But over time the middle class grew in size and power, so that by the nineteenth century many of the Western governments were excellent credit risks.

By the time financial markets boomed in the second half of the nineteenth century, the Western countries did not owe huge sums to foreign creditors, as poor countries today commonly do. To the contrary, they were large capital exporters. They therefore by and large escaped much of the temptation to default on foreigners, and because the holders of government debt were politically powerful, political leaders had even more reason to steer clear of extremes. That circumstance, plus their large middle class, gave them a historical advantage the poorer countries today lack.

Can poor countries today repeat the same process? Even without a large middle class, a typical poor country may develop rules such as limits on state spending or caps on public indebtedness. By themselves, however, these rules will do little to keep the government from borrowing too much, for no political constituency will demand that these rules be enforced. The same will hold for many of the other laws that poor countries adopt to regulate capital markets and financial transactions. Laws and rules may exist, but they are likely to be abandoned whenever the costs of enforcing them—and especially the political costs—are large. Crises will thus be more likely to bombard poorer countries and more likely to do damage when they strike, because the rules that could have prevented them or reduced their impact will go unenforced.

Rules can become actual institutions only if there is a political will to enforce them. The ultimate cause of the problem in poorer countries is the lack of politically powerful groups willing to bear the pain needed to secure financial markets. If countries like Argentina want to stabilize their financial systems, they must foster political support for financial markets that will endure even in bad times. And that task cannot be accomplished overnight. New rules can be adopted in an instant, but developing the political backing for them—and especially if that backing is to last through tough times—may take decades. It took that long for the world's rich nations to build support for financial markets, and if history is any guide, the poorer countries of the world will not have an easier time.

Not that we should abandon all hope here. Despite all the hurdles today, there are poorer countries such as India and China that have nonetheless managed to embark on a path of self-sustaining growth and financial development. Their experience suggests that long-term change is no naive dream, and other striking success stories in places like Ireland or Korea may well push politicians in developing countries toward policies that support financial development. After all, they demonstrate that reform can bring the great reward of rapid economic growth, and rapid growth appeals to politicians because it expands the resources under their control and makes their regime more stable. Both of these outcomes may become tempting alternatives to the current corruption and instability that bedevil many poor countries today.

This new path will not be easy to adopt, and it will be threatened by shocks, which give rich countries both opportunities and responsibilities. One thing rich countries could do to help the process along would be to forgive poor countries' debts, for such a move would encourage politicians in poorer nations to adopt policies that are favorable to financial markets. Today, poor countries that are deeply in debt usually face a dilemma: if they stay poor, they do not have to do much about repaying their debt, but if they grow rich they have to pay it back. Hence foreign debt discourages countries from seeking policies conducive to growth. By forgiving the poor countries' debts, rich nations can help keep more of the gains of economic development within the poor countries and thereby make the rewards of growth even more attractive.

There are other policies too that rich nations could pursue to hasten the financial development of poor countries, although all of them demand perseverance. Investing in educational infrastructure and other public goods that augment human capital, for instance, would have vast payoffs. While investment in human capital would take time to mature, it would help nurture the middle class and create a virtuous circle. A larger middle class could then assist the transformation of poor countries by giving politicians further incentives to promote financial development. Encouraging democracy would have a similar effect. Without democracy, the middle class will have little influence over the financial policies that politicians choose. Whatever rich nations do, they must never forget how important domestic political pressures are in developing countries.

Financial markets take decades or even generations to develop, but they can be ruined overnight. To enjoy their benefits, we must nurture good institutions and shun bad ones. As we make these choices, history is our most powerful tool, whether we want to break from the past or build upon it.

Notes

The source of the epigraph to the book is Francis Ponge, "Proèmes," in *Oeuvres complètes,* 2 vols. (Paris, 1999), 1: 181.

Introduction

1. The quotation is from B. Murphy 2002; see also Ivanovich 2001; Bernstein 2002; Flood 2005.
2. Nicolardot 1887, 1:80–104; Voltaire 1953–1977, letters 15248 (21 March 1770) and D16950 (9 January 1771); Westfall 1980, 861–862; R. L. Allen 1993. Neither Newton nor Voltaire died a pauper—far from it—but like Sandra both seemed deeply upset by their losses.
3. Bordo et al. 2001; Shiller 2001.
4. For the crises as turning points in the development of financial institutions, see, for example, Hubbard 1991; White 2000; Davis and Gallman 2001; Neal and Quinn 2003.
5. Financial crises do seem to exacerbate economic downturns. The evidence is complicated by the possibility that downturns themselves bring on financial crises; but if one takes this possibility into account, there is still statistical support for the claim that crises make recessions and depressions significantly worse. See Bordo et al. 2001.
6. For a brief assessment of the long-term effect of New Deal and Third Reich regulations, see Ritschl 2003, 414; Whaples 2003, 171.
7. Among the fine works on financial crises are Kindelberger 1978; Bordo et al. 2001; Eichengreen 2002, 2003; Neal and Weidenmier 2002. For the lack of any economic theory that can single out what sort of financial institutions will be most likely to survive crises and promote economic growth, see Allen and Gale 2000, 25–44, 310–311; Allen and Gale 2001.
8. Beck et al. 2000; Demirguc-Kunt and Levine 2001; Beck and Levine 2002; Levine 2002.
9. One might argue that a corporate bankruptcy does not really break a financial contract because stockholders are not guaranteed any dividends

when they purchase shares. But the bankruptcy does wipe out the shareholders' equity in the firm. Thereafter they own nothing, at least in our simplified description, and in that respect they are like creditors faced with default.

1. The Political Economy of Financial Crises

1. Lowenstein 2000.
2. Opening a bank account in Uruguay has been the easiest way for small-scale middle-class investors in Argentina to send money abroad. Initially most Argentines carried cash across the border to open an account in Uruguay, but that strategy entailed the expenses of transportation, loss of time from work, and the potential risk of theft or confiscation. Though not large, these costs could be an obstacle, particularly for a modest investor living far from the border. Although it eventually became possible to open such an account in Buenos Aires, not all banks had this capability, and boats to Uruguay were still filled with Argentines bearing suitcases full of money. Personal communication, Federico Echenique.
3. "Argentina's Collapse: A Decline without Parallel" 2002; "Foreign Creditors Join the Pyre" 2002.
4. North and Weingast 1989; Olson 2000; Ferguson 2001; Stasavage 2003.
5. Sargent and Wallace 1981.
6. Great Britain, Statistical Office 1951, 265; B. R. Mitchell 1981, 762; Roubini 2001. The figures for British and Argentine debt concern the central governments only, not local or provincial governments. One reason there is no simple formula that tells where the danger zone begins is that governments can victimize financial markets in a variety of ways. Modeling any one of the predatory actions a government can take turns out to be a complex matter, which has to take into account a variety of factors and historical contingencies. For an illustration, see the following studies of government default: Eaton and Gersovitz 1981; Grossman and Van Huyck 1988; Bulow and Rogoff 1989; Atkeson 1991; Manasse, Roubini, and Schimmelpfennig 2003; Kraay and Nehru 2004.
7. A model of the choices facing political leaders here not only must balance the state's revenues and expenses; it also has to take into account the political costs of tax increases and spending cuts. If the state pays back its loans, for example, it will face higher expenses in the future, expenses that will be both financial and political. Default may therefore be attractive, but it is not necessarily a panacea. It will make lenders react, and their reactions can include withholding loans or services, charging higher interest rates or fees in the future, and imposing penalties such as the seizure of the assets

that the state or its citizens may have in other countries. One further complication is that some of these costs of default may be pushed off onto future governments and future generations and thus pose little problem for the government in power.

8. Will and Wong 1991, 508; Hoffman and Rosenthal 1997, 36; Wong 1997, 88–99; Huang 1974, 62, 275, 294. Huang's figures imply that the Chinese empire spent 54 percent of its budget on the military in the sixteenth century; compare the European figures in Hoffman and Rosenthal. The Chinese budget was smaller too. Huang's figures for total tax revenues in the sixteenth century came to 9 grams of silver per person. Contemporary French figures (Hoffman 1994, 238) ranged from 9 to 22 grams of silver per person, and they climbed even higher in the seventeenth century.

9. Wong 1997, 131–133.

10. The efforts to raise money and troops outside Castile eventually provoked revolts in Catalonia and Portugal; Elliott 1963, 324–329, 333–345.

11. See Von Glahn 1996, 248–251, for debasements undertaken for seigneurage revenue during military crises in early seventeenth-century China and much earlier episodes of issuing paper money without adequate backing. For numerous European examples, see Sargent and Velde 2002. To these Chinese examples one could add cases of default on obligations owed salt merchants who advanced the government money, but these pale by comparison with what happened in Europe; Huang 1974, 200–204.

12. Although large banks did not exist, there were pawnshops, rural moneylenders, and merchants who extended credit; Yang 1952; Fairbank and Twitchett 1978, 8: 149, 156; Wong 1997, 20, 133. Some of the merchants (notably those who dealt in salt) lent to the government; Huang 1974, 200–204.

13. Brewer 1989; North and Weingast 1989; Neal 1990; Velde and Weir 1992; Sargent and Velde 1995; Baskin and Miranti 1997; Stasavage 2003. As Stasavage (136–37) shows, the over 2 percent interest rate gap does not seem to result from different inflation rates or changes in loan demand.

14. Probably the biggest financial crisis was the South Sea Bubble in 1720, at the very beginning of the London market's development. Although Parliament investigated after it collapsed, the bubble did not originate in government predation. Neither did the other crises in the eighteenth century; Neal 1990, 62–117, 166–179; Baskin and Miranti 1997; Garber 2000.

15. Braudel 1975, 1: 501–517; Thompson 1994, 158–164.

16. Through the early seventeenth century, as Conklin 1998 shows, the Spanish debt consolidations fitted the sort of behavior modeled in Grossman

and Van Huyck 1988; Bulow and Rogoff 1989; Atkeson 1991. Spain sometimes renegotiated its debt, just as lenders expected.

17. Elliott 1963, 281–353.

18. Thompson 1994, 158–164.

19. Ehrenberg 1922, 2: 192–221; Lapeyre 1955; Elliott 1963, 283.

20. Hoffman, Postel-Vinay, and Rosenthal 2000, 194–195.

21. Sutherland 1986; Hoffman, Postel-Vinay, and Rosenthal 2000, 195–196.

22. Postel-Vinay 1998; Hoffman, Postel-Vinay, and Rosenthal 2000, 177–228.

23. Hoffman, Postel-Vinay, and Rosenthal 2000. Other barriers to a revival of long-term credit in Paris included legal reforms and the temptations notaries faced to move into the risky business of banking.

24. "Argentina's Collapse: A Decline without Parallel" 2002; Mussa 2002.

25. "Kirchner and Lula" 2005; "Argentina: Another Country" 2005.

26. "Argentina's Collapse: A Decline without Parallel" 2002.

27. One could imagine, for instance, that political leaders might use revenues from a tax increase for something more popular with citizens—or more appealing to the leaders themselves—than repaying the government's creditors.

28. "Argentina's Collapse: A Decline without Parallel" 2002; "Argentina's Collapse: Return to the Dark Ages" 2002.

29. De Vries and Van der Woude 1997, 119–126; Israel 1998, 985–988.

30. Brewer 1989; North and Weingast 1989; Stasavage 2003; Sussman and Yafeh 2005. When we speak of risk premium here, we mean the spread between the interest rate paid on English government debt and that paid on loans issued by the creditworthy Dutch government.

31. We say potential income, because there is the possibility (as in eighteenth-century Poland) that the representative assembly will refuse to increase taxes: Ferguson 2001, 83.

32. Hoffman and Norberg 1994; Hoffman and Rosenthal 1997; Rosenthal 1998.

33. Wright 1942, 1: table 4.6; J. S. Levy 1983, figs. 6.1 and 6.4; Schroeder 1986, 12.

34. Hoffman and Rosenthal 2002. There were other reasons for the diminishing frequency of war as well, among them a change in international relations; Schroeder 1994. As for the greater costs of defeat in the nineteenth century, it is worth noting that no monarch in Austria, France, Prussia, or Spain lost his throne because of defeat in battle during the years 1500–1799, provided we rule out revolutions and conflicts that were at least in part civil wars. But if we do the same calculation for the years 1800–1919,

the chances of being deposed after a military loss jump to between 20 and 67 percent.

35. Hoffman and Rosenthal 1997, 2002; Rosenthal 1998.

36. Because the relationship between politics and danger zones is so complex, we should not expect to see a simple relationship between a country's debt level and the interest rate it pays, which will reflect the risk of inflation and default. This interest rate will also be determined by the strategies potential lenders adopt.

37. Collier and Gunning 1999; Ndulu and O'Connell 1999.

2. Information and Crises

1. Eichenwald 2002a; Glater 2002. The rise in restatements was not the result of an increase in the number of publicly traded firms, for that number actually declined during the same period.

2. Leonhardt 2002.

3. Mason 2002; Von Sternberg 2002. The executive quoted here was identified as a safety worker in one of the newspaper stories, but the other one noted that he had spent eighteen years in charge of the Enron human resources office in Minneapolis.

4. Andrews 2002.

5. Buffett 2002; McGeehan 2002.

6. Mauduit and Orange 2002.

7. By accuracy we do not mean that investors have to know returns exactly; rather, their estimates of the distribution of returns must be unbiased.

8. Smith, Suchanek, and Williams 1988; Bossaerts 2002.

9. For an earlier argument about the role of asymmetric information in explaining crises, see Mishkin 1991. A bubble can also arise if sophisticated, rational investors with limited wealth learn at different times that a financial asset is overvalued; see Abreu and Brunnermeier 2003.

10. Eichenwald 2002a, 2002b; Morgenson 2004; Barrionuevo 2006; "Enron Prosecution Scorecard" 2006. In July 2006 the *Houston Chronicle's* website listed criminal indictments against 26 former Enron employees; of these, 2 have been acquitted, 1 has had the charges dropped, 20 have pleaded guilty or been convicted, and 3 are awaiting new trials. Not all of those charged have been accused of self-enrichment.

11. "Enron: The Twister Hits" 2002; "Economics Focus: Taken for a Ride" 2002.

12. Abowd and Kaplan 1999.

13. Bebchuk, Fried, and Walker 2002. For a more nuanced view, see K. J. Murphy 1999.

14. For the economics of what was happening here, see Stiglitz and Weiss 1981.
15. Hoffman, Postel-Vinay, and Rosenthal 2001.
16. Akerlof 1970.
17. Altman 2002.
18. See Hoffman, Postel-Vinay, and Rosenthal 2001, esp. 200–201.
19. "Enron: The Twister Hits" 2002; "Consistently Right about Enron" 2002; Ackman 2002; CNN 2002; Ratner and Waters 2002.
20. Snowden 1995.
21. Ibid. The insurance companies survived because they had more diversified assets than the mortgage companies and longer-term liabilities too.
22. Ibid.
23. Roeder 2002.
24. Norris 2000; "Enron: The Twister Hits" 2002.
25. Morgenson 2004. Surveys of investors conducted at Yale University showed signs of rising confidence for both institutional and individual investors during much of 2003; see Yale University 2004.
26. Bossaerts 2002.
27. Barberis, Shleifer, and Vishny 1998; Barberis and Thaler 2003.
28. Snowden 1995, 216–221. As Snowden points out, it was not regulations that limited the scope of the building associations' lending.
29. Udry 1994.
30. Snowden 1995. For the interest rate gap, see Snowden 1987 but also the cautionary words of Eichengreen 1987.
31. Smith, Suchanek, and Williams 1988.
32. The prices here, which are in percentage of par value, are taken from Neal 1990, 62–117, 231–157, whose excellent analysis is the source for our account of the South Sea Bubble. As Neal points out, there were other issues in the South Sea Bubble besides information—in particular, a credit crunch in London.
33. Neal 1990, 80–88; Baskin and Miranti 1997, 110–111.
34. Dawson 1990, 102–123.
35. Morgan and Thomas 1962, 80–87; Dawson 1990, 102–122; Neal 1996.
36. Rippy 1947, 123; Morgan and Thomas 1962, 82–87; Dawson 1990, 102–122; Neal 1996.
37. Shiller 2001.
38. Hoppit 1986; Neal 1990, 169–171; Harris 1994; Baskin and Miranti 1997, 116–121; Ferguson 2001, 114.
39. Hill and Labate 2002; Labaton 2002. Initially investors remained confident that stocks would recover (Shiller 2001, 235–241), but eventually their attitudes began to change (Karmin and Sesit 2002).

40. For evidence of such beliefs prior to the Internet bubble, see Shiller 2001.

41. Snowden 1995, 230.

42. Davis and Gallman 2001, 642.

43. For Junius, see Chernow 1990, 26–27.

44. The paragraphs that follow are based on Chernow 1990, 3–70; Strouse 1999, 5, 13, 50, 196–199; and Carosso 1987.

45. De Long 1991.

3. Crises and the Middle Class

1. King 1983; Dickenson 1985.

2. Flanery 1985; Greenhouse 1985; Robbins 1985; Sinclair 1985. We thank Rod Kiewiet for the information about individual farmers who had financed sales.

3. "Iowa Governor Invokes Provision to Delay Foreclosures" 1985; Coleman 1985; Flanery 1985; Greenhouse 1985.

4. Hoffman had this experience in 1979 when buying a car for his first job after graduate school. For a simple example that uses this sort of problem (what economists call an "indivisibility") to show how inequality may never correct itself, see Ray 1998, 226–237. For further references and evidence that the constraints on credit can be severe, see Aghion, Caroli, and Garcia-Penalosa 1999, 1624–28; Woodruff 2001. One might object that rental markets would arise to solve the problem, but often they function poorly because of fears that renters will secretly damage or abscond with whatever they rent. In the United States, you cannot rent a truck or car without a credit card or a deposit, and in poorer countries it is often difficult to rent farm animals.

5. Over the last century the middle class has also grown to encompass wages earners who save for retirement and retirees who slowly draw down their accumulated wealth.

6. Advanced capital markets will reduce the risk by creating financial instruments such as mutual funds or the sort of insurance markets discussed by Shiller 2003. But in our simple model or imaginary world, instruments of this sort do not yet exist. That is one reason why (so we argue later) the middle class will favor financial innovation.

7. For inequality in England, see Lindert 2000, 176–185. Precise evidence about how much the rich actually own in Latin America is practically nonexistent, since they are not eager to reveal the magnitude of their fortunes. The distribution of income there is more unequal, however, than on any other continent, and the same holds for the ownership of land, a major asset. Furthermore, the distribution of land ownership is even more skewed toward the rich in Latin America than is income; Gasparini 2003.

8. Davies and Shorrocks 2000, 637–641, 664; Kennickell 2000, table 5; Lindert 2000, 181–192; Piketty, Postel-Vinay, and Rosenthal 2006. Davies and Shorrocks have the richest 1 percent in France holding 26 percent of the wealth—more than in Denmark—but Piketty, Postel-Vinay, and Rosenthal research arrives at a lower figure of 21 percent.

9. The evidence here comes from Archives Départementales de la Sarthe 1858–1871.

10. Lamoreaux 1994.

11. Bayard, Félix, and Hammon 2000; Hoffman, Postel-Vinay, and Rosenthal 2000.

12. Bercé, Boubli, and Folliot 1988; Chagniot 1988, 266–268; Hoffman, Postel-Vinay, and Rosenthal 2000, 156; Hoffman, Postel-Vinay, and Rosenthal 2004. The annuities that Chartres sold, called tontines, allowed the purchasers who lived the longest to share the remaining benefits, thereby providing a handsome prize for surviving a long time.

13. Recently services of this sort have trickled down to the level of high-income professionals, particularly in the United States.

14. World Bank 2002, 35–36, 92–94; Rajan and Zingales 2003, 31. The cost of foreclosure is measured as a fraction of the house's value in both Italy and Great Britain.

15. Rohter 2003.

16. Condominium law did not develop in France until the interwar period, and not until the 1950s in the United States.

17. For examples from the past and from developing countries, see Hoffman 1996, 69–71; Ray 1998, 561–565.

18. R. C. Allen 1992, 102–104. For the development of analogous loan contracts in France, see Schnapper 1957.

19. Engerman and Sokoloff 2002, 80–82.

20. Cf. Haber 1991; Banerjee, Besley, and Guinnane 1994; Hoffman, Postel-Vinay, and Rosenthal 2000.

21. Mérida: J. Levy 2004; Rio de Janeiro: Ryan forthcoming; for Lyons and Limoges, the data come from research we are conducting on the evolution of financial markets in France. The surviving evidence may leave out some informal lending in both France and Latin America, but for legal reasons the omissions are likely to be insignificant in both regions. If we consider the stock of outstanding debts, the advantage the European borrowers had would be even greater, for the average term of their loans was five years, versus only one year in Latin America.

22. For another example of how inequality affects institutions, see Engerman and Sokoloff 2001, 2002.

23. Flanery 1985; Greenhouse 1985; "Hawkeye Agrees on Debt Program" 1986; "Hawkeye Bank Sale" 1986.

24. What follows is based on Rajan and Zingales 2003.

25. For evidence about the amount of money that Latin Americans invest in the United States, see Sokoloff and Zolt 2004.

26. Rosenthal 1994.

27. See, for example, Bernstein 2002.

28. Tittle et al. v. Enron et al. 2002; Bernstein 2002; Cheng 2002. The estimates concern managers' gains in the three-year period 1999–2001 and bankruptcies of publicly traded corporations between January 2001 and an unspecified date before August 2002. They do not take into account the cost of stock when purchased, but in many cases this cost was small. Nor do they include penalties or damages paid in subsequent legal proceedings. For further details, see the Cheng article. Given our argument, some readers might wonder why the share of wealth held by the rich declined during the Great Depression. The reason is that it was such a large crisis—an international one—that diversification no longer offered the rich any protection. Other readers might contend that modern securities markets would discourage managers from cashing in their holdings. For a theoretical argument why that need not be so when investors have different beliefs, see Bolton, Scheinkman, and Xiong 2003.

29. The fact that assets fetch a low price during crises does not necessarily mean that severe crises are worse for the middle class. A bigger crisis means that more assets have to be liquidated and hence that asset prices will be lower. But as the economy recovers, the rich will want to sell more assets from their portfolios, and prices will be lower then too, a situation that will facilitate the recovery of the middle class. That price effect, however, has to be balanced against the time it takes the members of the middle class who have fallen into poverty to save enough to reenter the asset markets. That time may be quite long given the assumptions we make—in particular, the assumption that physical assets are lumpy or indivisible.

30. Unfortunately, intermediaries cannot always do this, in part because the financial markets needed for such insurance simply do not exist; Shiller 2003.

31. Gueslin 1985; Hoffman, Postel-Vinay, and Rosenthal 2000, 229–272; Postel-Vinay 1998.

32. Haber 1991; Maurer 2002; Maurer and Haber 2002; Haber, Razo, and Maurer 2003.

33. Parker 2002; Sharrock 2002; Argentina Ministry of Economy and Production, Secretariat of Economic Policy 2006.

34. J. Mitchell 2003; Thomson and Lapper 2003; "Argentina Macroeconomic Report" 2003a, 2003b; personal communication, Federico Echenique.

4. What Happens after Crises

1. Carosso 1970, 23–50; Davis and Gallman 2001, 300–312.
2. It did so by preventing banks from competing over the interest rates they could offer depositors and by making it more difficult to establish new banks. In addition, commercial banks could no longer compete with investment banks in the underwriting business in a way that would work to the advantage of investors and entrepreneurs. For details, see White 2000, 765–767; Mahoney 2001; Rajan and Zingales 2003, 220–224. Deposit insurance also subsidized small banks at the expense of larger, more diversified ones; Calomiris and White 1995.
3. "Japanese Banks" 1998; "Japan's Long Winter" 1999; Dekle and Kletzer 2003; Desai 2003, 70–85.
4. "Japan's Long Winter" 1999; Dekle and Kletzer 2003; Desai 2003.
5. Shiller 2003.
6. For the relevant psychological literature and its application to finance and politics, see Noll and Krier 1990; Kahneman et al. 1993; Redelmeier and Kahneman 1996; Ariely, Kahneman, and Loewenstein 2000; Camerer 2001; Barberis and Thaler 2003; and Kuran and Sunstein 1999, which draws on psychology and economic models of how individuals learn from one another's actions.
7. Lindert 1996, 16–19; Persson and Tabellini 2000, 121–123.
8. Lindert 1996; Lindert 2004, chap. 7.
9. For evidence that the sort of programs at issue here do not slow growth in wealthy democracies, see Lindert 2004.
10. For a similar argument, see Acemoglu and Robinson 2001.
11. Aberbach, Dollar, and Sokoloff 1994.
12. Our evidence here comes from Lindert 1980, table 3; Lindert 1983, table A3; Engerman and Sokoloff 2002, table 6; and from research Gilles Postel-Vinay is doing on social mobility in France.
13. Eichengreen 1992, 67–152; Lindert 2000; Morrisson 2000, 249–251; Ferguson 2001, 148–151, 196–200; Piketty, Postel-Vinay, and Rosenthal 2006.
14. Acemoglu and Robinson 2000; Lindert 2004; Lizzeri and Persico 2004.
15. Eichengreen 1992, 92; Morrisson 2000, 249–251; Lindert 2004, tables 1.1 and 1.2. The figures on social spending here (from table 1.2 of Peter Lindert's book) exclude sums devoted to education.
16. For returns from education, adjustments to tax policies, and the lack of a

connection between economic growth and total spending on social programs, see Lindert 2004. For the incentives faced by politicians to adopt growth-enhancing policies, see the comparative evidence in Kiewiet 2000.

17. Grinnath, Wallis, and Sylla 1997; Sylla 2000, 522–523; Wallis 2001.

18. For available evidence about the extent of the suffrage and levels of inequality in some of the nine states, see Soltow 1975; Kousser 1984; Engerman and Sokoloff 2001. For comparative evidence about the narrower franchise and greater inequality in Britain, see Lindert 2000 and 2004, table 4.1. For bondholders in Britain, who also benefited from a return to the gold standard that offset losses to inflation, see Ferguson 2001, 194–200.

19. Sylla 2000, 520–521.

20. Ibid., 522–523; Wallis 2001.

21. Sylla 2000.

5. Financial Intermediaries and the Demand for Change

1. Demirguc-Kunt and Levine 2001.

2. North and Weingast 1989; Quinn 2001; Temin and Voth 2004.

3. Lefebvre-Teillard 1985, 180–181.

4. For this and the following paragraphs, see Bruck 1988; "Milken Saw Chances and He Took Them" 1989; Ippolito and James 1992; Fischel 1995, 1–28, 309–310; Freedland 1995; Holmstrom and Kaplan 2001; Rajan and Zingales 2003, 59–63, 71–73.

5. Milken and Drexel Burnham Lambert undoubtedly sought to protect the market dominance they had gained in the junk bond market. Whatever one might think about such behavior, it does not detract from the importance of their financial innovation.

6. When an intermediary creates a new institution, he gains a temporary monopoly that puts him ahead of his competitors. The resulting temporary jump in his profits is an incentive to innovate, and under certain conditions it will be larger under competition. See Aghion et al. 2001.

7. Fischel 1995, 23–28.

8. For a way to arrange credit dealings without state enforcement, see Greif 2006.

9. Bortz and Haber 2002; Riguzzi 2002; Haber and Kantor 2003.

10. Between 1820 and 1870, real GDP per capita in Belgium grew at a 1.44 percent annual rate, which was higher than in any other western European country; Maddison 2001, 186.

11. Van Der Wee and Verbreyt 1997; Brion and Moreau 1998.

12. The material on Antwerp is derived from De Roover 1953, 95–96;

Wee 1963, 339–354; Wee 1977, 322–332; De Vries and Van der Woude 1997, 130–131. Some of the short-term debt—particularly the promissory notes—did not actually trade regularly; the principle of negotiability, however, would later become quite important for trading other instruments.

13. Craig 2003; Feder 2003.

14. Akerlof and Romer 1993; White 2000, 790–792.

15. Akerlof and Romer 1993; White 2000, 790–792.

16. Shiller 2003 proposes bringing this kind of insurance within reach for the middle class, but as yet it is hard to find parties willing to provide the insurance by selling the new securities Shiller seeks to create.

17. This paragraph is based on two literatures. The first is a portion of the growing literature in behavioral finance, which employs insights from psychology, experiments, and questionnaires to revise the way economists model how investors update their beliefs about the future and how they act on their beliefs; Shleifer 2000, 154–174; Shiller 2001; Barberis and Thaler 2003. The second source is Bossaerts 2002, who uses experiments but eschews psychology. He focuses instead on the erroneous initial beliefs that investors bring to markets. Also relevant here are several recent theoretical papers: Abreu and Brunnermeier 2003; Goeree, Palfrey, and Rogers 2003.

18. For this and the following paragraphs, see Edwards 1999; Lowenstein 2000.

19. Edwards 1999, 199, 203, 206.

20. What follows is based on Lüthy 1959–1961, 2: 464–592; Velde and Weir 1992.

21. Velde and Weir 1992; Hoffman, Postel-Vinay, and Rosenthal 2001, 221–224.

22. What we say about the Law affair is based on Neal 1990; and Hoffman, Postel-Vinay, and Rosenthal 2001 and the sources they cite.

6. Governments and the Demand for Reform

1. Yang 1952, 5, 92–101; Gernet 1956, 149–165; Will and Wong 1991, 355, 372; Kuran 2003.

2. Botticini 2000.

3. Sapienza 2004.

4. See, for example, FinAid 2006.

5. For this and what follows, see "Crony Capitalism" 2003; Wallison 2003; Labaton and Dash 2006.

6. Both organizations also have important allies, ranging from the investment banks that market their securities to the homeowners and developers

who benefit from their mortgage subsidies; as a result, privatization will not be easy.

7. For the shift in opinion among economists, see Shleifer 1998.

8. See Baskin and Miranti 1997, 197–204; Rajan and Zingales 2003, 160–161; and Simon 1989, who provides statistical evidence for the impact of the 1933 Securities Act.

9. Mahoney 2001.

10. Maurer 2002; Maurer and Haber 2002; Haber, Razo, and Maurer 2003, 83–93.

11. Burgess and Pande 2003.

12. Cf. Allen and Gale 2000 and Demirguc-Kunt and Levine 2001, on differences in financial systems; and Lindert 2004 on the wide variation in social transfers, which are often substitutes for private financial services.

13. Rajan and Zingales 2003, 212–216.

14. The evolution of per-capita income in western Europe is instructive here. Over the past three decades, the poorer countries in western Europe have tended to catch up with the richer ones, and the overall tendency has been toward convergence, despite enormous differences in the role governments play from country to country. In the last three decades, for instance, Britain and other countries have privatized and significantly reduced the government's role in the economy, while the Scandinavian nations have maintained a very large welfare state. Both, however, have maintained very high levels of income. Western Europe also does well relative to the United States, particularly if one looks at income per hour worked, which takes into account the value of what economists call "leisure" (essentially, time off the job). Such leisure time, which Europeans seem to agree to, does not enter into the per-capita income figures even though people value it highly. Finally, the most recent statistical tests (done by Peter Lindert) suggest that economic growth in these European democracies is not slowed by all the welfare spending. The reason, Lindert argues, is that the government programs and the taxes that support them are designed to avoid negative effects on growth. That result is in fact what we would expect in democracies with a large middle class. See Organization for Economic Cooperation and Development 2001; Crafts 2002, chap. 2 and table 18; Gordon 2002; Blanchard 2004; Lindert 2004, 1: 227–307 and 2: 82–99, 172–193.

15. Haber, Razo, and Maurer 2003, 42–51, 83–93.

16. Caprio and Peria 2000; Barth, Caprio, and Levine 2001, chap. 2; World Bank 2002, 84–85, 202.

17. Many of the bankers were in fact merchants themselves. Historians might

consider any talk of a middle class in medieval or early modern cities to be something of an anachronism, but it is not, provided we keep in mind the definition in force in this book (which concerns the mount of wealth a person has and the diversification of his portfolio) and not get distracted by the common use of the term "middle class" to describe nineteenth- and twentieth-century societies.

18. Troesken and Geddes 2003; Cutler and Miller 2006.

19. Noll and Krier 1990.

20. Lindert 2004, table 1.2. These figures include spending on housing, another form of assistance to the impoverished, but they omit pensions for government workers and soldiers.

21. Calomiris 1998.

22. Bates 2001.

Conclusion

1. One might argue that international markets offer substitutes for local institutions when governments suffer from poor public finances. For instance, with access to international capital markets, bankers need no longer depend on domestic public bonds for liquid assets to hold as reserves. But this substitution is minor and can arise only if the state allows banks to hold foreign assets as reserves—and it is unlikely to do so when its credit position is poor.

2. See Morduch 1999; Karlan 2005.

3. Fogel 2004.

4. See Feldstein 2005 for a discussion and references.

5. For the French pensions, see France, Caisse Nationale d'Assurance Vieillesse 2006. Compare the $6,328 per-capita GDP in Poland (calculated using current exchange rates) in 2004 in Organization for Economic Cooperation and Development 2006, which works out to roughly 5,000 Euros at 2004 exchange rates. A similar contrast holds for Mexico and the United States; see Porter and Malkin 2005.

References

Aberbach, J. D., D. Dollar, and K. L. Sokoloff, eds. 1994. *The Role of the State in Taiwan's Development.* Armonk, N.Y.

Abowd, J. M., and D. S. Kaplan. 1999. "Executive Compensation: Six Questions That Need Answering." *Journal of Economic Perspectives* 13, 4: 145–168.

Abreu, D., and M. K. Brunnermeier. 2003. "Bubbles and Crashes." *Econometrica* 71, 1: 173–204.

Acemoglu, D., and J. A. Robinson. 2000. "Why Did the West Extend the Franchise? Democracy, Inequality, and Growth in Historical Perspective." *Quarterly Journal of Economics* 115, 4: 1167–99.

——— 2001. "A Theory of Political Transitions." *American Economic Review* 91, 4: 938–963.

Ackman, D. 2002. "Merrill on Enron: Unknowingly, We Went Along." www.forbes.com (accessed 22 August).

Aghion, P., E. Caroli, and C. Garcia-Penalosa. 1999. "Inequality and Economic Growth: The Perspective of the New Growth Theories." *Journal of Economic Literature* 37, 4: 1615–60.

Aghion, P., C. Harris, P. Howitt, and J. Vickers. 2001. "Competition, Imitation and Growth with Step-by-Step Innovation." *Review of Economic Studies* 68: 467–492.

Akerlof, G. A. 1970. "The Market for 'Lemons': Quality Uncertainty and the Market Mechanism." *Quarterly Journal of Economics* 84, 3: 488–500.

Akerlof, G. A., and P. M. Romer. 1993. "Looting: The Economic Underworld of Bankruptcy for Profit." *Brookings Papers on Economic Activity,* ed. W. C. Brainard and G. L. Perry. Washington, D.C., 2: 1–60, 70–73.

Allen, F., and D. Gale. 2000. *Comparing Financial Systems.* Cambridge, Mass.

——— 2001. "Banking and Markets." Working Paper, Wharton Financial Institutions Center, University of Pennsylvania.

Allen, R. C. 1992. *Enclosure and the Yeoman: The Agricultural Development of the South Midlands, 1450–1850.* Oxford.

Allen, R. L. 1993. *Irving Fisher: A Biography.* Cambridge, Mass.

Altman, D. 2002. "How to Tie Pay to Goals, instead of the Stock Price." *New York Times,* 8 September: Business 4.

Andrews, E. L. 2002. "U.S. Businesses Dim as Models for Foreigners." *New York Times,* 27 June: A1.

Archives Départementales de la Sarthe. 1858–1871. Série H, "Domaine de Bonnétable."

"Argentina: Another Country." 2005. *The Economist,* 23 July: 34–35.

"Argentina Macroeconomic Report." 2003a. April report, Economic Section, U.S. Embassy, Buenos Aires.

———— 2003b. August report, Economic Section, U.S. Embassy, Buenos Aires.

Argentina Ministry of Economy and Production, Secretariat of Economic Policy. 2006. "Poverty and Indigence. Greater Buenos Aires." http://www.mecon.gov.ar/ (accessed 12 March).

"Argentina's Collapse: A Decline without Parallel." 2002. *The Economist,* 2 March: 26–28.

"Argentina's Collapse: Return to the Dark Ages." 2002. *The Economist,* 27 April: 35–36.

Ariely, D., D. Kahneman, and G. Loewenstein. 2000. "Joint Comment on 'When Does Duration Matter in Judgment and Decision Making' (Ariely & Loewenstein 2000)." *Journal of Experimental Psychology* 129, 4: 524–529.

Atkeson, A. 1991. "International Lending with Moral Hazard and Risk of Repudiation." *Econometrica* 59, July 1991: 1069–89.

Banerjee, A. V., T. Besley, and T. W. Guinnane. 1994. "The Neighbor's Keeper: The Design of a Credit Cooperative with Theory and a Test." *Quarterly Journal of Economics* 109, 2: 491–515.

Barberis, N., A. Shleifer, and R. Vishny. 1998. "A Model of Investor Sentiment." *Journal of Financial Economics* 49: 307–343.

Barberis, N., and R. Thaler. 2003. "A Survey of Behavioral Finance." In *Handbook of the Economics of Finance,* ed. G. Constantinides, M. Harris, and R. Stulz. Amsterdam.

Barrionuevo, A. 2006. "Who Will Steal the Enron Show?" *New York Times,* 29 January: sec. 3, 1, 8–9.

Barth, J. R., G. Caprio, and R. Levine. 2001. "Banking Systems around the Globe: Do Regulation and Ownership Affect Performance and Stability?" *Prudential Regulation and Supervision: What Works and What Doesn't,* ed. F. S. Mishkin. Chicago.

Baskin, J. B., and P. J. Miranti. 1997. *A History of Corporate Finance.* Cambridge.

Bates, R. H. 2001. *Prosperity and Violence: The Political Economy of Development.* New York.

Bayard, F., J. Félix, and P. Hammon. 2000. *Dictionnaire des surintendants et contrôleurs généraux des finances du XVIe siècle à la Révolution française de 1789.* Paris.

Bebchuk, L., J. Fried, and D. Walker. 2002. "Managerial Power and Rent Extraction in the Design of Executive Compensation." *University of Chicago Law Review* 69: 751–846.

Beck, T., A. Demirguc-Kunt, R. Levine, and V. Maksimovic. 2000. "Financial Structure and Economic Development: Firm, Industry, and Country Evidence." Manuscript, Carlson School of Management, University of Minnesota.

Beck, T., and R. Levine. 2002. "Industry Growth and Capital Allocation: Does Having a Market- or Bank-Based System Matter?" *Journal of Financial Economics* 64: 147–180.

Bercé, F., L. Boubli, and F. Folliot. 1988. *Le Palais Royal: Catalogue of an Exposition at the Musée Carnavalet, 9 May–4 September 1988.* Paris.

Bernstein, A. 2002. "The Fall of Enron: Routine 401(k) Decision Became Costly Flashpoint." *Houston Chronicle,* 22 January: A1.

Blanchard, O. 2004. "The Economic Future of Europe." NBER Working Paper, National Bureau of Economic Research. Cambridge, Mass.

Bolton, P., J. Scheinkman, and W. Xiong. 2003. "Executive Compensation and Short-Termist Behavior in Speculative Markets." Paper presented 26 March at California Institute of Technology.

Bordo, M., B. Eichengreen, D. Klingebiel, and M. S. Martinez-Peria. 2001. "Is the Crisis Problem Growing More Severe?" *Economic Policy* 32: 51–82.

Bortz, J. L., and S. H. Haber. 2002. "The New Institutional Economics and Latin American Economic History." In *The Mexican Economy, 1870–1930: Essays on the Economic History of Institutions, Revolution, and Growth,* ed. J. L. Bortz and S. H. Haber. Stanford, Calif.: 1–22.

Bossaerts, P. L. 2002. *The Paradox of Asset Pricing.* Princeton.

Botticini, M. 2000. "A Tale of 'Benevolent Governments': Private Credit Markets, Public Finance, and the Role of Jewish Lenders in Medieval and Renaissance Italy." *Journal of Economic History* 60, 1: 164–189.

Braudel, F. 1975. *The Mediterranean and the Mediterranean World in the Age of Philip II.* 2 vols. New York.

Brewer, J. 1989. *The Sinews of Power: War, Money, and the English State, 1688–1783.* New York.

Brion, R., and J. L. Moreau. 1998. *The Société Générale de Belgique, 1822–97.* Antwerp.

Bruck, C. 1988. *The Predators' Ball: The Junk-Bond Raiders and the Man Who Staked Them.* New York.

Buffett, W. E. 2002. "Who Really Cooks the Books?" *New York Times,* 24 July: A21.

Bulow, J., and K. Rogoff. 1989. "A Constant Recontracting Model of Sovereign Debt." *Journal of Political Economy* 97, February: 155–178.

Burgess, R., and R. Pande. 2003. "Do Rural Banks Matter? Evidence from the Indian Social Banking Experiment." Working Paper, Department of Economics, London School of Economics.

Calomiris, C. 1998. "The Asian Economic Crisis in Historical Perspective." www.eh.net (accessed 4 November 2003).

Calomiris, C. W., and E. N. White. 1995. "The Origins of Federal Deposit Insurance." In *The Regulated Economy,* ed. C. Goldin and G. D. Libecap. Chicago: 145–188.

Camerer, C. F. 2001. "Prospect Theory in the Wild: Evidence from the Field." In *Choices, Values, and Frames,* ed. D. Kahneman and A. Tversky. Cambridge: 288–300.

Caprio, G., and M. S. M. Peria. 2000. "Avoiding Disaster: Policies to Reduce the Risk of Banking Crises." Paper, World Bank, Washington, D.C.

Carosso, V. P. 1970. *Investment Banking in America: A History.* Cambridge, Mass.

——— 1987. *The Morgans: Private International Bankers, 1854–1913.* Cambridge, Mass.

Chagniot, J. 1988. *Nouvelle histoire de Paris: Paris au XVIIIe siècle.* Paris.

Cheng, I. 2002. "Survivors Who Laughed All the Way to the Bank: Barons of Bankruptcy Part I." *Financial Times,* 31 July: 10.

Chernow, R. 1990. *The House of Morgan: An American Banking Dynasty and the Rise of Modern Finance.* New York.

CNN. 2002. "Merrill Execs Take Fifth: Brokerage Firm Says It Trusted Enron in Deals Questioned by Congressional Investigators." money.cnn.com (accessed 22 August).

Coleman, M. 1985. "Reagan Farm Policy Makes Political Fodder in the Midwest." *Washington Post,* 12 April: A3.

Collier, P., and J. W. Gunning. 1999. "Why Has Africa Grown Slowly?" *Journal of Economic Perspectives* 13, 3: 3–22.

Conklin, J. 1998. "The Theory of Sovereign Debt and Spain under Philip II." *Journal of Political Economy* 106: 485–513.

"Consistently Right about Enron." 2002. *Pennsylvania Gazette,* March–April: www.upenn.edu (accessed 22 August).

"Consumer Price Index, All Midwest Urban Consumers." 2006. U.S. Department of Labor, Bureau of Labor Statistics. www.bls.gov (accessed 8 March).

Crafts, N. 2002. *Britain's Relative Economic Performance, 1870–1999.* London.

Craig, S. 2003. "How One Firm Uses Strict Governance to Fix Its Troubles." *Wall Street Journal,* 21 August: A1.

"Crony Capitalism." 2003. *The Economist*, 28 June: 70–71.

Cutler, D., and G. Miller. 2006. "Water, Water Everywhere: Municipal Finance and Water Supply in American Cities." In *Corruption and Reform: Lessons from America's Economic History*, ed. E. L. Glaeser and C. Goldin. Chicago: 153–183.

Davies, J. B., and A. F. Shorrocks. 2000. "The Distribution of Wealth." In *Handbook of Income Distribution*, ed. A. B. Atkinson and F. Bourguignon. Amsterdam: 605–675.

Davis, L. E., and R. E. Gallman. 2001. *Evolving Financial Markets and International Capital Flows: Britain, the Americas, and Australia, 1865–1914*. Cambridge.

Dawson, F. G. 1990. *The First Latin American Debt Crisis: The City of London and the 1822–25 Loan Bubble*. New Haven.

Dekle, R., and K. Kletzer. 2003. "The Japanese Banking Crisis and Economic Growth: Theoretical and Empirical Implications of Deposit Guarantees and Weak Financial Regulation." Paper, Santa Cruz Center for International Economics, University of California, Santa Cruz.

De Long, J. B. 1991. "Did J. P. Morgan's Men Add Value? An Economist's Perspective on Financial Capitalism." In *Inside the Business Enterprise: Historical Perspectives on the Use of Information*, ed. P. Temin. Chicago: 205–249.

Demirguc-Kunt, A., and R. Levine, eds. 2001. *Financial Structure and Economic Growth: A Cross-Country Comparison of Banks, Markets, and Development*. Cambridge, Mass.

De Roover, R. A. 1953. *L'évolution de la lettre de change, XIVe–XVIIIe siècles*. Paris.

Desai, P. 2003. *Financial Crisis, Contagion, and Containment*. Princeton.

De Vries, J., and A. Van der Woude. 1997. *The First Modern Economy: Success, Failure, and Perseverance of the Dutch Economy, 1500–1815*. Cambridge.

Dickenson, J. R. 1985. "Iowa Governor Activates Debt-Moratorium Law: Farmers Can Seek One-Year Reprieve from Foreclosure." *Washington Post*, 2 October: A3.

Eaton, J., and M. Gersovitz. 1981. "Debt with Potential Repudiation: Theoretical and Empirical Analysis." *Review of Economic Studies* 48, 2: 289–309.

"Economics Focus: Taken for a Ride." 2002. *The Economist*, 13 July: 64.

Edwards, F. R. 1999. "Hedge Funds and the Collapse of Long-Term Capital Management." *Journal of Economic Perspectives* 13, 2: 189–210.

Ehrenberg, R. 1922. *Das Zeitalter der Fugger*. 2 vols. Jena.

Eichengreen, B. 1987. "Agricultural Mortgages in the Populist Era: Reply to Snowden." *Journal of Economic History* 47, 3: 757–760.

——— 1992. *Golden Fetters: The Gold Standard and the Great Depression, 1919–1939*. Oxford.

────── 2002. *Financial Crises and What to Do about Them*. Oxford.

────── 2003. *Capital Flows and Crises*. Cambridge, Mass.

Eichenwald, K. 2002a. "Enron Panel Finds Inflated Profits and Self-Dealing." *New York Times*, 3 February: A1.

────── 2002b. "Ex-Enron Official Admits Payments to Finance Chief." *New York Times*, 22 August: A1.

Elliott, J. H. 1963. *Imperial Spain, 1469–1716*. New York.

Engerman, S. L., and K. L. Sokoloff. 2001. "The Evolution of Suffrage Institutions in the New World." Working Paper, National Bureau of Economic Research. Cambridge, Mass.

────── 2002. "Factor Endowments, Inequality, and Paths of Development among New World Economies." *Economia* 3, 1: 41–109.

"Enron: The Twister Hits." 2002. *The Economist*, 19 January: 57–59.

"Enron Prosecution Scorecard." 2006. *Houston Chronicle*. www.chron.com (accessed 21 July).

Fairbank, J. K., and D. Twitchett, eds. 1978. *The Cambridge History of China*. 15 vols. Cambridge.

Feder, B. J. 2003. "WorldCom Report Recommends Sweeping Changes for Its Board." *New York Times*, 26 August: C1–2.

Feldstein, M. 2005. "Structural Reform of Social Security." *Journal of Economic Perspectives* 19, 2: 33–55.

Ferguson, N. 2001. *The Cash Nexus: Money and Power in the Modern World*. New York.

FinAid. 2006. "Student Aid Lobbying and Advocacy Groups." www.finaid.org (accessed 21 March).

Fischel, D. R. 1995. *Payback: The Conspiracy to Destroy Michael Milken and His Financial Fevolution*. New York.

Flandreau, M. 1998. "Caveat Emptor: Coping with Soverein Risk without the Multilaterals." Centre for Economic Policy Research Discussion Paper. London.

Flanery, J. A. 1985. "Hawkeye Chief Says Sales Add to Ag Land Glut." *Omaha World Herald*, 6 December: 1.

Flood, M. 2005. "The Fall of Enron: Pension Settlement Gets Final Approval." *Houston Chronicle*, 25 May: Business 1.

Fogel, R. 2004. *The Escape from Hunger and Premature Death, 1700–2100: Europe, America, and the Third World*. Cambridge.

"Foreign Creditors Join the Pyre." 2002. *The Economist*, 3 January. www.economist.com (accessed 10 May).

France, Caisse Nationale d'Assurance Vieillesse. 2006. "La base nationale de législation, barèmes." www.legislation.cnav.fr (accessed 3 April).

Freedland, J. 1995. "Saint Michael." *The Guardian,* 16 November: T2.

Garber, P. M. 2000. *Famous First Bubbles: The Fundamentals of Early Manias.* Cambridge, Mass.

Gasparini, L. 2003. "Different Lives: Inequality in Latin America and the Caribbean." World Bank report. Washington, D.C.

Gernet, J. 1956. *Les aspects économiques du Bouddhisme dans la société chinoise du Ve au Xe siècle.* Paris.

Glater, J. D. 2002. "Recomputing Earnings with Lawbook and Eraser." *New York Times,* 2 July: C8.

Goeree, J., T. Palfrey, and B. Rogers. 2003. "Social Learning with Private and Common Values." Social Science Working Paper 1187, California Institute of Technology.

Gordon, R. J. 2002. "Two Centuries of Economic Growth: Europe Chasing the American Frontier." Paper prepared for Economic History Workshop, Northwestern University.

Great Britain, Statistical Office. 1951. *Annual Abstract of Statistics 87 (1938–1949).* London.

Greenhouse, S. 1985. "Iowa Bank Seeks Loan Pact." *New York Times,* 6 December: D3.

Greif, A. 2006. *Institutions and the Path to the Modern Economy.* Cambridge.

Grinnath, A., III, J. Wallis, and R. Sylla. 1997. "Debt, Default, and Revenue Structure: The American State Debt Crisis in the Early 1840s." Working Paper H0097, National Bureau of Economic Research. Cambridge, Mass.

Grossman, H. I., and J. B. Van Huyck. 1988. "Sovereign Debt as a Contingent Claim: Excusable Default, Repudiation, and Reputation." *American Economic Review* 78, 5: 1088–97.

Gueslin, A. 1985. *Le crédit agricole.* Paris.

Haber, S. H. 1991. "Industrial Concentration and the Capital Markets: A Comparative Study of Brazil, Mexico, and the United States, 1830–1930." *Journal of Economic History* 51, 3: 559–580.

Haber, S. H., and S. Kantor. 2003. "Getting Privatization Wrong: The Mexican Banking System, 1991–2002." Manuscript, Department of Political Science, Stanford University.

Haber, S. H., A. Razo, and N. Maurer. 2003. *The Politics of Property Rights: Political Instability, Credible Commitments, and Economic Growth in Mexico, 1876–1929.* Cambridge.

Harris, R. 1994. "The Bubble Act: Its Passage and Its Effects on Business Organization." *Journal of Economic History* 54, 3: 610–627.

"Hawkeye Agrees on Debt Program." 1986. *New York Times,* 12 December: D4.

"Hawkeye Bank Sale." 1986. *New York Times,* 24 June: D4.

Hill, A., and J. Labate. 2002. "NYSE Calls for Tougher Governance Rules." *Financial Times*, 7 June: 21.

Hoffman, P. T. 1994. "Early Modern France, 1450–1700." In *Fiscal Crises, Liberty, and Representative Government, 1450–1789*, ed. P. T. Hoffman and K. Norberg. Stanford, Calif.: 226–252.

———— 1996. *Growth in a Traditional Society*. Princeton.

Hoffman, P. T., and K. Norberg. 1994. "Conclusion." In *Fiscal Crises, Liberty, and Representative Government, 1450–1789*, ed. P. T. Hoffman and K. Norberg. Stanford, Calif.: 299–310.

Hoffman, P. T., G. Postel-Vinay, and J. L. Rosenthal. 2000. *Priceless Markets: The Political Economy of Credit in Paris, 1660–1870*. Chicago.

———— 2001. *Des marchés sans prix: Une économie politique du crédit à Paris, 1660–1870*. Paris.

———— 2004. "Révolution et évolution: Les marchés de crédit notarié en France 1780–1840." *Annales: Histoire et sciences sociales* 59: 387–424.

Hoffman, P. T., and J. L. Rosenthal. 1997. "The Political Economy of Warfare and Taxation in Early Modern Europe: Historical Lessons for Economic Development." In *The Frontiers of the New Institutional Economics*, ed. J. N. Drobak and J. V. C. Nye. San Diego: 31–55.

———— 2002. "Divided We Fall: The Political Economy of Warfare and Taxation." Manuscript, California Institute of Technology.

Holmstrom, B., and S. N. Kaplan. 2001. "Corporate Governance and Merger Activity in the U.S.: Making Sense of the 1980s and 1990s." *Journal of Economic Perspectives* 15: 121–144.

Hoppit, J. 1986. "Financial Crises in Eighteenth-Century England." *Economic History Review* 39: 39–58.

Huang, R. 1974. *Taxation and Governmental Finance in Sixteenth-Century Ming China*. Cambridge.

Hubbard, R. G. 1991. Introduction. In *Financial Markets and Financial Crises*, ed. R. G. Hubbard. Chicago: 1–10.

"Iowa Governor Invokes Provision to Delay Foreclosures on Farms." 1985. *New York Times*, 2 October: B8.

Ippolito, R. A., and W. H. James. 1992. "LBOs, Reversions, and Implicit Contracts." *Journal of Finance* 47, 1: 139–167.

Israel, J. I. 1998. *The Dutch Republic: Its Rise, Greatness and Fall, 1477–1806*. Oxford.

Ivanovich, D. 2001. "Enron's 401(k) Claims Disputed; Senate Panel Hears of Employees' Losses." *Houston Chronicle*, 19 December: A1.

"Japanese Banks: A Funny Sort of Crisis." 1998. *The Economist*, 31 October: 81.

"Japan's Long Winter." 1999. *The Economist*, 17 April. www.economist.com (accessed 9 August 2006).

Kahneman, D., B. L. Fredrickson, C. A. Schreiber, and D. A. Redelmeir. 1993. "When More Pain Is Preferred to Less: Adding a Better End." *Psychological Science* 4, 6: 401–405.

Karlan, D. 2005. "Social Connections and Group Banking." Economic Growth Center Discussion Paper, Yale University.

Karmin, C., and M. R. Sesit. 2002. "Prescient Professor Favors Market Timing." *Wall Street Journal,* 29 July: C1.

Kennickell, A. B. 2000. "An Examination of Changes in the Distribution of Wealth from 1989 to 1998: Evidence from the Survey of Consumer Finances." Survey of Consumer Finances Working Paper, Federal Reserve Board, Washington, D.C.

Kiewiet, D. R. 2000. "Economic Retrospective Voting and Incentives for Policymakers." *Electoral Studies* 19: 427–444.

Kindelberger, C. P. 1978. *Manias, Panics, and Crashes: A History of Financial Crises.* New York.

King, S. S. 1983. "Credit Crunch on Farmers Eases, Bankers Say." *New York Times,* 21 December: A1.

"Kirchner and Lula: Different Ways to Give the Fund the Kiss Off; Argentina, Brazil and the IMF." 2005. *The Economist,* 24 December: 49–50.

Kousser, J. M. 1984. "Suffrage." In *Encyclopedia of American Political History: Studies of the Principal Movements and Ideas,* ed. J. P. Greene. New York. 3: 1236–58.

Kraay, A., and V. Nehru. 2004. "When Is External Debt Sustainable?" World Bank Policy Research Paper, World Bank, Washington, D.C.

Kuran, T. 2003. "Levant: Islamic Rule." In *Oxford Encycopedia of Economic History,* ed. J. Mokyr. Oxford. 3: 309–314.

Kuran, T., and C. R. Sunstein. 1999. "Availability Cascades and Risk Regulation." *Stanford Law Review* 51, 4: 683–768.

Labaton, S. 2002. "Will Reforms with Few Teeth Be Able to Bite?" *New York Times,* 22 September: Money and Business 4.

Labaton, S., and E. Dash. 2006. "New Report Criticizes Big Lender: Fannie Mae Said to Inflate Profit." *New York Times,* 24 February: C1.

Lamoreaux, N. R. 1994. *Insider Lending: Banks, Personal Connections and Economic Development in Industrial New England.* Cambridge.

Lapeyre, H. 1955. *Une famille de marchands: Les Ruiz. Contribution à l'étude du commerce entre la France et l'Espagne au temps de Philippe II.* Paris.

Lefebvre-Teillard, A. 1985. *La société anonyme au XIXe siècle: Du Code de commerce à la loi de 1867, histoire d'un instrument juridique du développement capitaliste.* Paris.

Leonhardt, D. 2002. "Anger at Executives' Profits Fuels Support for Stock Curb." *New York Times,* 9 July: A1.

Levine, R. 2002. "Bank-Based or Market-Based Financial Systems: Which Is Better?" *Journal of Financial Intermediation* 11: 398–428.

Levy, J. 2004. "Yucatán's Arrested Development: Credit Markets and Social Networks in Mérida between 1850 and 1899." Ph.D. diss., Department of Economics, University of California, Los Angeles.

Levy, J. S. 1983. *War in the Modern Great Power System, 1945–1975.* Lexington, Ky.

Lindert, P. 1980. "English Occupations, 1670–1811." *Journal of Economic History* 40, 4: 685–712.

—— 1983. "Who Owned Victorian England." Working Paper, Agricultural History Center, University of California, Davis.

—— 1996. "What Limits Social Spending?" *Explorations in Economic History* 33, 1: 1–34.

—— 2000. "Three Centuries of Inequality in Britain and America." In *Handbook of Income Distribution,* ed. A. B. Atkinson and F. Bourguignon. Amsterdam. 1: 167–216.

—— 2004. *Growing Public: Social Spending and Economic Growth since the Eighteenth Century.* 2 vols. Cambridge.

Lizzeri, A., and N. Persico. 2004. "Why Did the Elites Extend the Suffrage? Democracy and the Scope of Government, with an Application to Britain's 'Age of Reform.'" *Quarterly Journal of Economics* 19, 2: 707–765.

Lowenstein, R. 2000. *When Genius Failed: The Rise and Fall of Long-Term Capital Management.* New York.

Lüthy, H. 1959–1961. *La banque protestante en France de la Révocation de l'Edit de Nantes à la Révolution.* 2 vols. Paris.

Maddison, A. 2001. *The World Economy: A Millennial Perspective.* Paris.

Mahoney, P. G. 2001. "The Political Economy of the Securities Act of 1933." *Journal of Legal Studies* 30: 1–31.

Manasse, P., N. Roubini, and A. Schimmelpfennig. 2003. "Predicting Sovereign Debt Crises." Working Paper, International Monetary Fund, Washington, D.C.

Mason, J. 2002. "Former Enron Workers Air Complaints on CNN." *Houston Chronicle,* 21 January: A10.

Mauduit, L., and M. Orange. 2002. "Les opérations qui jettent le doute sur les comptes de Vivendi." *Le Monde,* 3 July: 18.

Maurer, N. 2002. "The International Consequences of External Credibility: Banking Regulation and Banking Performance in Porfirian Mexico." In *The Mexican Economy, 1870–1930: Essays on the Economic History of Institutions, Revolution, and Growth,* ed. J. L. Bortz and S. H. Haber. Stanford, Calif.: 50–92.

Maurer, N., and S. H. Haber. 2002. "Institutional Change and Economic Growth: Banks, Financial Markets, and Mexican Industrialization, 1878–1913." In *The Mexican Economy, 1870–1930: Essays on the Economic History of Institutions, Revolution, and Growth*, ed. J. L. Bortz and S. H. Haber. Stanford, Calif.: 23–49.

McGeehan, P. 2002. "Goldman Chief Urges Reforms in Corporations." *New York Times*, 6 June: A1.

"Milken Saw Chances and He Took Them." 1989. *St. Louis Post Dispatch*, 31 March: Business 9D.

Mishkin, F. S. 1991. "Asymmetric Information and Financial Crises: A Historical Perspective." In *Financial Markets and Financial Crises*, ed. R. G. Hubbard. Chicago: 69–108.

Mitchell, B. R. 1981. *European Historical Statistics, 1750–1975*. New York.

Mitchell, J. 2003. "Argentina—Another Central Bank Boss Takes the Reins—The Resignation of Yet Another Central Bank President Raises the Issue of Independence." *The Banker*, 1 January. Lexus/Nexus (accessed 9 August 2006).

Morduch, J. 1999. "The Microfinance Promise." *Journal of Economic Literature* 37, 4: 1569–1614.

Morgan, E. V., and W. A. Thomas. 1962. *The Stock Exchange: Its History and Functions*. London.

Morgenson, G. 2004. "Trials, Trials, Trials, and Then What?" *New York Times*, 8 June: C1.

Morrisson, C. 2000. "Historical Perspectives on Income Distribution: The Case of Europe." In *Handbook of Income Distribution*, ed. A. B. Atkinson and F. Bourguignon. Amsterdam. 1: 217–260.

Murphy, B. 2002. "Laid-off Workers Lash Out at Lay." *Houston Chronicle*, 19 June: Business 1.

Murphy, K. J. 1999. "Executive Compensation." In *Handbook of Labor Economics*, ed. O. Ashenfelter and D. Card. Amsterdam. 3B: 2485–2563.

Mussa, M. 2002. "Argentina and the Fund: From Triumph to Tragedy." Working Paper, Institute for International Economics, Washington, D.C.

Ndulu, B. J., and S. A. O'Connell. 1999. "Governance and Growth in Sub-Saharan Africa." *Journal of Economic Perspectives* 13, 3: 41–66.

Neal, L. 1990. *The Rise of Financial Capitalism: International Capital Markets in the Age of Reason*. Cambridge.

——— 1996. "The First Latin American Debt Crisis and the Stock Market Crash of 1825." Unpublished paper, Department of Economics, University of Illinois, Urbana.

Neal, L., and S. Quinn. 2003. "Markets and Institutions in the Rise of London as a Financial Center in the Seventeenth Century." In *Finance, Intermediaries, and Economic Development*, ed. S. L. Engerman, P. T. Hoffman, J. L. Rosenthal, and K. L. Sokoloff. Cambridge: 11–33.

Neal, L., and M. Weidenmier. 2002. "Crises in the Global Economy from Tulips to Today: Contagion and Consequences." Working Paper, National Bureau of Economic Research. Cambridge, Mass.

Nicolardot, L. 1887. *Ménage et finances de Voltaire.* 2 vols. Paris.

Noll, R. G., and J. E. Krier. 1990. "Some Implications of Cognitive Psychology for Risk Regulation." *Journal of Legal Studies* 19: 747–779.

Norris, F. 2000. "Levitt to Leave S.E.C. Early; Bush to Pick 4." *New York Times,* 21 December: C1, 5.

North, D. C., and B. Weingast. 1989. "Constitutions and Commitment: Evolution of the Institutions Governing Public Choice in Seventeenth-Century England." *Journal of Economic History* 49: 803–832.

Olson, M. 2000. *Power and Prosperity: Outgrowing Communist and Capitalist Dictatorships.* New York.

Organization for Economic Cooperation and Development. 2001. "OECD Science, Technology and Industry Scoreboard 2001—Towards a Knowledge-based Economy: Economic Structure and Productivity: Differences in Income and Productivity in the OECD." www1.oecd.org (accessed 9 November 2003).

——— 2006. "Annual National Accounts—Comparative tables based on exchange rates and PPPs." www.oecd.org (accessed 23 March).

Parker, S. 2002. "Argentina's Economic Future." *Voice of America.* Transcript. 8 December.

Persson, T., and G. Tabellini. 2000. *Political Economics: Explaining Economic Policy.* Cambridge, Mass.

Piketty, T., G. Postel-Vinay, and J. L. Rosenthal. 2006. "Wealth Concentration in a Developing Economy: Paris and France, 1807–1994." *American Economic Review* 96, 1: 236–256.

Porter, E., and E. Malkin. 2005. "Mexicans at Home Abroad: Will Millions Retire Here or Go South of Border?" *New York Times,* 4 August: C1.

Postel-Vinay, G. 1998. *La terre et l'argent: L'agriculture et le crédit en France du XVIIIe au début du XXe siècle.* Paris.

Quinn, S. 2001. "The Glorious Revolution's Effect on English Private Finance: A Microhistory, 1680–1705." *Journal of Economic History* 61, 3: 593–615.

Rajan, R., and L. Zingales. 2003. *Saving Capitalism from the Capitalists: Unleashing the Power of Financial Markets to Create Wealth and Spread Opportunity.* New York.

Ratner, J., and R. Waters. 2002. "Wall Street's Faithful Bull: Man in the News Jack Grubman." *Financial Times,* 17 August: Comment and Analysis 8.

Ray, D. 1998. *Development Economics*. Princeton.

Redelmeir, D. A., and D. Kahneman. 1996. "Patients' Memories of Painful Medical Treatments: Real-Time and Retrospective Evaluations of Two Minimally Invasive Procedures." *Pain* 66: 3–8.

Riguzzi, P. 2002. "The Legal System, Institutional Change, and Financial Regulation in Mexico, 1870–1910: Mortgage Contracts and Long-Term Credit." In *The Mexican Economy, 1870–1930: Essays on the Economic History of Institutions, Revolution, and Growth,* ed. J. L. Bortz and S. H. Haber. Stanford, Calif.: 120–160.

Rippy, J. F. 1947. "Latin America and the British Investment 'Boom' of the 1820's." *Journal of Modern History* 19, 2: 122–129.

Ritschl, A. 2003. "Germany: Modern Germany." In *Oxford Encylopedia of Economic History,* ed. J. Mokyr. Oxford. 2: 409–417.

Robbins, W. 1985. "Farms' Crisis Endangering Rural Towns." *New York Times,* 14 October: A1.

Roeder, D. 2002. "Andersen Gets Death Sentence." *Chicago Sun-Times,* 16 June: News 1.

Rohter, L. 2003. "Brazil to Let Squatters Own Homes: Formal Property Rights Could Benefit Millions of Slum Dwellers." *New York Times,* 19 April: A7.

Rosenthal, J. L. 1994. "Rural Credit Markets and Aggregate Shocks: The Experience of Nuits St. Georges, 1756–1776." *Journal of Economic History* 54, 2: 288–306.

——— 1998. "The Political Economy of Absolutism Reconsidered." In *Analytic Narratives,* ed. R. H. Bates, A. Greif, M. Levi, J. L. Rosenthal, and B. Weingast. Princeton: 64–108.

Roubini, N. 2001. "Debt Sustainability: How to Assess Whether a Country Is Insolvent." Manuscript, Stern School of Business, New York University.

Ryan, J. Forthcoming. "Credit Where Credit Is Due: Lending and Borrowing in Nineteenth-Century Rio de Janeiro, 1820–1900." Ph.D. diss., Department of Economics, University of California, Los Angeles.

Sapienza, P. 2004. "The Effects of Government Ownership on Bank Lending." *Journal of Financial Economics* 72: 357–384.

Sargent, T. J., and F. R. Velde. 1995. "Macroeconomic Features of the French Revolution." *Journal of Political Economy* 103, 3 June: 474–518.

——— 2002. *The Big Problem of Small Change*. Princeton.

Sargent, T. J., and N. Wallace. 1981. "Some Unpleasant Monetarist Arithmetic." *Federal Reserve Bank of Minnesota Quarterly Review* 5, Fall: 1–17.

Schnapper, B. 1957. *Les rentes au XVIe siècle: Histoire d'un instrument de crédit.* Paris.

Schroeder, P. W. 1986. "The 19th-Century International System: Changes in the Structure." *World Politics* 39, 1: 1–26.

—— 1994. *The Transformation of European Politics, 1763–1848.* Oxford.

Sharrock, D. 2002. "Middle Classes Become Argentina's Dispossessed." *The Times,* 20 December: Overseas News 18.

Shiller, R. J. 2001. *Irrational Exuberance.* New York.

—— 2003. *The New Financial Order: Risk in the Twenty-first Century.* Princeton.

Shleifer, A. 1998. "State versus Private Ownership." *Journal of Economic Perspectives* 12, 4: 133–150.

—— 2000. *Inefficient Markets: An Introduction to Behavioral Finance.* Oxford.

Simon, C. J. 1989. "The Effect of the 1933 Securities Act on Investor Information and the Performance of New Issues." *American Economic Review* 79, 3: 295–318.

Sinclair, W. 1985. "Farm Failures Threaten to Reshape Rural U.S.; Long-Predicted Crisis Seems at Hand." *Washington Post,* A1.

Smith, V. L., G. L. Suchanek, and A. Williams. 1988. "Bubbles, Crashes, and Endogenous Expectations in Experimental Spot Asset Markets." *Econometrica* 56, 5: 1119–51.

Snowden, K. A. 1987. "Mortgage Rates and American Capital Market Development in the Late Nineteenth Century." *Journal of Economic History* 47, 3: 671–691.

—— 1995. "The Evolution of Interregional Mortgage Lending Channels, 1870–1940: The Life Insurance–Mortgage Company Connection." In *Coordination and Information: Historical Perspectives on the Organization of Enterprise,* ed. N. R. Lamoreaux and D. M. G. Raff. Chicago: 209–247.

Sokoloff, K. L., and E. Zolt. 2004. "Taxation and Inequality: Some Evidence from the Americas." Paper delivered at meeting of All University of California Group in Economic History, University of California, Los Angeles.

Soltow, L. 1975. *Men and Wealth in the United States, 1850–1870.* New Haven.

Stasavage, D. 2003. *Public Debt and the Birth of the Democratic State: France and Great Britain, 1688–1789.* Cambridge.

Stiglitz, J. E., and A. Weiss. 1981. "Credit Rationing in Markets with Imperfect Information." *American Economic Review* 71, 3: 393–410.

Strouse, J. 1999. *Morgan: American Financier.* New York.

Sussman, N., and Y. Yafeh. 2005. "Constitutions and Commitment: Evidence on the Relationship between Institutions and the Cost of Capital." Paper, Hebrew University of Jerusalem.

Sutherland, D. 1986. *France 1789–1815: Revolution and Counter-revolution.* New York.

Sylla, R. 2000. "Experimental Federalism: The Economics of American Government, 1789–1914." In *The Cambridge Economic History of the United States,* ed. S. L. Engerman and R. E. Gallman. Cambridge. 2: 483–541.

Temin, P., and H. J. Voth. 2004. "Banking as an Emerging Technology: Hoare's Bank 1702–42." Working Paper 04-01, Department of Economics, Massachusetts Institute of Technology.

Thompson, I. A. A. 1994. "Polity, Fiscality, and Fiscal Crisis." In *Fiscal Crises, Liberty, and Representative Government, 1450–1789,* ed. P. T. Hoffman and K. Norberg. Stanford, Calif.: 140–180.

Thomson, A., and R. Lapper. 2003. "Argentina to Lift Savings Curb." *Financial Times,* 28 March: World News 12.

Tittle et al. v. Enron et al. 2002. Complaint filed 8 April with the United States District Court for the Southern District of Texas, Houston Division. Keller Rohrback L. L. P., counsel.

Troesken, W., and R. Geddes. 2003. "Municipalizing American Waterworks, 1897–1914." *Journal of Law, Economics, and Organization* 19: 373–400.

Udry, C. 1994. "Risk and Insurance in a Rural Credit Market: An Empirical Investigation in Northern Nigeria." *Review of Economic Studies* 61, 3: 495–526.

"Value of Farm Real Estate." 2006. U.S. Department of Agriculture, Economic Research Service. www.ers.usda.gov (accessed 7 March).

Van Der Wee, H., and M. Verbreyt. 1997. *The General Bank, 1822–1897: A Continuing Challenge.* Tielt.

Velde, F., and D. Weir. 1992. "The Financial Market and Government Debt Policy in France, 1746–1793." *Journal of Economic History* 52: 1–40.

Voltaire. 1953–1977. *Voltaire's Correspondence,* ed. Theodore Besterman. 135 vols. Geneva.

Von Glahn, R. 1996. *Fountain of Fortune: Money and Monetary Policy in China, 1000–1700.* Berkeley, Calif.

Von Sternberg, B. 2002. "Wellstone Hearing Focuses on Retirement Accounts." *Star Tribune,* 22 February: News 8A.

Wallis, J. 2001. "What Caused the Crisis of 1839." Working Paper, National Bureau of Economic Research. Cambridge, Mass.

Wallison, P. J. 2003. "Fannie Mae and Freddie Mac." www.aei.org (accessed 6 August).

Wee, H. v. d. 1963. *The Growth of the Antwerp Market and the European Economy (Fourteenth–Sixteenth Centuries).* The Hague.

——— 1977. "Monetary, Credit and Banking Systems." In *The Cambridge Economic History of Europe,* ed. M. Poston, D. C. Coleman, and P. Mathias. Cambridge. 5: 290–393.

Westfall, R. S. 1980. *Never at Rest: A Biography of Isaac Newton.* Cambridge.

Whaples, R. 2003. "United States: Modern Period." In *Oxford Encyclopedia of Economic History,* ed. J. Mokyr. Oxford. 5: 167–174.

White, E. N. 2000. "Banking and Finance in the Twentieth Century." In *The*

Cambridge Economic History of the United States, ed. S. L. Engerman and R. E. Gallman. Cambridge. 3: 743–802.

Will, P.-E., and R. Bin Wong. 1991. *Nourish the People: The State Civilian Granary System in China, 1650–1850.* Ann Arbor.

Wong, R. B. 1997. *China Transformed: Historical Change and the Limits of European Experience.* Ithaca.

Woodruff, C. 2001. "Review of de Soto's *The Mystery of Capital.*" *Journal of Economic Literature* 39: 1215–23.

World Bank. 2002. *World Development Report 2002: Building Institutions for Markets.* New York.

Wright, Q. 1942. *A Study of War.* 2 vols. Chicago.

Yale University. 2004. "Yale School of Management Stock Market Confidence Indexes." icf.som.yale.edu (accessed 26 March).

Yang, L. S. 1952. *Money and Credit in China: A Short History.* Cambridge, Mass.

Index